175 Best
Small-Batch
Baking
Recipes

175 Best Small-Batch Baking Recipes

Treats for 1 or 2

Jill Snider

Robert ROSE

175 Best Small-Batch Baking Recipes

Text copyright © 2017 Jill Snider
Photographs copyright © 2017 Robert Rose Inc.
Cover and text design copyright © 2017 Robert Rose Inc.

Some of the recipes in this book appeared, in a slightly different form, in *Bake Something Great* (2011), published by Robert Rose Inc.

For complete cataloguing information, see page 247.

Disclaimers

The recipes in this book have been carefully tested by our kitchen and our tasters. To the best of our knowledge, they are safe and nutritious for ordinary use and users. For those people with food or other allergies, or who have special food requirements or health issues, please read the suggested contents of each recipe carefully and determine whether or not they may create a problem for you. All recipes are used at the risk of the consumer.

We cannot be responsible for any hazards, loss or damage that may occur as a result of any recipe use.

For those with special needs, allergies, requirements or health problems, in the event of any doubt, please contact your medical adviser prior to the use of any recipe.

Design and production: Kevin Cockburn/PageWave Graphics Inc.
Editor: Tracy Bordian
Proofreader: Gillian Watts
Indexer: Gillian Watts
Photographer: Colin Erricson
Associate photographer: Matt Johannsson
Food stylists: Kathryn Robertson & Jill Snider
Prop stylist: Charlene Erricson

Front cover image: Oatmeal Candy Cookies (page 35)

The publisher gratefully acknowledges the financial support of our publishing program by the Government of Canada through the Canada Book Fund.

Canada

Published by Robert Rose Inc.
120 Eglinton Avenue East, Suite 800, Toronto, Ontario, Canada M4P 1E2
Tel: (416) 322-6552 Fax: (416) 322-6936
www.robertrose.ca

Printed and bound in Canada

1 2 3 4 5 6 7 8 9 FP 25 24 23 22 21 20 19 18 17

Contents

Acknowledgments

I'd like to express my sincere thanks to the many talented and devoted people who helped to put this book together.

To my publisher, Bob Dees, who even though I started out quite skeptical convinced me that this was a great idea and the way many people bake today. It was his vision that turned a market need into a small-batch baking cookbook.

To the terrific team at PageWave Graphics—Joseph Gisini, Kevin Cockburn and Daniella Zanchetta—who worked through editorial, design, layouts and production to bring this book together.

To Susanne McMahon, who accurately input the recipes, often while watching her kids play hockey and baseball games.

To Tracy Bordian for her eagle eyes while editing.

To Colin Erricson, the outstanding photographer I've worked with for many, many years, who always manages to make even the most difficult shots jump off the page.

To Charlene Erricson, who has to be one of the best prop stylists I have ever worked with.

I'd also like to thank my dear friend and fellow food stylist Carol Brown, who with great enthusiasm and professionalism helped me test and retest recipes and critique them until perfect.

Thanks as well to all my friends, neighbors and co-workers who tasted and commented on the recipes.

Introduction

As the ultimate comfort food, homemade baking is at the top of my list. There is nothing quite like baked goods fresh from the oven.

These days many people don't have a lot of storage space, so being able to bake only the amount you intend to use and enjoy fresh, with no leftovers to worry about, is such a bonus. The recipes in this book take the guesswork out of trying to downsize traditional recipes, which can often be disastrous. It isn't always possible to reduce the quantities in a recipe by half or more and end up with the same result you'd expect from the original recipe. Many ingredients simply don't divide neatly; for example, 1 egg, $\frac{1}{4}$ tsp (1 mL) baking powder, 1 can (10 oz/300 mL) sweetened condensed milk, 1 oz (30 g) chocolate.

In the pages that follow, you'll find small-batch recipes for many of your favorite cookie and bar recipes; fabulous quick breads, including muffins, loaves, scones, shortcakes and coffee cakes; wonderful cupcakes, mini cakes and cheesecakes for family and entertaining; flaky pastry that will hold a variety of fillings for pies and tarts; and spectacular desserts that include cobblers, crisps and puddings. I've also included a selection of gluten-free goodies that everyone will love—whether or not you are following a gluten-free diet.

There are other benefits to small-batch baking, too: recipes require smaller quantities of ingredients, baking time is considerably less and cleanup is a breeze. Almost all of the recipes in this book can be mixed by hand, using a whisk or wooden spoon rather than an electric mixer.

I've done the testing, adjusting and retesting for you. I've also provided storage and freezing instructions for people who prefer to bake ahead and save some to enjoy later on. Whether you are an experienced or novice baker, this book will help you enjoy everyday favorites as well as special-occasion treats.

Happy baking—and eating!

Baking for Success

Baking can be foolproof when you have the proper equipment and ingredients to work with and you follow the recipes exactly.

Equipment

Kitchen scale

Invest in a scale that has the ability to tare out the bowl weight. For small amounts of certain ingredients like chocolate, weighing is easier and more accurate.

Measuring cups and spoons

You'll need an accurate set of graduated dry ingredient measures and spoons, as well as glass or plastic measuring cups for liquid ingredients.

Electric mixer

Although most of the small-batch recipes in this book can be mixed using a whisk or wooden spoon, you will need an electric mixer to make cheesecakes, whipped cream and frostings. A handheld mixer is best for small quantities.

Food processor

A food processor is a valuable time-saving tool for chopping, puréeing and blending. Both mini processors and regular processors work well, so use whatever you already have.

Culinary torch

Although not essential, a culinary torch is a handy gadget for melting sugar on crème brûlée as well as crisping the tops of some puddings. The broiling element in your oven can also do the job.

Parchment paper

This is something I can't live without. When you use parchment to line your pans and cookie sheets, nothing will stick. For loaves and bars, I also use it to lift the entire product out of the pan for easy cutting. It also makes pan cleanup simple. Follow individual recipes for recommendations.

Pastry blender

For some doughs, shortbreads and crusts for bars and pastry, a pastry blender is used to cut cold butter into the flour mixture. I prefer pastry blenders with flexible wires versus stiff ones. You can also use a food processor or two knives.

Spatulas

Rubber spatulas are used for folding in ingredients as well as cleaning bowls to get all the batter/dough into the pan. Silicone spatulas are great, as they can be used with hot mixtures as well as cold. Always keep a few spatulas on hand. Small metal offset spatulas are handy for spreading batter into a pan and frosting cakes.

Wire whisk

I use wire whisks a lot in place of an electric mixer. Small- and medium-sized whisks are best.

Wooden spoons

Because wooden spoons are slightly stiffer than whisks, they are ideal for mixing doughs and creaming together ingredients.

Wire cooling racks

Almost every baked good should be placed on a wire rack to cool, either in the pan or individually. Doing so allows the air to circulate and speeds cooling.

Bowls

A variety of bowls in different sizes is a must in any kitchen. Glass and metal bowls are preferable. Small microwave-safe bowls work well for melting things like chocolate and butter.

Zester/grater

A fine-toothed grater (such as those made by Microplane) is ideal for zesting citrus. Graters with three or four sides often include a fine grater that will work as well.

Rolling pin, cloth and cover

These are great for rolling out pastry and cookie dough. The cloth and cover, although not essential, make rolling out dough a breeze. The dough doesn't stick, and you don't have to worry about it becoming tough because you've added flour to keep the dough from sticking.

Baking sheets

These are a must for baking cookies. I prefer metal pans over nonstick. Nonstick surfaces are easily scratched; they are also darker, which causes cookies to bake more quickly. If you do use nonstick baking sheets, reduce the oven temperature by 25°F (10°C). I always line baking sheets with parchment paper.

Loaf pans

I use traditional loaf pans for bars and squares as well as mini loaf pans for quick breads and small cakes. Although several sizes are available for each, I routinely use the following:

Standard loaf pans:
9 by 5 inches (23 by 12.5 cm)
8 by 4 inches (20 by 10 cm)

Mini loaf pans:
Metal: $5\frac{1}{2}$ by $2\frac{3}{4}$ inches (14 by 7 cm)
Metal or foil: $5\frac{1}{2}$ by $3\frac{1}{4}$ inches (14 by 8 cm)

Muffin pans

Regular muffin pans with six $\frac{1}{2}$-cup (125 mL) cups are great for small-batch baking. If all you have is a 12-cup pan, it is best to fill the unused cups with water to ensure even cooking and prevent the pan from burning. Muffin pans can also be used for cupcakes and tarts. Jumbo muffin pans, although not essential, make great mini pies.

Cake pans

I use small 6-inch (15 cm) or 5-inch (12.5 cm) round cake pans, and 6-inch (15 cm) square pans for layer cakes and coffee cakes.

Springform pans

I use small 6-inch (15 cm) pans with removable rims for cheesecakes.

Tart pans with removable bottoms

Small 6-inch (15 cm) tart pans are ideal for desserts like flans and tarts. Mini 3-inch (7.5 cm) pans are ideal for baking pecan tarts.

Pie plates

Small 6-inch (15 cm) pie plates—metal or ceramic or ovenproof glass—are ideal for small pies. (They are really cute, too.)

Baking dishes

I use small baking dishes and casseroles for scaled-down desserts and puddings. See individual recipes for sizes.

Ramekins

I use ramekins for desserts such as crème brûlée and custards. See individual recipes for sizes.

Baking Ingredients

I highly recommend using quality ingredients. Your finished product is only as good as what you put into it. This is especially true for things like chocolate, cocoa powder, nuts, yogurt and butter. For small-batch baking, bulk stores are a great source for ingredients like nuts, coconut, chocolate and spices; you can buy just the amounts you require as you need them.

Flours

For simplicity I have used all-purpose or whole-wheat flour in all of the recipes. For best results and freshness, I recommend buying reputable brands and storing flour in a cool, dark place in airtight containers.

Sugars

Sugar is a common ingredient used in almost all baking. Use the type specified in each recipe for best results.

Granulated sugar: This sugar is most commonly called for in the recipes in this book. For some shortbreads, superfine sugar (also known as fruit sugar or instant-dissolving sugar) is recommended.

Brown sugar: Brown sugar is less refined than granulated sugar. The darker the color, the more molasses and moisture it contains. Golden and dark brown sugar are generally interchangeable in recipes (dark brown provides a more caramel-like flavor). I like to use golden brown sugar, but the choice is yours.

Confectioners' (icing) sugar: Confectioners' sugar is powdered sugar with a little cornstarch added. It is used in icings and some shortbreads and as a sweetener for whipping cream. It is wise to sift it before using, as it tends to clump during storage.

Other sweeteners: Fancy molasses, liquid honey, corn syrup and pure maple syrup all work well. Follow the recommendation in each recipe for best results.

Eggs

Eggs contribute to leavening, texture, color, flavor, volume and richness in recipes. All the recipes in this book were tested using large eggs. Where scaling down the amount of egg was a problem (say, when the original recipe called for only one egg), I call for an egg yolk. The leftover egg white can be used in other recipes (they also make delicious omelets!). Remove eggs from the refrigerator about 1 hour before using, to bring to room temperature. If eggs are to be separated, however, this is easier to do when they are cold.

Leavening agents

Baking soda and baking powder cause doughs and batters to rise, giving baked goods a light, tender texture. Check the best-before date on your packaging and always use fresh.

Dairy products

Milk: All recipes were tested using reduced-fat (2%) milk. Whole (3.25%) milk and low-fat (1%) milk will also work, so use whatever you have on hand.

Buttermilk: Buttermilk is available in most supermarkets, but you can also make your own. To make 1 cup (250 mL) buttermilk, combine milk with 1 tbsp (15 mL) vinegar or lemon juice in a small bowl or measuring cup. Let stand for 5 minutes, then stir. You can also substitute an equal amount of plain yogurt.

Evaporated milk: Evaporated milk is sold in cans. It has a slightly caramel flavor that is delicious in custard-based desserts.

Sweetened condensed milk: Sweetened condensed milk is evaporated milk that has been reduced and sweetened. Whole- and low-fat versions work equally well. Recipes will usually call for half a 10 oz (300 mL) can ($^2/_3$ cup/150 mL) or less, so I've provided measurements. Store leftovers in an airtight container in the refrigerator.

Sour cream: Recipes were tested using 14% MF sour cream. Using low-fat sour cream is fine, but I don't recommend no-fat sour cream. You can substitute an equal amount of plain Greek yogurt if you like.

Cream cheese: Recipes were tested using regular (full-fat) cream cheese blocks. Using low-fat cream cheese is fine, but don't use the tubs of spreadable cream cheese—the consistency is too soft.

Butter: In my opinion, there is no substitute for pure butter. The choice of salted or unsalted is up to you. I usually use salted unless the recipe specifies otherwise. Unless it is to be melted, bring butter to room temperature before using, for easy mixing.

Oils

Vegetable or canola oil is used when required.

Chocolate

Chocolate is a staple in my kitchen. Semisweet, bittersweet and unsweetened chocolate squares or pieces are used throughout the recipes in this book. Chocolate chips are usually called for in recipes where they will hold their shape; squares are used for melting.

For an accurate measurement, it is best to weigh chocolate.

To melt chocolate, chop the squares into pieces. For the small quantities, I find it easiest to melt chocolate in the microwave. Simply place chocolate in a microwave-safe bowl and heat on Medium for 45 seconds to 1 minute, until almost melted, stirring halfway through. After heating, stir again until smooth. (You can also melt chocolate in a small saucepan over low heat, stirring often, until smooth.)

Cocoa powder: Cocoa powder is an unsweetened powder made from chocolate liquor with most of the cocoa butter removed. It tends to clump during storage, so sift after measuring for easy blending.

Nuts

Nuts add flavor and texture to baked goods. As you can tell from my recipes, I love nuts. Bulk food stores are a great source for nuts, as you can buy only as much as you need to ensure you are always using fresh nuts (they can go rancid quickly). For optimum flavor, toast nuts on a baking sheet in a preheated 350°F (180°C) oven for 5 to 10 minutes, stirring often, until golden and fragrant. Use salted or unsalted nuts to suit your preference and feel free to substitute whatever nuts you have on hand.

Coconut

To ensure freshness, buy coconut as you need it (bulk food stores are a great source). Coconut should be soft and a bit chewy, not dry. Sweetened and unsweetened coconut are interchangeable in the recipes in this book.

Flavorings

Use pure (not artificial) extracts, especially vanilla. Pure extracts are more expensive, but the resulting flavor is well worth it.

Spices

Spices lose their flavor over time, so purchase small quantities in bulk food stores. Store spices in a cool, dark place for no longer than 6 months.

Dried fruits

To ensure freshness, buy dried fruit as needed. Fresh dried fruits are soft and somewhat moist.

Fresh fruits

For the best flavor and texture I like to use whatever fruit is in season. Remember that when a recipe calls for citrus zest and juice, you should remove the zest before juicing.

Frozen and canned fruits

Some frozen and canned fruits are better than others. Cranberries, for example, are great either fresh or frozen. Follow the recommendations in each recipe.

Baking Tips and Techniques

Be prepared. Before starting to bake, gather all your ingredients and equipment. There is nothing more frustrating than starting to mix the ingredients, only to realize you are missing something or don't have the right baking pan. Having everything at the ready also ensures that you won't accidentally omit an ingredient. Allow time for cold ingredients like butter and eggs to come to room temperature for easy mixing.

   Preheat your oven and prepare pan(s) as directed in each recipe at least 15 minutes ahead of baking. Most baked goods are baked on the middle rack unless specified otherwise.

Measuring accurately

- Use the correct measuring utensil for the ingredient.

- To measure dry ingredients like flour and granulated sugar, lightly spoon the item into a dry measuring cup (do not shake or pack it down). Then, using a spatula or knife, level off the top. The exception is brown sugar, which should be packed firmly into the measuring cup, then leveled off.

- For dry ingredients like baking soda, baking powder and spices, use measuring spoons the same as you would dry measuring cups. Fill to the top of the spoon, then level off with a spatula or knife.

- Measure liquids in glass liquid measuring cups with spouts. Verify the measure at eye level.

- Measure butter using the gauge on the package.

- If the preparation method (chopped, melted, sliced) is listed before the food—such as "chopped nuts"—it means that you prepare the food before measuring it. If the preparation is listed after the food—as in "butter, melted"—you measure first, then prepare.

Follow the recipe

Changing one of the ingredients or adjusting the amount can often have disastrous results. In most recipes I have provided variations and substitutions that will work. By following the recipe for measurements, ingredients and methods, you are sure to succeed.

Mixing

When a combination of several dry ingredients will be mixed with liquid or creamed mixtures, it is smart to first whisk together the dry ingredients (flour, baking powder, baking powder, salt, spice) and set them aside. Then combine the other ingredients as specified in the recipe and stir together as directed.

Baking

- Unless otherwise specified, the recipes were tested in metal pans. Reduce the oven temperature by 25°F (10°C) if using glass or nonstick pans.

- I prefer to bake on only one rack at a time, which is almost always possible for small-batch baking.

- Oven temperature can vary and fluctuate per oven, so set the timer for the minimum time indicated. You can always bake longer but you can't fix an overbaked product. Tips to indicate doneness for each recipe are given. Tips for when and how to remove items from pans for cooling are also indicated.

- Although all my recipes were tested in a regular oven, the small batches may be suited to toaster ovens. Follow manufacturer's directions for temperature and time accuracy.

Gluten-free baking

- Although only a small percentage of the population has been diagnosed with celiac disease, a growing number of people are choosing to avoid the gluten in wheat, barley and rye because of an allergy or sensitivity, or simply because they feel it promotes a healthier lifestyle. I've included a chapter on gluten-free baking that features muffins, cakes and cookies—recipes that everyone will love, whether they eat wheat or not.

- Baking your own homemade treats has several benefits. Many packaged gluten-free foods are high in sugar and low in fiber. They are usually expensive and, in my opinion, often not very yummy. Baking only the amount you are going to use means you don't have to eat the same thing for the next four days to finish it up.

- Many grocery stores and bulk food stores stock a rapidly growing number of gluten-free ingredients, making gluten-free baking even easier.

Cookies

Frosted Carrot Cake Cookies

◆

These cookies taste like bite-size morsels of carrot cake. Better still, you don't need a plate and fork to eat them.

MAKES 8 MEDIUM OR 6 LARGE COOKIES (SEE TIPS, OPPOSITE)

- Preparation: 20 minutes
- Baking: 12 minutes
- Freezing: excellent

Tips

Parchment paper makes cleanup easy. It also solves the problem of cookies sticking to the pan. Washable silicone sheets also work well.

Be sure to peel the carrots. If peel is left on, sometimes it will show up as green flecks in baked cookies.

- **Preheat oven to 350°F (180°C)**
- **Baking sheet, greased or lined with parchment paper (see Tips, left)**

COOKIES

2/3 cup	all-purpose flour	150 mL
1/8 tsp	baking soda	0.5 mL
Pinch	salt	Pinch
1/4 tsp	ground cinnamon	1 mL
Pinch	ground nutmeg	Pinch
Pinch	ground cloves	Pinch
1/4 cup	butter, softened	60 mL
1/4 cup	granulated sugar	60 mL
2 tbsp	packed brown sugar	30 mL
1	egg	1
1/2 cup	finely shredded peeled carrots (see Tips, left)	125 mL
1/4 cup	chopped pecans	60 mL

FROSTING

2 tbsp	cream cheese, softened	30 mL
1 tbsp	butter, softened	15 mL
1/2 cup	confectioners' (icing) sugar, sifted	125 mL
	Chopped pecans, optional	

1. *Cookies:* In a small bowl, whisk together flour, baking soda, salt, cinnamon, nutmeg and cloves. Set aside.
2. In a medium bowl, using a wooden spoon, beat together butter and granulated and brown sugars. Add egg, beating until creamy. Gradually add flour mixture, stirring well. Stir in carrots and pecans.
3. Drop dough by heaping tablespoonfuls (22 mL) about 2 inches (5 cm) apart on prepared baking sheet.
4. Bake in preheated oven for 8 to 12 minutes or until golden. Let cool for 5 minutes on sheet, then transfer to a wire rack and cool completely.

Tips

Omit the frosting for fewer calories; note, however, that by giving up calories you are also losing some appearance, texture and flavor.

To make large cookies, drop dough by large spoonfuls (2 tbsp/30 mL). Bake for 10 to 14 minutes, as directed.

Frosted cookies will keep in an airtight container at room temperature for up to 1 week or can be frozen for up to 3 months (separate layers with waxed paper). Thaw and bring to room temperature before serving.

5. *Frosting:* In a small bowl, using a wooden spoon, beat together cream cheese and butter until smooth. Gradually add confectioners' sugar, beating well.

6. *Assembly:* Spread frosting evenly over tops of cookies. Sprinkle with chopped pecans, if desired.

Make Ahead: Dough can be refrigerated in an airtight container for up to a week or frozen for up to 3 months. Thaw in the refrigerator overnight or for 1 hour at room temperature before baking.

Variations

Substitute walnuts for the pecans, or omit them for a nut-free cookie.

Substitute an equal amount of raisins, coconut or dried cranberries for the nuts.

QUICK TIP

There is no need for an electric mixer when making small batches of cookies. You can get the butter-sugar mixture to a light, creamy consistency by beating it with a wooden spoon.

Cranberry Almond Oatmeal Cookies

◆

Dried fruit makes this old-fashioned oatmeal cookie chewy, and nuts provide a pleasing crunch.

MAKES 8 MEDIUM OR 6 LARGE COOKIES (SEE TIPS, OPPOSITE)

- Preparation: 15 minutes
- Baking: 14 minutes
- Freezing: excellent

Tips

I prefer combining the dry ingredients on a piece of waxed paper instead of dirtying a bowl. Then I use the paper as a funnel when adding them to the butter mixture.

There is no need for an electric mixer when making small batches of cookies. You can get the butter-sugar mixture to a light, creamy consistency by beating it with a wooden spoon.

- **Preheat oven to 350°F (180°C)**
- **Baking sheet, greased or lined with parchment paper (see Quick Tip, right)**

⅓ cup	all-purpose flour	75 mL
¼ tsp	baking powder	1 mL
Pinch	salt	Pinch
¼ tsp	ground cinnamon	1 mL
¼ cup	butter, softened	60 mL
¼ cup	packed brown sugar	60 mL
2 tbsp	granulated sugar	30 mL
1	egg	1
¼ tsp	pure almond extract	1 mL
½ cup	quick-cooking rolled oats	125 mL
⅓ cup	dried cranberries	75 mL
¼ cup	slivered almonds	60 mL

1. In a small bowl, whisk together flour, baking powder, salt and cinnamon (see Tips, left). Set aside.
2. In a medium bowl, using a wooden spoon, beat together butter and brown and granulated sugars. Add egg and almond extract, beating until creamy. Gradually add flour mixture, stirring well. Stir in oats, cranberries and almonds.
3. Drop dough by tablespoonfuls (15 mL) about 2 inches (5 cm) apart on prepared baking sheet. Flatten slightly with fingers.
4. Bake in preheated oven for 10 to 14 minutes or until golden. Let cool for 5 minutes on sheet, then transfer to a wire rack and cool completely.

Tips

To make large cookies, drop dough by large spoonfuls (2 tbsp/30 mL). Bake for 10 to 14 minutes, as directed.

Cooled cookies will keep in an airtight container at room temperature for up to 1 week or can be frozen for up to 3 months. Thaw and bring to room temperature before serving.

Make Ahead: Dough can be refrigerated in an airtight container for up to a week or frozen for up to 3 months. Thaw overnight in the refrigerator or for 1 hour at room temperature before baking.

Variations

Substitute chopped dried cherries or apricots for the cranberries.

Substitute pecans for the almonds.

QUICK TIP

Parchment paper makes cleanup easy. It also solves the problem of cookies sticking to the pan.

Raspberry Coconut Pinwheels

◆

This is a cheat's way to make pinwheel cookies. There's no rolling and cutting, unlike traditional refrigerated pinwheel cookies.

MAKES 8 MEDIUM OR 6 LARGE COOKIES (SEE TIPS, OPPOSITE)

- Preparation: 20 minutes
- Baking: 14 minutes
- Freezing: excellent

Tips

Bring butter to room temperature before using, for easy blending.

Use sweetened or unsweetened coconut—the choice is yours.

Seedless jam has a more intense flavor than jam with seeds.

- **Preheat oven to 375°F (190°C)**
- **Baking sheet, greased or lined with parchment paper**

¾ cup	all-purpose flour	175 mL
2 tbsp	quick-cooking rolled oats (see Quick Tip, right)	30 mL
¼ tsp	baking soda	1 mL
Pinch	salt	Pinch
¼ cup	butter, softened (see Tips, left)	60 mL
¼ cup	packed brown sugar	60 mL
3 tbsp	granulated sugar	45 mL
1	egg	1
¼ tsp	pure almond extract	1 mL
½ cup	flaked coconut (see Tips, left)	125 mL
1½ tbsp	raspberry jam (see Tips, left)	22 mL

1. In a small bowl, whisk together flour, oats, baking soda and salt. Set aside.
2. In a medium bowl, using a wooden spoon, beat together butter, brown and granulated sugars, egg and almond extract, until creamy. Gradually add flour mixture and coconut, stirring well. Set aside 3 tbsp (45 mL) of the dough for topping.
3. Drop dough by tablespoonfuls (15 mL) about 2 inches (5 cm) apart on prepared baking sheet. Using a floured finger, make a small indentation in each cookie. Fill indentation with ¼ tsp (1 mL) jam. Top jam with ½ tsp (2 mL) reserved dough, not quite covering it.
4. Bake in preheated oven for 10 to 14 minutes or until golden. Let cool for 5 minutes on sheet, then transfer to a wire rack and cool completely.

Tips

To make large cookies, drop dough by large spoonfuls (2 tbsp/30 mL). Bake for 10 to 14 minutes, as directed.

Cooled cookies will keep in an airtight container at room temperature for up to 1 week or can be frozen for up to 3 months. Thaw and bring to room temperature before serving.

Make Ahead: Dough can be refrigerated in an airtight container for up to a week or frozen for up to 3 months. Thaw in the refrigerator overnight or for 1 hour at room temperature before baking.

Variations

Use any jam you have. Blueberry, strawberry and apricot are all good.

QUICK TIP

Use quick-cooking rolled oats (not large-flake rolled oats) for the nicest texture.

Black Forest Cookies

◆

These scrumptious cookies have all the flavors of Black Forest cake, but in bite-size form.

MAKES 12 MEDIUM OR 8 LARGE COOKIES (SEE TIPS, BELOW)

- Preparation: 15 minutes
- Baking: 12 minutes
- Freezing: excellent

Tips

Use pure vanilla extract for baking. Its flavor far surpasses artificial versions.

To ensure even baking, bake only 8 cookies per sheet.

To make large cookies, drop dough by large spoonfuls (2 tbsp/30 mL). Bake for 10 to 14 minutes, as directed.

- **Preheat oven to 350°F (180°C)**
- **Baking sheet, ungreased**

7 tbsp	all-purpose flour	105 mL
¼ tsp	baking powder	1 mL
¼ tsp	baking soda	1 mL
Pinch	salt	Pinch
¼ cup	butter, softened	60 mL
3 tbsp	packed brown sugar	45 mL
2 tbsp	granulated sugar	30 mL
1	egg	1
¼ tsp	pure vanilla extract (see Tips, left)	1 mL
½ cup	quick-cooking rolled oats	125 mL
⅓ cup	white chocolate chips	75 mL
¼ cup	semisweet chocolate chips	60 mL
¼ cup	dried cherries, coarsely chopped (see Quick Tip, right)	60 mL
3 tbsp	slivered almonds	45 mL

1. In a small bowl, whisk together flour, baking powder, baking soda and salt. Set aside.
2. In a medium bowl, using a wooden spoon, beat together butter, brown and granulated sugars, egg and vanilla, until creamy. Gradually add flour mixture, stirring well. Stir in oats, white and semisweet chocolate chips, cherries and almonds.
3. Drop dough by heaping tablespoonfuls (22 mL) about 2 inches (5 cm) apart on baking sheet (see Tips, left).
4. Bake in preheated oven for 8 to 12 minutes or until golden (see Tips, left). Let cool for 5 minutes on sheet, then transfer to a wire rack and cool completely.

Tip

Cooled cookies will keep in an airtight container at room temperature for up to 1 week or can be frozen for up to 3 months. Thaw and bring to room temperature before serving.

Make Ahead: Dough can be refrigerated in an airtight container for up to a week or frozen for up to 3 months. Thaw overnight in the refrigerator or for 1 hour at room temperature before baking.

Variations

Substitute dried cranberries for the cherries. There is no need to chop the cranberries, as they are smaller.

For a sweeter flavor, use maraschino cherries, chopped and patted dry with a paper towel.

Substitute white chocolate chips for the semisweet chocolate chips.

QUICK TIP

Dried fruits such as apricots, raisins, cranberries and cherries are soft when fresh. Store them in the freezer to retain freshness. If dried fruit seems hard, place in a bowl, cover with boiling water and let stand for 5 minutes, until softened. Drain well and pat dry with paper towels.

Key Lime Coconut Macaroons

◆

These easy-to-make cookies will be particularly appealing to coconut lovers.

MAKES ABOUT 12 COOKIES

- Preparation: 10 minutes
- Baking: 25 minutes
- Freezing: not recommended

Tips

. . . .

Half a 14 oz (300 mL) can of sweetened condensed milk equals 2/3 cup (150 mL). Store leftover milk in an airtight container in the refrigerator for use in another recipe.

When zesting and juicing a lime, remove zest first, then warm the fruit in a microwave oven for 5 seconds before squeezing, to obtain the most juice.

Drizzle melted chocolate overtop cookies for an attractive finish.

Cooled cookies will keep in an airtight container at room temperature for up to 1 week.

- **Preheat oven to 325°F (160°C)**
- **Baking sheet, lined with parchment paper**

2/3 cup	sweetened condensed milk (see Tips, left)	150 mL
2 tbsp	freshly squeezed Key lime juice	30 mL
2 tbsp	all-purpose flour	30 mL
1¼ cups	sweetened shredded coconut	300 mL
1 tsp	freshly grated Key lime zest (see Tips, left)	5 mL

1. In a medium bowl, whisk together sweetened condensed milk and lime juice. Using a wooden spoon, gradually add flour, stirring until well blended. Stir in coconut and lime zest.
2. Drop dough by heaping tablespoonfuls (22 mL) about 1 inch (2.5 cm) apart on prepared baking sheet.
3. Bake in preheated oven for 20 to 25 minutes or until golden around edges. Let cool for 15 minutes on baking sheet, then transfer to a wire rack and cool completely.

Variations

For a slightly less sweet cookie, use unsweetened coconut.

Substitute Persian limes for the Key limes.

Mixed Seed and Fruit Spice Cookies

◆

Flax seeds give these cookies a wonderful crunch and unique flavor while adding nutritional value.

MAKES 12 MEDIUM OR 8 LARGE COOKIES (SEE TIPS, BELOW)

- Preparation: 20 minutes
- Baking: 12 minutes
- Freezing: excellent

Tips

Flax seeds are a good source of soluble fiber and omega-3 fatty acids. Consumption of omega-3 fatty acids has been linked with lower rates of heart disease and stroke. Store flax seeds in the freezer to prevent rancidity.

To make large cookies, drop dough by large spoonfuls (2 tbsp/30 mL). Bake for 10 to 14 minutes, as directed.

Cooled cookies will keep in an airtight container at room temperature for up to 1 week or can be frozen for up to 3 months. Thaw and bring to room temperature before serving.

Use your favorite dried fruits. Raisins or dried mango, cherries, dates and strawberries are all great.

- **Preheat oven to 350°F (180°C)**
- **Baking sheet, greased or lined with parchment paper**

7 tbsp	all-purpose flour	105 mL
3 tbsp	ground flax seeds (see Tips, left)	45 mL
¼ tsp	baking powder	1 mL
⅛ tsp	baking soda	0.5 mL
Pinch	salt	Pinch
¼ tsp	ground cinnamon	1 mL
¼ tsp	ground cloves	1 mL
⅛ tsp	ground nutmeg	0.5 mL
2 tbsp	butter, softened	30 mL
¼ cup	packed brown sugar	60 mL
1	egg	1
2 tbsp	corn syrup	30 mL
¼ cup	chopped dried apricots	60 mL
¼ cup	chopped dried cranberries	60 mL
2 tbsp	sunflower seeds	30 mL
1½ tbsp	sesame seeds	22 mL
1 tbsp	whole flax seeds	15 mL

1. In a small bowl, whisk together flour, ground flax seeds, baking powder, baking soda, salt, cinnamon, cloves and nutmeg. Set aside.
2. In a medium bowl, using a wooden spoon, beat together butter, brown sugar, egg and corn syrup, until creamy. Gradually add flour mixture, stirring well. Stir in apricots, cranberries, sunflower seeds, sesame seeds and whole flax seeds.
3. Drop dough by heaping tablespoonfuls (22 mL) about 2 inches (5 cm) apart on prepared baking sheet.
4. Bake in preheated oven for 8 to 12 minutes or until lightly browned. Let cool for 5 minutes on sheet, then transfer to a wire rack and cool completely.

Make Ahead: Dough can be refrigerated in an airtight container for up to a week or frozen for up to 3 months. Thaw overnight in the refrigerator or for 1 hour at room temperature before baking.

White Chocolate Nut Crisps

◆

Lots of crunchy nuts and creamy white chocolate make these cookies irresistible.

MAKES 8 MEDIUM OR 6 LARGE COOKIES (SEE TIPS, BELOW)

- Preparation: 20 minutes
- Baking: 18 minutes
- Freezing: excellent

Tips

Use pure vanilla extract for baking. Its flavor far surpasses artificial versions.

You can substitute ½ cup (125 mL) white chocolate chips for the white chocolate chunks.

Washable silicone sheets also work well here instead of parchment paper.

For chewy cookies, bake about 14 minutes or until golden around the edges. For crisp cookies, bake about 18 minutes or until tops of cookies are also light golden.

To make large cookies, drop dough by large spoonfuls (2 tbsp/30 mL). Bake for 15 to 19 minutes, as directed.

Cooled cookies will keep in an airtight container at room temperature for up to 1 week or can be frozen for up to 3 months. Thaw and bring to room temperature before serving.

- **Preheat oven to 300°F (150°C)**
- **Baking sheet, greased or lined with parchment paper**

½ cup	all-purpose flour	125 mL
¼ tsp	baking soda	1 mL
Pinch	salt	Pinch
3 tbsp	butter, softened	45 mL
¼ cup	packed brown sugar	60 mL
3 tbsp	granulated sugar	45 mL
1	egg yolk	1
¼ tsp	pure vanilla extract	1 mL
2½ oz	white chocolate, cut into chunks (½ cup/125 mL)	75 g
¼ cup	coarsely chopped macadamia nuts	60 mL
2 tbsp	chopped pecans	30 mL

1. In a small bowl, whisk together flour, baking soda and salt. Set aside.
2. In a medium bowl, using a wooden spoon, beat together butter, brown and granulated sugars, egg yolk and vanilla, until creamy. Gradually add flour mixture, stirring well. Stir in white chocolate chunks, macadamia nuts and pecans.
3. Drop dough by heaping tablespoonsfuls (22 mL) about 2 inches (5 cm) apart on prepared baking sheet.
4. Bake in preheated oven for 14 to 18 minutes or until golden. Let cool for 5 minutes on sheet, then transfer to a wire rack and cool completely.

Make Ahead: Dough can be refrigerated in an airtight container for up to a week or frozen for up to 3 months. Thaw overnight in the refrigerator or for 1 hour at room temperature before baking.

Variations

Use your favorite nuts. Slivered almonds, cashews and Brazil nuts are all good.

Replace the white chocolate with semisweet chocolate.

Sesame Snap Wafers

Make these your own by trying different seeds for a new look and taste.

MAKES ABOUT 12 COOKIES

- Preparation: 10 minutes
- Baking: 10 minutes
- Freezing: not recommended

Tips

Use pure vanilla extract for baking. Its flavor far surpasses artificial versions.

Many types and varieties of seeds are available in bulk food stores (where it is also ideal to buy small amounts).

These cookies will flatten and spread during baking, so be sure to leave enough room between them.

Cooled cookies will keep in an airtight container at room temperature for up to 2 weeks.

- **Preheat oven to 350°F (180°C)**
- **Baking sheet, lined with parchment paper or lightly greased aluminum foil**

2½ tbsp	all-purpose flour	37 mL
Pinch	baking powder	Pinch
2 tbsp	butter, softened	30 mL
¼ cup	packed brown sugar	60 mL
1	egg yolk	1
¼ tsp	pure vanilla extract (see Tips, left)	1 mL
5 tbsp	toasted sesame seeds	75 mL

1. In a small bowl, whisk together flour and baking powder. Set aside.
2. In a medium bowl, using a wooden spoon, beat together butter, brown sugar and egg yolk, until creamy. Stir in sesame seeds.
3. Drop by heaping teaspoonfuls (7 mL) about 2 inches (5 cm) apart on prepared baking sheet (see Tips, left).
4. Bake in preheated oven for 7 to 10 minutes or until lightly browned. Let cool for 5 minutes on sheet, then transfer to a wire rack and cool completely.

Variations

You can experiment with different seeds. Half black and half white sesame seeds looks nice. Or try substituting an equal quantity of hemp seeds. You can also use a mixture of seeds. Try 2 tbsp (30 mL) each sesame and chia seeds and 1 tbsp (15 mL) flax seeds—it looks attractive and tastes great.

Crunchy Cereal Cookies

◆

Breakfast couldn't taste better. These cookies are delicious any time of the day.

MAKES 8 MEDIUM OR 6 LARGE COOKIES (SEE TIPS, OPPOSITE)

- Preparation: 20 minutes
- Baking: 14 minutes
- Freezing: excellent

Tips

Use pure vanilla extract for baking. Its flavor far surpasses artificial versions.

There is no need for an electric mixer when making small batches of cookies. You can get the butter-sugar mixture to a light, creamy consistency by beating it with a wooden spoon.

- **Preheat oven to 350°F (180°C)**
- **Baking sheet, ungreased**

½ cup	all-purpose flour	125 mL
⅛ tsp	baking soda	0.5 mL
⅛ tsp	cream of tartar	0.5 mL
Pinch	salt	Pinch
⅓ cup	packed brown sugar	75 mL
2½ tbsp	butter, softened	37 mL
2½ tbsp	vegetable oil	37 mL
1	egg yolk	1
¼ tsp	pure vanilla extract (see Tips, left)	1 mL
⅓ cup	crisp rice cereal	75 mL
2½ tbsp	quick-cooking rolled oats	37 mL
2½ tbsp	sliced almonds	37 mL
1½ tbsp	unsweetened flaked coconut	22 mL
1½ tbsp	sunflower seeds	22 mL
1½ tbsp	wheat germ (see Quick Tip, right)	22 mL

1. In a small bowl, whisk together flour, baking soda, cream of tartar and salt. Set aside.
2. In a medium bowl, using a wooden spoon, beat together brown sugar, butter, oil, egg yolk and vanilla, until creamy. Gradually add flour mixture, stirring well. Stir in cereal, oats, almonds, coconut, sunflower seeds and wheat germ, until well combined.
3. Drop dough by heaping tablespoonfuls (22 mL) about 2 inches (5 cm) apart on baking sheet.
4. Bake in preheated oven for 10 to 14 minutes or until light golden. Let cool for 5 minutes on sheet, then transfer to a wire rack and cool completely.

Tips

To make large cookies, drop dough by large spoonfuls (2 tbsp/30 mL). Bake as directed.

Cooled cookies will keep in an airtight container at room temperature for up to 1 week or can be frozen for up to 3 months. Thaw and bring to room temperature before serving.

Make Ahead: Dough can be refrigerated in an airtight container for up to a week or frozen for up to 3 months. Thaw in the refrigerator overnight or for 1 hour at room temperature before baking.

Variations

Other crisp cereals, such as crushed corn flakes, work well in place of the rice cereal.

Substitute pecans or walnuts for the almonds.

Substitute pumpkin seeds for the sunflower seeds.

Substitute hemp seeds for the wheat germ.

QUICK TIP

I like to use toasted wheat germ, which is sold in bottles. It has a nice nutty flavor and pleasing texture. Store wheat germ in the freezer to keep it fresh.

Chocolate Chunk and Pumpkin Seed Drops

◆

These spiced drop cookies taste and resemble small, mounded brownies.

MAKES ABOUT 8 COOKIES

- Preparation: 20 minutes
- Baking: 20 minutes
- Freezing: excellent

Tips

Cocoa powder tends to clump in storage, so press it through a fine-mesh sieve to remove any lumps.

Add some zip by using hot smoked paprika.

- **Preheat oven to 350°F (180°C)**
- **2 baking sheets, greased or lined with parchment paper**

¾ cup	raw pumpkin seeds	175 mL
1¼ cups	all-purpose flour	300 mL
¼ cup	unsweetened cocoa powder, sifted (see Tips, left)	60 mL
¾ tsp	salt	3 mL
¼ tsp	baking soda	1 mL
¼ tsp	ground cinnamon	1 mL
⅛ tsp	smoked paprika (see Tips, left)	0.5 mL
½ cup	butter, softened	125 mL
¾ cup	packed brown sugar	175 mL
⅔ cup	granulated sugar	150 mL
1	egg	1
⅔ cup	bittersweet chocolate chunks	150 mL
	Flaky sea salt	

1. Scatter pumpkin seeds onto a baking sheet.
2. Bake in preheated oven for 8 to 10 minutes, stirring occasionally, until light golden. Let pan cool on a wire rack.
3. In a small bowl, whisk together flour, cocoa powder, salt, baking soda, cinnamon and paprika. Set aside.
4. In a medium bowl, using a wooden spoon, beat together butter, brown and granulated sugars and egg, until creamy. Gradually add flour mixture, stirring well. Stir in chocolate chunks and toasted pumpkin seeds, until well combined.

Tips

To allow room for spreading, divide the balls between two baking sheets (half on each sheet). If you want to bake both trays at the same time, rotate sheets in the oven halfway through.

Cooled cookies will keep in an airtight container at room temperature for up to 1 week or can be frozen for up to 3 months. Thaw and bring to room temperature before serving.

5. Drop dough in 8 equal portions, about $1/3$ cup (75 mL) each onto prepared baking sheet, spacing about 3 inches (7.5 cm) apart (see Tips, left). Sprinkle lightly with sea salt.

6. Bake in preheated oven for 15 to 20 minutes or until lightly browned and firm around the edges but still soft in the center. Let cool 5 minutes on sheet, then transfer to a wire rack and cool completely.

Make Ahead: Dough can be refrigerated in an airtight container for up to a week or frozen for up to 3 months. Thaw in the refrigerator overnight or for 1 hour at room temperature before baking.

Variations

Substitute semisweet chocolate for the bittersweet.

Omit paprika if desired.

Hermit Cookies

◆

I'm not sure where the name originated, but these heritage cookies, which usually contain raisins and walnuts, have been around for a long time. They were my grandmother's favorite.

MAKES ABOUT 12 COOKIES

- Preparation: 20 minutes
- Baking: 14 minutes
- Freezing: excellent

Tips

I like the flavor of Medjool dates or honey dates, especially when they are soft and fresh.

Some dates will stick to your knife when chopping. Lightly oil the blade or spray it with cooking spray to help prevent sticking.

If you are a ginger lover you can replace the dates with candied ginger and use ground ginger instead of cinnamon.

Cooled cookies will keep in an airtight container at room temperature for up to 1 week or can be frozen for up to 3 months. Thaw and bring to room temperature before serving.

- **Preheat oven to 375°F (190°C)**
- **Baking sheet, greased or lined with parchment paper**

⅔ cup	all-purpose flour	150 mL
⅛ tsp	baking soda	0.5 mL
Pinch	salt	Pinch
¼ tsp	ground cinnamon	1 mL
⅛ tsp	ground nutmeg	0.5 mL
Pinch	ground cloves	Pinch
3½ tbsp	butter, softened	52 mL
¼ cup	packed brown sugar	60 mL
2½ tbsp	granulated sugar	37 mL
1	egg	1
⅓ cup	raisins	75 mL
⅓ cup	chopped pitted dates (see Tips, left)	75 mL
¼ cup	coarsely chopped walnuts	60 mL

1. In a small bowl, sift together flour, baking soda, salt, cinnamon, nutmeg and cloves. Set aside.
2. In a medium bowl, using a wooden spoon, beat together butter, brown and granulated sugars and egg, until creamy. Gradually add flour mixture, stirring well. Add raisins, dates and walnuts. Stir well.
3. Drop dough by heaping tablespoonfuls (22 mL) about 2 inches (5 cm) apart on prepared baking sheet.
4. Bake in preheated oven for 10 to 14 minutes or until golden. Let cool for 5 minutes on sheet, then transfer to a wire rack and cool completely.

Make Ahead: Dough can be refrigerated in an airtight container for up to a week or frozen for up to 3 months. Thaw overnight in the refrigerator or for 1 hour at room temperature before baking.

Variations

Use all dates or all raisins to suit your preference.

Omit the nuts.

Vary the amount of spices to suit your taste.

Oatmeal Candy Cookies

◆

Although moms prefer that their kids not eat candy, it's easier to justify when it's combined with an oatmeal cookie.

MAKES ABOUT 8 COOKIES

- Preparation: 15 minutes
- Baking: 14 minutes
- Freezing: excellent

Tips

. . . .

If you like the nutty flavor of whole wheat flour, you can substitute an equal quantity for the all-purpose flour. When trying out this substitution for the first time, I prefer to use a half-and-half mixture to see if I like the flavor.

The most common brands of candy-coated chocolate pieces are M&M's, Smarties and Reese's Pieces. They are available in bulk stores and most stores that carry candies and snacks.

Cooled cookies will keep in an airtight container for up to 1 week or can be frozen for up to 3 months. Thaw and bring to room temperature before serving.

- **Preheat oven to 350°F (180°C)**
- **Baking sheet, greased or lined with parchment paper**

¼ cup	all-purpose flour (see Tips, left)	60 mL
½ tsp	baking powder	2 mL
⅛ tsp	baking soda	0.5 mL
Pinch	salt	Pinch
2 tbsp	butter, softened	30 mL
2 tbsp	granulated sugar	30 mL
2 tbsp	packed brown sugar	30 mL
1	egg yolk	1
¼ tsp	vanilla extract	1 mL
¼ cup	quick-cooking rolled oats	60 mL
¼ cup	candy-coated chocolate pieces (see Tips, left)	60 mL
2 tbsp	unsweetened flaked coconut	30 mL

1. In a small bowl, whisk together flour, baking powder, baking soda and salt. Set aside.
2. In a medium bowl, using a wooden spoon, beat together butter, granulated and brown sugars, egg yolk and vanilla, until creamy. Gradually add flour mixture, stirring well. Stir in oats, candies and coconut.
3. Drop dough by heaping tablespoonfuls (22 mL) about 2 inches (5 cm) apart on prepared baking sheet.
4. Bake in preheated oven for 10 to 14 minutes or until golden. Let cool for 5 minutes on sheet, then transfer to a wire rack and cool completely.

Make Ahead: Dough can be refrigerated in an airtight container for up to a week or frozen for up to 3 months. Thaw overnight in the refrigerator or for 1 hour at room temperature before baking.

Variation

Replace the candy pieces with chopped chocolate-covered nuts or halved baking gumdrops. Baking gumdrops are available at bulk stores; they are smaller than regular gumdrops and don't melt when heated.

Milk Chocolate Peanut Butter Cookies

◆

These chocolate cookies have a mild peanut butter taste. They're perfect with a glass of milk for an after-school treat.

MAKES 8 MEDIUM OR 6 LARGE COOKIES (SEE TIPS, BELOW)

- Preparation: 15 minutes
- Baking: 16 minutes
- Freezing: excellent

Tips

Check the best-before date on peanut butter. It can go rancid quickly.

If you prefer more crunch, substitute ¼ cup (60 mL) crunchy peanut butter for the creamy.

To make large cookies, drop dough by large spoonfuls (2 tbsp/30 mL). Bake for 16 minutes, as directed.

Cooled cookies will keep in an airtight container at room temperature for up to 1 week or can be frozen for up to 3 months. Thaw and bring to room temperature before serving.

- **Preheat oven to 350°F (180°C)**
- **Baking sheet, ungreased or lined with parchment paper**

⅔ cup	all-purpose flour	150 mL
¼ tsp	baking soda	1 mL
¼ cup	butter, softened	60 mL
3 tbsp	creamy peanut butter (see Tips, left)	45 mL
¼ cup	granulated sugar	60 mL
¼ cup	packed brown sugar	60 mL
1	egg yolk	1
¾ cup	milk chocolate chips	175 mL

1. In a small bowl, whisk together flour and baking soda. Set aside.
2. In a medium bowl, using a wooden spoon, beat together butter, peanut butter, granulated and brown sugars and egg yolk, until creamy. Gradually add flour mixture, stirring well. Add chocolate chips and stir until evenly distributed.
3. Drop dough by heaping tablespoonfuls (22 mL) about 2 inches (5 cm) apart on prepared baking sheet.
4. Bake in preheated oven for 12 to 16 minutes or until light golden. Let cool for 5 minutes on sheet, then transfer to a wire rack and cool completely.

Make Ahead: Dough can be refrigerated in an airtight container for up to a week or frozen for up to 3 months. Thaw in the refrigerator overnight or for 1 hour at room temperature before baking.

Variations

Add ¼ cup (60 mL) chopped peanuts along with the chocolate chips in Step 2.

For a stronger chocolate flavor use semisweet chocolate chips.

Butterscotch Cashew Slices

◆

With a roll of dough in the refrigerator, you can bake these as you need them and enjoy them fresh.

MAKES ABOUT 12 COOKIES

- Preparation: 20 minutes
- Chilling: 3 hours
- Baking: 12 minutes
- Freezing: excellent

Tips

For easy shaping, place dough on parchment paper, plastic wrap or waxed paper and roll up.

Use a sharp serrated knife to slice these cookies. When slicing, rotate the roll frequently to avoid flattening one side and ensure evenly shaped round cookies.

Be sure to leave space between the cookies on the baking sheet. They will flatten and spread during baking.

Underbake for chewy cookies (9 minutes) and bake a little longer (12 minutes) for crisp ones.

• **Baking sheet, greased or lined with parchment paper**

¾ cup	all-purpose flour	175 mL
¼ tsp	baking soda	1 mL
Pinch	salt	Pinch
¼ cup	butter, softened	60 mL
2 tbsp	granulated sugar	30 mL
2 tbsp	packed brown sugar	30 mL
1	egg	1
¼ tsp	pure vanilla extract	1 mL
½ cup	butterscotch chips	125 mL
¼ cup	chopped cashews	60 mL

1. In a small bowl, whisk together flour, baking soda and salt. Set aside.
2. In a medium bowl, using a wooden spoon, beat together butter and granulated and brown sugars. Add egg and vanilla, beating until light and creamy. Gradually add flour mixture, stirring well. Stir in butterscotch chips and cashews.
3. With floured hands, shape dough into a cylinder 6 inches (15 cm) long (see Tips, left). Wrap and refrigerate until firm, at least 3 hours or overnight.
4. When ready to bake, preheat oven to 350°F (180°C).
5. Unwrap dough and cut into ½-inch (1 cm) slices. Arrange slices about 2 inches (5 cm) apart on prepared baking sheet (see Tips, left).
6. Bake in preheated oven for 9 to 12 minutes or until golden around the edges (see Tips, left). Let cool for 5 minutes on sheet, then transfer to a wire rack and cool completely.

Make Ahead: Dough can be refrigerated in an airtight container for up to 3 weeks or frozen for up to 3 months. Thaw in refrigerator overnight before baking.

Variations

Substitute chocolate chips for the butterscotch chips. Use your favorite nut in place of the cashews.

Apricot Fig Pinwheels

I speak from experience when I say that even people who claim they don't like figs love these cookies.

MAKES ABOUT 18 COOKIES

- Preparation: 30 minutes
- Chilling: 4 hours
- Baking: 10 minutes
- Freezing: excellent

Tip

Be sure to cut the woody stems off the figs before chopping.

• Baking sheet, greased or lined with parchment paper

$\frac{1}{2}$ cup	all-purpose flour	125 mL
$\frac{1}{2}$ tsp	baking powder	2 mL
Pinch	salt	Pinch
2 tbsp	butter, softened	30 mL
$\frac{1}{4}$ cup	granulated sugar	60 mL
1	egg yolk	1
$\frac{1}{4}$ tsp	pure vanilla extract	1 mL
3 tbsp	finely chopped dried figs (see Quick Tip, right)	45 mL
2 tbsp	sweetened flaked coconut	30 mL
2 tbsp	apricot jam (see Tip, right)	30 mL

1. In a small bowl, whisk together flour, baking powder and salt. Set aside.
2. In a medium bowl, using a wooden spoon, beat together butter, sugar, egg yolk and vanilla, until light and creamy. Gradually add flour mixture, stirring well.
3. Turn dough out onto a clean work surface lightly dusted in flour. Using your hands, knead dough until smooth.
4. Shape dough into a flat disk and place between two sheets of waxed paper. Roll out dough into a 6- by 7-inch (15 by 18 cm) rectangle. Set aside.
5. In a small bowl, using a wooden spoon, combine figs, coconut and jam, stirring well.
6. Remove top sheet of waxed paper. Spread jam mixture evenly over dough, leaving a $\frac{1}{2}$-inch (1 cm) border along one long side. Starting with the opposite long side and using the bottom sheet of waxed paper to help you, roll up the dough tightly, jelly-roll fashion. Press edge to seal and, using your hands, shape roll into a nice cylinder. Wrap and refrigerate until firm, at least 4 hours.
7. When ready to bake, preheat oven to 375°F (190°C).

Use a thick jam, not a light, sugar-reduced spread, which is too soft to work in these cookies.

8. Unwrap dough and cut into ¼-inch (0.5 cm) slices. Arrange slices about 2 inches (5 cm) apart on prepared baking sheet.

9. Bake in preheated oven for 7 to 10 minutes or until golden around edges. Let cool for 5 minutes on sheet, then transfer to a wire rack and cool completely.

Make Ahead: Dough can be refrigerated in an airtight container for up to 3 weeks or frozen for up to 3 months. Thaw in refrigerator overnight before baking.

Variations

Substitute chopped dried apricots or nuts for the figs.

Substitute orange marmalade or peach jam for the apricot jam.

QUICK TIP

Use whatever variety of fig you prefer. Golden Calimyrna figs look the best with apricot jam. If you're using Black Mission figs, substitute an equal quantity of raspberry jam for the apricot.

Lemon Lime Slices

◆

Tender, light and crisp—
enjoy these cookies with
a cup of tea or bowl
of sherbet.

MAKES ABOUT
12 COOKIES

- Preparation: 20 minutes
- Chilling: 3 hours
- Baking: 12 minutes
- Freezing: excellent

Tips

For easy shaping, place
dough on parchment paper,
plastic wrap or waxed paper
and roll up.

Use a sharp serrated knife
to slice these cookies.
When slicing, rotate the
roll frequently to avoid
flattening one side and
ensure evenly shaped
round cookies.

When juicing citrus, remove
zest first, then warm the
fruit in a microwave oven for
5 seconds before squeezing,
to obtain the most juice.

For an all-lemon flavor,
substitute more lemon zest
and juice for the lime.

These make great sandwich
cookies. Spread lemon or
lime curd or lemon icing
between two cookies.

• Baking sheet, greased or lined with parchment paper

7 tbsp	all-purpose flour	105 mL
1 tbsp	cornstarch	15 mL
Pinch	salt	Pinch
3 tbsp	butter, softened	45 mL
4 tsp	confectioners' (icing) sugar, sifted	20 mL
1 tsp	freshly grated lemon zest (see Tips, left)	5 mL
1 tsp	freshly grated lime zest	5 mL
1½ tsp	freshly squeezed lemon juice	7 mL
1½ tsp	freshly squeezed lime juice	7 mL
2 tbsp	colored coarse sugar (yellow and green)	30 mL

1. In a small bowl, sift together flour, cornstarch and salt. Set aside.
2. In a medium bowl, using a wooden spoon, beat together butter, confectioners' sugar, lemon and lime zest, and lemon and lime juices, until light and creamy. Gradually add flour mixture, stirring well. Shape dough into a cylinder 5 inches (12.5 cm) long.
3. Spread coarse sugar over a sheet of waxed paper. Roll dough in sugar until evenly coated. Wrap and refrigerate until firm, at least 3 hours or overnight.
4. When ready to bake, preheat oven to 350°F (180°C).
5. Unwrap dough and cut into ¼-inch (0.5 cm) slices. Arrange slices about 1 inch (2.5 cm) apart on prepared baking sheet.
6. Bake in preheated oven for 8 to 12 minutes or until golden around the edges. Let cool for 10 minutes on sheet, then transfer to a wire rack and cool completely.

Make Ahead: Dough can be refrigerated in an airtight container for up to 3 weeks or frozen for up to 3 months. Thaw in refrigerator overnight before baking.

Variations
Substitute ¼ cup (60 mL) poppy seeds for the lime zest and juice.

Sugar Cookies

◆

There are many variations of sugar cookies, each slightly different in flavor and texture. This is my favorite recipe. Not only does it taste great, the dough is easy to work with.

MAKES ABOUT 12 COOKIES

- Preparation: 20 minutes
- Baking: 15 minutes
- Freezing: excellent

Tips

To prevent dough from sticking, roll out between 2 sheets of parchment paper.

Use different-sized cookie cutters if you prefer. Bake smaller shapes for less time than larger ones.

Cooled cookies will keep in an airtight container at room temperature for up to 1 week or frozen for up to 3 months. Thaw and bring to room temperature before serving.

- **Preheat oven to 325°F (160°C)**
- **2-inch (5 cm) cookie cutters**
- **Baking sheet, ungreased**

1 cup	all-purpose flour	250 mL
¼ tsp	baking powder	1 mL
Pinch	salt	Pinch
¼ cup	butter, softened	60 mL
½ cup	granulated sugar	125 mL
1	egg yolk	1
1½ tsp	freshly grated lemon zest	7 mL
1½ tsp	freshly squeezed lemon juice	7 mL

1. In a small bowl, whisk together flour, baking powder and salt. Set aside.
2. In a medium bowl, using a wooden spoon, beat together butter and sugar until light, about 2 minutes. Add egg yolk, lemon zest and juice. Stir well. Gradually add flour mixture, stirring until smooth (work dough with hands if necessary to reach desired consistency).
3. On a lightly floured surface, roll out dough to ¼ inch (0.5 cm) thick (see Tips, left). Cut into desired shapes, using floured cookie cutters. Space shapes about 1 inch (2.5 cm) apart on baking sheet.
4. Bake in preheated oven for 10 to 15 minutes or until light golden around edges. Let cool for 5 minutes on sheet, then transfer to a wire rack and cool completely.

Make Ahead: Dough can be refrigerated in an airtight container for up to a week or frozen for up to 3 months. Thaw in the refrigerator overnight or for 1 hour at room temperature before baking.

Variations

Change the cookie shape to match the occasion. Cut out bunnies and eggs for Easter, hearts for Valentine's Day, and trees, stars and bells for Christmas.

Sprinkle cookies with regular or colored sugar before baking, or leave them plain and decorate with icing and sprinkles once baked and cooled.

Viennese Fingers

These luscious treats are sandwich cookies shaped like fingers and filled with a coffee-flavored icing. When my niece got married, she requested a huge box of these cookies for a wedding present.

MAKES ABOUT 12 COOKIES

- Preparation: 25 minutes
- Baking: 7 minutes
- Freezing: excellent

Tips

Use pure vanilla extract for baking. Its flavor far surpasses artificial versions.

The dough should be soft enough that it can be pushed easily through a cookie press. If it is too stiff, stir in another 1 tbsp (15 mL) softened butter. If it is too soft, add a little flour.

- Preheat oven to 375°F (190°C)
- Cookie press fitted with 1/2-inch (1 cm) star-shaped nozzle (see Tips, right)
- Baking sheet, ungreased

COOKIES

1/2 cup	all-purpose flour	125 mL
Pinch	baking powder	Pinch
1/4 cup	butter, softened	60 mL
2 tbsp	confectioners' (icing) sugar, sifted	30 mL
1/4 tsp	pure vanilla extract (see Tips, left)	1 mL

FILLING

1 tbsp	butter, softened	15 mL
1/4 cup	confectioners' (icing) sugar, sifted	60 mL
1/2 tsp	instant coffee granules	2 mL
1/2 tsp	hot water	2 mL

1. *Cookies:* In a small bowl, whisk together flour and baking powder. Set aside.
2. In a medium bowl, using a wooden spoon, beat together butter, confectioners' sugar and vanilla. Gradually add flour mixture, stirring until smooth.
3. Pack dough into cookie press (see Tips, left). Press dough into 24 strips about 1 1/2 inches (4 cm) long, spacing about 1 inch (2.5 cm) apart on baking sheet.
4. Bake in preheated oven for 5 to 7 minutes or until just starting to brown around the edges. Let cool for 5 minutes on sheet, then transfer to a wire rack and cool completely.
5. *Filling:* Meanwhile, in a small bowl, using a wooden spoon, beat together butter and confectioners' sugar. In another bowl, combine coffee granules and hot water. Pour into sugar mixture and stir until smooth (if necessary, add a little milk or water to reach a spreadable consistency).

Tips

Although the cookie press makes an attractive strip, you can also make fingers without a press that are just as delicious. Shape dough into 24 balls and roll each into a 1-inch (2.5 cm) log; flatten slightly.

Filled cookies will keep in an airtight container at room temperature for up to 1 week or can be frozen for up to 3 months (separate layers with waxed paper). Thaw and bring to room temperature before serving.

6. *Assembly:* Divide cookies into 2 equal batches. Spread about $1\frac{1}{2}$ tsp (7 mL) filling over flat side of each cookie in one batch. Sandwich with remaining cookies, flat sides together. Press lightly together.

Make Ahead: Dough can be refrigerated in an airtight container for up to a week or frozen for up to 3 months. Thaw in the refrigerator overnight or for 1 hour at room temperature before baking.

Variations

Substitute raspberry jam or chocolate-hazelnut spread for the coffee filling.

For a fancier presentation, dip ends of cookies in melted chocolate.

Chocolate Caramel Pecan Rounds

◆

These will remind you of the famous Turtles chocolates.

MAKES ABOUT 12 COOKIES

- Preparation: 30 minutes
- Chilling: 15 to 30 minutes
- Baking: 14 minutes
- Cooking (topping): 1 minute
- Standing: 1 hour
- Freezing: excellent

Tips

If dough seems too soft for rolling, add 1 to 2 tbsp (15 to 30 mL) more flour in Step 1.

Dip the cutter in flour between cuts so the dough doesn't stick to it.

This dough is very forgiving. You can reroll scraps after cutting the first batch of rounds.

- Preheat oven to 350°F (180°C)
- 2½-inch (6 cm) round cookie cutter
- Baking sheet, ungreased

COOKIES

½ cup	butter, softened	125 mL
3 tbsp	granulated sugar	45 mL
¼ tsp	pure vanilla extract	1 mL
1 cup	all-purpose flour	250 mL
Pinch	salt	Pinch

TOPPING

12	vanilla caramels	12
1 tbsp	milk	15 mL
⅓ cup	chopped pecans	75 mL
½ oz	semisweet chocolate, chopped and melted	15 g

1. *Cookies:* In a medium bowl, using a wooden spoon, beat together butter, sugar and vanilla. Gradually add flour and salt, stirring well (see Tips, left). Refrigerate dough for 15 to 30 minutes for easy rolling.
2. On a lightly floured surface, roll out dough to ¼ inch (0.5 cm) thick (see Tips, left). Using cookie cutter dipped in flour, cut into rounds. Space rounds about 1 inch (2.5 cm) apart on baking sheet.
3. Bake in preheated oven for 10 to 14 minutes or until golden around the edges. Let cool for 10 minutes on sheet, then transfer to a wire rack and cool completely.
4. *Topping:* In a small microwave-safe bowl, combine caramels and milk. Microwave on Medium for 1 minute, stirring after 30 seconds, until melted and smooth. Place pecans in a small bowl.

Tip

Cookies will keep in an airtight container at room temperature for up to 1 week or can be frozen for up to 3 months. Thaw and bring to room temperature before serving.

5. *Assembly:* Dip top of each cookie first in caramel mixture, covering about one-third, then in pecans. Place on a sheet of waxed paper. Drizzle chocolate overtop. Set aside for about 1 hour to set.

Make Ahead: Dough can be refrigerated in an airtight container for up to a week or frozen for up to 3 months. Omit chocolate drizzle if freezing. Thaw in the refrigerator overnight or for 1 hour at room temperature before baking.

Variations

Place a pecan half on top of cookie before drizzling with chocolate.

Substitute unsalted peanuts or cashews for the pecans.

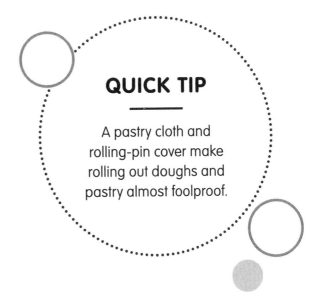

QUICK TIP

A pastry cloth and rolling-pin cover make rolling out doughs and pastry almost foolproof.

Peanut Butter and Banana Sandwich Cookies

◆

These sandwich cookies are much loved by those who have no allergy concerns (just remember not to put them in school lunches).

MAKES ABOUT 12 COOKIES

- Preparation: 25 minutes
- Baking: 14 minutes
- Freezing: excellent

Tips

The banana should be soft and ripe for easy mixing (and the riper the banana, the better the flavor). If it isn't, mash it with a fork before mixing into the dough.

These also taste great plain, without the frosting.

- **Preheat oven to 350°F (180°C)**
- **Baking sheet, greased or lined with parchment paper**

COOKIES

1¼ cups	all-purpose flour	300 mL
¼ tsp	baking soda	1 mL
Pinch	salt	Pinch
½ cup	butter, softened	125 mL
½ cup	granulated sugar	125 mL
¼ cup	ripe banana (see Tips, left)	60 mL
½ cup	chopped peanuts	125 mL

FROSTING

2 tbsp	butter, softened	30 mL
2 tbsp	creamy peanut butter	30 mL
1 cup	confectioners' (icing) sugar, sifted	250 mL
1 tbsp	milk	15 mL

1. *Cookies:* In a small bowl, whisk together flour, baking soda and salt. Set aside.
2. In a medium bowl, using a wooden spoon, beat together butter, sugar and banana. Gradually add flour mixture, stirring until smooth. Stir in peanuts.
3. Drop dough by tablespoonfuls (15 mL), spacing about 2 inches (5 cm) apart, on prepared baking sheet.
4. Bake in preheated oven for 10 to 14 minutes or until golden around the edges. Let cool for 5 minutes on sheet, then transfer to a wire rack and cool completely.
5. *Frosting:* In a small bowl, using a wooden spoon, beat together butter and peanut butter until smooth. Gradually add confectioners' sugar and milk, beating until smooth and spreadable.

Frosted cookies will keep in an airtight container at room temperature for up to 1 week or can be frozen for up to 3 months (separate layers with waxed paper). Thaw and bring to room temperature before serving.

6. *Assembly:* Divide cookies into 2 equal batches. Spread about 1 tbsp (15 mL) frosting over flat side of each cookie in one batch. Place remaining cookies on top, flat sides together. Press lightly together.

Make Ahead: Dough can be refrigerated in an airtight container for up to a week or frozen for up to 3 months. Thaw in the refrigerator overnight or for 1 hour at room temperature before baking.

Variations

For a peanut-free cookie, substitute almond or hazelnut butter for the peanut butter, and chopped almonds or hazelnuts for the peanuts.

QUICK TIP

The cookies are crisp and crunchy but will soften a little after they are filled. If you prefer a crisp cookie, fill them no more than a day ahead.

Crunchy Almond Crescents

◆

Marzipan may seem expensive, but one bite of these easy-to-make cookies will assure you that it's well worth the price. These are a great accompaniment to a bowl of fresh fruit or sherbet.

MAKES ABOUT 8 COOKIES

- Preparation: 20 minutes
- Chilling: 30 minutes
- Baking: 12 minutes
- Freezing: excellent

Tips
. . . .

Be sure to use marzipan rather than almond paste. It is usually softer and easier to work with, as confectioners' sugar and corn syrup have been added to the almond paste.

Parchment paper makes cleanup easy and solves the problem of cookies sticking to the pan. Washable silicone sheets also work well.

Cooled cookies will keep in an airtight container at room temperature for up to 4 weeks or can be frozen for up to 3 months. Thaw and bring to room temperature before serving.

- **Preheat oven to 375°F (190°C)**
- **Baking sheet, greased or lined with parchment paper**

3½ oz	marzipan	100 g
½ cup	confectioners' (icing) sugar, sifted	125 mL
3 tbsp	all-purpose flour	45 mL
1	egg white	1
½ cup	finely chopped almonds	125 mL

1. In a medium bowl, break marzipan into small pieces. Add confectioners' sugar and flour. Knead with hands until combined. Using a wooden spoon, stir in egg white until combined. Cover and refrigerate dough for 30 minutes.
2. Spread almonds on a sheet of waxed paper. Drop chilled dough by tablespoonfuls (15 mL) onto almonds and roll until evenly coated. Shape into crescents and place on prepared baking sheet, spacing 2 inches (5 cm) apart.
3. Bake in preheated oven for 8 to 12 minutes or until very light golden brown. Let cool for 10 minutes on sheet, then transfer to a wire rack and cool completely.

Make Ahead: Dough can be refrigerated in an airtight container for up to a week or frozen for up to 3 months. Thaw overnight in the refrigerator or for 1 hour at room temperature before baking.

Variations

To dress up these cookies, drizzle melted chocolate on top or dip both ends in melted chocolate.

Sprinkle with confectioners' sugar just before serving.

Sesame Wafers

◆

Almost a candy, these are similar in texture and taste to the commercial Sesame Snaps you can buy.

MAKES ABOUT 8 COOKIES

- Preparation: 15 minutes
- Baking: 14 minutes
- Freezing: excellent

Tips

Use pure vanilla extract for baking. Its flavor far surpasses artificial versions.

Do not put more than 6 cookies on a baking sheet—they spread considerably during baking.

The dough is quite sticky. Be prepared to wash your hands often while making these cookies.

Cooled cookies will keep in an airtight container at room temperature for up to 1 week.

- **Preheat oven to 350°F (180°C)**
- **Baking sheet, greased or lined with parchment paper**

3 tbsp	butter, softened	45 mL
¼ cup	granulated sugar	60 mL
1 tsp	grated lemon zest	5 mL
2 tsp	egg white	10 mL
¼ tsp	pure vanilla extract (see Tips, left)	1 mL
1 tbsp	all-purpose flour	15 mL
Pinch	salt	Pinch
½ cup	sesame seeds	125 mL

1. In a medium bowl, using a wooden spoon, beat butter and sugar until light and creamy, about 3 minutes. Add lemon zest, egg white and vanilla, beating until creamy. Add flour, salt and sesame seeds, stirring until ingredients are well moistened.

2. Shape dough into 1-inch (2.5 cm) balls. Place on prepared baking sheet, spacing about 3 inches (7.5 cm) apart (see Tips, left). Using a wet offset spatula or fingers, press balls flat.

3. Bake in preheated oven for 10 to 14 minutes or until golden. Place sheet on a wire rack and let cool completely.

Make Ahead: Dough can be refrigerated in an airtight container for up to a week or frozen for up to 3 months. Thaw overnight in the refrigerator or for 1 hour at room temperature before baking.

> ## Variation
>
> For a pretty presentation, use a mixture of black and white sesame seeds. They are sold in well-stocked supermarkets and by Asian grocers.

Four-Nut Biscotti

You can prepare these biscotti several ways: leave them plain, drizzle with melted semisweet or white chocolate or dip the ends in melted chocolate.

MAKES ABOUT 12 BISCOTTI

- Preparation: 20 minutes
- Baking: 22 minutes
- Drying: 30 minutes
- Freezing: excellent

Tip

The glaze gives the biscotti a nice appearance and taste, but it can be omitted.

- **Preheat oven to 350°F (180°C)**
- **Baking sheet, greased or lined with parchment paper**

BISCOTTI

¾ cup	all-purpose flour	175 mL
⅛ tsp	baking powder	0.5 mL
Pinch	salt	Pinch
¼ cup	butter, softened	60 mL
¼ cup	granulated sugar	60 mL
3 tbsp	packed brown sugar	45 mL
1	egg yolk	1
¼ tsp	pure almond extract	1 mL
2 tbsp	each coarsely chopped hazelnuts, pecans, pistachios and slivered almonds (see Quick Tip, right)	30 mL

GLAZE

1	egg white	1
1 tbsp	water	15 mL
2 tbsp	turbinado or coarse sugar	30 mL

1. *Biscotti:* In a small bowl, whisk together flour, baking powder and salt. Set aside.
2. In a medium bowl, using a wooden spoon, beat together butter and granulated and brown sugars. Add egg yolk and almond extract and beat well. Gradually add flour mixture, stirring until smooth. Stir in nuts.
3. Spoon dough onto prepared baking sheet and, with floured hands, shape into an 8-inch (20 cm) long cylinder, leaving top slightly rounded. Set aside.
4. *Glaze:* In a small bowl, whisk together egg white and water. Brush over top of dough. Sprinkle with sugar.
5. Bake in preheated oven for 18 to 22 minutes or until lightly browned around the edges. Let cool for 15 minutes on sheet, then transfer to a cutting board. Using a serrated knife, cut dough into ½-inch (1 cm) slices. Place slices cut side up on baking sheet.

Cooled cookies will keep in an airtight container at room temperature for up to 4 weeks or can be frozen for up to 3 months. Thaw and bring to room temperature before serving.

6. Return sheet to oven. Turn off oven and leave biscotti for 30 minutes to dry. Let biscotti cool for 5 minutes on sheet, then transfer to a wire rack and cool completely.

Make Ahead: Dough can be refrigerated in an airtight container for up to a week or frozen for up to 3 months. Thaw overnight in the refrigerator or for 1 hour at room temperature before baking.

Variation

Use your favorite nuts, keeping the total amount to $1/2$ cup (125 mL).

QUICK TIP

For maximum flavor, toast nuts on a baking sheet in a 350°F (180°C) oven for 5 minutes. It restores their freshness as well.

Chocolate-Wrapped Ginger Biscotti

◆

A dark chocolate dough wrapped around a lighter-colored ginger dough makes an attractive two-toned biscotti.

MAKES ABOUT 12 BISCOTTI

- Preparation: 26 minutes
- Baking: 40 minutes
- Cooling: 15 minutes
- Freezing: excellent

Tip

Always sift cocoa powder, as it tends to clump in storage.

- **Preheat oven to 375°F (190°C)**
- **Baking sheet, greased or lined with parchment paper**

1 cup	all-purpose flour	250 mL
1 tsp	baking powder	5 mL
Pinch	salt	Pinch
3 tbsp	butter, softened	45 mL
⅓ cup	granulated sugar	75 mL
1	egg	1
1 tbsp	unsweetened cocoa powder, sifted (see Tip, left)	15 mL
2 tbsp	finely chopped crystallized ginger	30 mL
¼ cup	miniature semisweet chocolate chips	60 mL
⅛ tsp	ground ginger	0.5 mL

1. In a small bowl, whisk together flour, baking powder and salt. Set aside.
2. In a medium bowl, using a wooden spoon, beat together butter and sugar until creamy. Add egg and beat well. Gradually add flour mixture, stirring well. Divide dough into two equal portions and place in separate bowls.
3. Using a wooden spoon, stir cocoa powder and chopped ginger into one portion. Knead with your hands until thoroughly incorporated. Set aside. To the other portion, add chocolate chips and ground ginger. Knead with your hands until thoroughly incorporated. Set aside.
4. Between two sheets of waxed paper, roll chocolate dough into an 8- by 6-inch (20 by 15 cm) rectangle. Remove top sheet of waxed paper and set aside. Using your hands, shape ginger dough into an 8-inch (20 cm) cylinder. Place in center of chocolate dough and wrap chocolate dough around it. Transfer to prepared baking sheet, seam side down. Flatten slightly, leaving top slightly rounded.

Tip

Cooled cookies will keep in an airtight container at room temperature for up to 4 weeks or can be frozen for up to 3 months. Thaw and bring to room temperature before serving.

5. Bake in preheated oven for 20 to 25 minutes or until set. Let cool for 15 minutes on sheet, then transfer to a cutting board. Reduce oven temperature to 325°F (160°C). Using a serrated knife, cut dough into $\frac{1}{2}$-inch (1 cm) slices. Stand slices upright on baking sheet. Bake for 10 to 15 minutes or until crisp and centers are light golden. Let cool for 5 minutes on sheet, then transfer to a wire rack and cool completely.

Make Ahead: Dough can be refrigerated in an airtight container for up to a week or frozen for up to 3 months. Thaw overnight in the refrigerator or for 1 hour at room temperature before baking.

Variations

Substitute finely chopped chocolate for the miniature semisweet chocolate chips.

For a stronger ginger flavor, increase the amount of ground ginger to $\frac{1}{4}$ tsp (1 mL).

QUICK TIP

These doughs are best kneaded with your hands to evenly distribute the ingredients.

Jam Thumbprint Cookies

◆

Fill these thumbprint cookies with a variety of jams for a colorful cookie plate. These cookies can be baked ahead and filled with jam as you need them.

MAKES ABOUT 12 COOKIES

- Preparation: 20 minutes
- Baking: 20 minutes
- Freezing: excellent

Tips

Make sure you finely chop the nuts so your cookies have a nice even coating.

The egg white helps the nuts adhere to the cookie balls, so be sure to thoroughly dip the dough balls until evenly coated.

Filled cookies will keep in an airtight container at room temperature for up to 1 week. Unfilled cookies can be frozen for up to 3 months. Thaw and bring to room temperature before filling with jam and serving.

- **Preheat oven to 300°F (150°C)**
- **Baking sheet, greased or lined with parchment paper**

²/₃ cup	all-purpose flour	150 mL
Pinch	salt	Pinch
¹/₃ cup	butter, softened	75 mL
2½ tbsp	packed brown sugar	37 mL
1	egg, separated	1
¼ tsp	pure vanilla extract	1 mL
½ cup	finely chopped pecans (see Tips, left)	125 mL
2 tbsp	raspberry jam or jelly (approx.)	30 mL

1. In a small bowl, whisk together flour and salt. Set aside.
2. In a medium bowl, using a wooden spoon, beat together butter, brown sugar, egg yolk and vanilla, until light and creamy. Gradually add flour mixture, stirring well.
3. Using your hands, shape dough into 12 balls, each about 1 inch (2.5 cm) around. Set aside.
4. In a small bowl, whisk egg white lightly. In another bowl, place chopped nuts. Dip cookie balls first into the egg white, then into the nuts, rolling to cover completely. Place on prepared baking sheet. Using your thumb, make an indentation in the center of each cookie.
5. Bake in preheated oven for 5 minutes. Indent the centers again and bake for 10 to 15 minutes longer or until firm. Let cool for 5 minutes on sheet, then transfer to a wire rack and cool completely.
6. Fill center of each cooled cookie with about ½ tsp (2 mL) jam.

Make Ahead: Dough can be refrigerated in an airtight container for up to a week or frozen for up to 3 months. Thaw overnight in the refrigerator or for 1 hour at room temperature before baking.

Variations

Substitute walnuts or hazelnuts for the pecans.

Use other jams, such as strawberry, apricot or blueberry.

Swedish Butter Balls

These melt-in-your mouth delights are loaded with nuts.

MAKES ABOUT 12 COOKIES

- Preparation: 15 minutes
- Baking: 10 minutes
- Freezing: excellent

Tips

For optimum flavor, toast whole nuts on a baking sheet in a 350°F (180°C) oven for 5 to 10 minutes, stirring often, until golden and fragrant.

Store nuts in the freezer or purchase just before using to assure freshness.

For an attractive presentation, serve in small, colorful paper cups.

Cooled cookies will keep in an airtight container at room temperature for up to 1 week or can be frozen for up to 3 months. Thaw and bring to room temperature before serving.

- **Preheat oven to 400°F (200°C)**
- **Baking sheet, ungreased or lined with parchment paper**

⅓ cup	butter, softened	75 mL
2½ tbsp	confectioners' (icing) sugar, sifted	37 mL
¼ tsp	pure vanilla extract	1 mL
⅔ cup	all-purpose flour	150 mL
¼ cup	finely chopped pecans (see Tips, left)	60 mL
	Confectioners' (icing) sugar, sifted	

1. In a medium bowl, using a wooden spoon, beat together butter, confectioners' sugar and vanilla until creamy. Gradually add flour, stirring well. Stir in pecans.
2. Using your hands, shape dough into 1-inch (2.5 cm) balls. Place on prepared baking sheet.
3. Bake in preheated oven for 7 to 10 minutes or until very light golden brown. Let cool for 10 minutes on sheet, then transfer to a wire rack and cool completely.
4. Roll in confectioners' sugar to coat.

Make Ahead: Dough can be refrigerated in an airtight container for up to a week or frozen for up to 3 months. Thaw overnight in the refrigerator or for 1 hour at room temperature before baking.

Variations

Substitute hazelnuts, almonds or walnuts for the pecans. Hazelnuts and almonds can be either blanched or natural.

Cherry Mandelbrot

◆

Mandelbrot, or almond bread, is shaped and baked like a loaf. Similar to biscotti, it is then sliced and rebaked to make crisp cookies. This version is lower in fat and provides more dietary fiber than most.

MAKES ABOUT 12 COOKIES

- Preparation: 25 minutes
- Baking: 42 minutes
- Cooling: 10 minutes
- Drying: 20 minutes
- Freezing: excellent

- **Preheat oven to 350°F (180°C)**
- **9- by 5-inch (23 by 12.5 cm) loaf pan, lined with parchment paper**
- **Baking sheet, ungreased**

½ cup	all-purpose flour	125 mL
½ cup	whole wheat flour	125 mL
2 tbsp	wheat germ	30 mL
1 tsp	baking powder	5 mL
Pinch	salt	Pinch
¼ tsp	ground cinnamon	1 mL
1 tbsp	butter, softened	15 mL
⅓ cup	granulated sugar	75 mL
1 tbsp	vegetable oil	15 mL
1	egg	1
1½ tsp	freshly grated orange zest (see Quick Tip, right)	7 mL
2 tbsp	freshly squeezed orange juice	30 mL
1 tbsp	plain yogurt	15 mL
¼ cup	sliced almonds	60 mL
¼ cup	dried cherries	60 mL

1. In a small bowl, whisk together all-purpose flour, whole wheat flour, wheat germ, baking powder, salt and cinnamon. Set aside.
2. In a medium bowl, using a wooden spoon, beat together butter, sugar, oil, egg, orange zest, orange juice and yogurt. Gradually add flour mixture, stirring well. Stir in almonds and cherries. Press dough evenly into bottom of prepared pan.

Cooled cookies will keep in an airtight container at room temperature for up to 1 week or can be frozen for up to 3 months. Thaw and bring to room temperature before serving.

3. Bake in preheated oven for 25 to 30 minutes or until top is golden. Cool for 10 minutes in pan set on a wire rack, then transfer to a cutting board. Using a serrated knife, cut dough into $1/2$-inch (1 cm) slices. Stand slices upright on baking sheet and bake for 8 to 12 minutes longer or until golden. Turn oven off and leave in oven for 15 to 20 minutes longer or until crisp. Transfer to a wire rack to cool completely.

Make Ahead: Dough can be refrigerated in an airtight container for up to a week or frozen for up to 3 months. Thaw overnight in the refrigerator or for 1 hour at room temperature before baking.

Variations

Substitute coarsely chopped hazelnuts or Brazil nuts for the almonds and dried cranberries for the cherries.

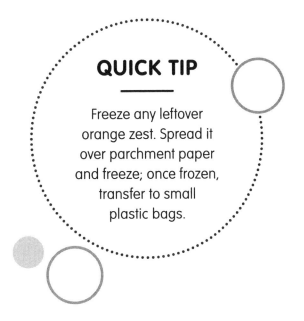

QUICK TIP

Freeze any leftover orange zest. Spread it over parchment paper and freeze; once frozen, transfer to small plastic bags.

Apricot Pecan Rugelach

These cookies, which are Jewish in origin, are a traditional favorite during the holiday season.

MAKES ABOUT 12 COOKIES

- Preparation: 20 minutes
- Chilling: 2½ hours
- Baking: 25 minutes
- Freezing: excellent

Tips

The cream cheese should be soft for mixing. If it's too hard, place on a piece of waxed paper and soften in a microwave on High for about 15 seconds.

Be sure to line your baking sheet with parchment paper, as the jam will leak out and stick to the baking sheet without it.

- **Preheat oven to 350°F (180°C)**
- **Baking sheet, lined with parchment paper**

DOUGH

¼ cup	butter, softened	60 mL
3 tbsp	cream cheese, softened (see Tips, left)	45 mL
1 tbsp	granulated sugar	15 mL
½ cup	all-purpose flour	125 mL

FILLING

¼ cup	apricot jam (see Quick Tip, right)	60 mL
¼ tsp	freshly squeezed lemon juice	1 mL
¼ cup	finely chopped pecans	60 mL
¼ tsp	ground cinnamon	1 mL

TOPPING

1	egg	1
2 tsp	coarse or regular granulated sugar	10 mL

1. *Dough:* In a small bowl, using a wooden spoon, beat together butter, cream cheese and sugar until smooth. Gradually add flour, stirring until smooth. Wrap dough in plastic wrap and refrigerate for 2 hours.
2. *Filling:* In a small bowl, combine jam and lemon juice. Set aside.
3. On a lightly floured surface, roll out dough into an 11-inch (27.5 cm) circle. Using a small offset spatula, carefully spread dough circle with the jam mixture. Top with the pecans and cinnamon. Using a long, sharp knife, cut the circle into 12 pie-shaped wedges.
4. Starting from the wide end, tightly roll up each wedge to form a crescent. Place crescents on prepared baking sheet, spacing about 2 inches (5 cm) apart. Refrigerate for 30 minutes.
5. Fifteen minutes before you are ready to bake, preheat oven to 350°F (180°C).

Tip

Cooled cookies will keep in an airtight container at room temperature for up to 1 week or can be frozen for up to 3 months. Thaw and bring to room temperature before serving.

6. *Topping:* In a small bowl, using a fork, beat egg lightly. Brush over surface of chilled cookies. Sprinkle sugar evenly overtop.

7. Bake in preheated oven for 20 to 25 minutes or until golden. Let cool for 15 minutes on baking sheet, then transfer to a wire rack and cool completely.

Make Ahead: Dough can be refrigerated in an airtight container for up to a week or frozen for up to 3 months. Thaw overnight in the refrigerator or for 1 hour at room temperature before baking.

Variations

Substitute chopped almonds or hazelnuts for the pecans.

Substitute raspberry jam for the apricot.

QUICK TIP

The flavor of these cookies depends on the jam. Choose a thick, tart jam with a nice fruit flavor. Be sure to chop any large pieces of fruit in the jam before combining with the lemon juice.

Cranberry Almond Biscotti

These biscotti are not too sweet and not too hard. The crisp, tender texture makes them enjoyable without needing to be dunked.

MAKES ABOUT 12 BISCOTTI

- Preparation: 20 minutes
- Baking: 46 minutes
- Cooling: 15 minutes
- Freezing: excellent

Tips

Bring butter to room temperature before using, for easy blending.

Use whichever type of butter you have on hand. Salted and unsalted both work well.

You can substitute chopped dried apricots for the cranberries.

Cooled cookies will keep in an airtight container at room temperature for up to 1 week or can be frozen for up to 3 months. Thaw and bring to room temperature before serving.

- **Preheat oven to 325°F (160°C)**
- **Baking sheet, greased or lined with parchment paper**

¾ cup	all-purpose flour	175 mL
½ tsp	baking powder	2 mL
Pinch	salt	Pinch
2½ tbsp	butter, softened (see Tips, left)	37 mL
¼ cup	granulated sugar	60 mL
1	egg yolk	1
1½ tsp	freshly grated orange zest	7 mL
1 tsp	freshly squeezed orange juice	5 mL
⅓ cup	dried cranberries	75 mL
3 tbsp	sliced almonds	45 mL

1. In a small bowl, whisk together flour, baking powder and salt. Set aside.
2. In a medium bowl, using a wooden spoon, beat together butter, sugar, egg yolk, orange zest and orange juice, until light and creamy. Gradually add flour mixture, stirring until smooth.
3. With floured hands, knead in cranberries and almonds. Shape dough into a 7-inch (18 cm) cylinder. Place on prepared baking sheet. Flatten to 2½ inches (6 cm) wide.
4. Bake in preheated oven for 23 to 28 minutes or until firm and golden around the edges. Cool for 15 minutes on sheet, then transfer to a cutting board. Using a serrated knife, cut dough into ½-inch (1 cm) slices. Place slices cut side down on baking sheet and bake for 8 minutes. Turn over and bake for 5 to 10 minutes longer, until crisp and golden. Let cool for 5 minutes on sheet, then transfer to a wire rack and cool completely.

Make Ahead: Dough can be refrigerated in an airtight container for up to a week or frozen for up to 3 months. Thaw overnight in the refrigerator or for 1 hour at room temperature before baking.

Variations

Substitute hazelnuts or pistachios for the almonds.

Substitute lemon zest and juice for the orange.

Marvelous Molasses Cookies

◆

There are many versions of molasses cookies. These are crisp, more like a gingersnap.

MAKES ABOUT 10 COOKIES

- Preparation: 20 minutes
- Chilling: 30 minutes
- Baking: 12 minutes
- Freezing: excellent

Tips

Use light (fancy) molasses (sometimes called table molasses) rather than blackstrap molasses, which has quite a strong flavor.

Cooled cookies will keep in an airtight container at room temperature for up to 1 week or can be frozen for up to 3 months. Thaw and bring to room temperature before serving.

- **Preheat oven to 375°F (180°C)**
- **Baking sheet, greased and lined with parchment paper**

½ cup + 1 tbsp	all-purpose flour	140 mL
½ tsp	baking soda	2 mL
⅛ tsp	each ground cloves, ginger and cinnamon	0.5 mL
Pinch	salt	Pinch
3 tbsp	butter, melted and cooled	45 mL
¼ cup	granulated sugar	60 mL
1 tbsp	light (fancy) molasses (see Tips, left)	15 mL
1	egg yolk	1
	Granulated sugar for coating	

1. In a small bowl, whisk together flour, baking soda, cloves, ginger, cinnamon and salt. Set aside.
2. In a medium bowl, using a wooden spoon, beat together butter, sugar, molasses and egg yolk, until creamy. Gradually add flour mixture, stirring well.
3. Cover and refrigerate the dough for about 30 minutes (this makes it easier to shape).
4. Using your hands, roll dough into balls of about 1 tbsp (15 mL) each. Roll balls in sugar until completely coated and place on prepared baking sheet, spacing about 2 inches (5 cm) apart.
5. Bake in preheated oven for 8 to 12 minutes or until firm. Let cool for 5 minutes on sheet, then transfer to a wire rack and cool completely.

Make Ahead: Dough can be refrigerated in an airtight container for up to a week or frozen for up to 3 months. Thaw overnight in the refrigerator or for 1 hour at room temperature before baking.

Variation

Roll the dough balls in coarse white sugar instead of granulated sugar.

Toffee Chocolate Almond Chippers

When you have a craving for something sweet and you can't decide between a cookie and a candy bar, these cookies fill the bill.

MAKES 8 MEDIUM OR 6 LARGE COOKIES

- Preparation: 15 minutes
- Baking: 14 minutes
- Freezing: excellent

Tips

I like to use Skor bars, but Heath bars are another good choice.

Refrigerate the chocolate bars for easy chopping. You can also put them in a heavy plastic bag and smash them with a mallet.

If you bake most chocolate chip cookies until they are golden around the edges but still pale in the center, they will be soft and chewy. If you bake until they are a light golden color overall, they will be crisp.

To make large cookies, drop by 2 tbsp (30 mL). Bake for 12 to 16 minutes, as directed.

Cooled cookies will keep in an airtight container at room temperature for up to 1 week or can be frozen for up to 3 months. Thaw and bring to room temperature before serving.

- Preheat oven to 350°F (180°C)
- Baking sheet, lined with parchment paper

½ cup	all-purpose flour	125 mL
¼ tsp	baking soda	1 mL
Pinch	salt	Pinch
2½ tbsp	butter, softened	37 mL
2 tbsp	granulated sugar	30 mL
2 tbsp	packed brown sugar	30 mL
1	egg	1
⅛ tsp	pure almond extract	0.5 mL
2 oz	chocolate-covered toffee bars, chopped (see Tips, left)	60 g
⅓ cup	semisweet chocolate chips	75 mL
⅓ cup	slivered almonds	75 mL

1. In a small bowl, whisk together flour, baking soda and salt. Set aside.
2. In a medium bowl, using a wooden spoon, beat together butter, granulated and brown sugars, egg and almond extract, until creamy. Gradually add flour mixture, stirring well. Stir in chopped toffee bars, chocolate chips and almonds, until well combined.
3. Drop dough by heaping tablespoonfuls (22 mL), spacing about 2 inches (5 cm) apart, on prepared baking sheet.
4. Bake in preheated oven for 10 to 14 minutes or until golden. Let cool for 5 minutes on sheet, then transfer to a wire rack and cool completely.

Make Ahead: Dough can be refrigerated in an airtight container for up to a week or frozen for up to 3 months. Thaw overnight in the refrigerator or for 1 hour at room temperature before baking.

Variations

Substitute pecans or cashews for the almonds.

For a milder chocolate taste, use milk chocolate chips.

Turn these into ice-cream sandwich cookies with a filling of chocolate or butterscotch ripple ice cream.

Judie's Chocolate Chip Cookies

These decadent soft cookies are overloaded with chocolate chips. My sister Judie's special ingredient is lard.

MAKES 12 MEDIUM OR 8 LARGE COOKIES

- Preparation: 20 minutes
- Baking: 12 minutes
- Freezing: excellent

Tips

If you prefer a little less chocolate, reduce the chips to ⅔ cup (150 mL).

For a milder chocolate flavor, use milk chocolate chips.

For chewy cookies, underbake (8 minutes for medium; 10 minutes for large). For crisp cookies, bake longer (12 minutes for medium, 14 minutes for large). Keep in mind that the cookies will continue to bake a little after they come out of the oven.

To make large cookies, drop by heaping tablespoons (22 mL). Bake for 12 to 14 minutes, as directed.

Cooled cookies will keep in an airtight container at room temperature for up to 1 week or can be frozen for up to 3 months. Thaw and bring to room temperature before serving.

- **Preheat oven to 375°F (190°C)**
- **Baking sheet, greased or lined with parchment paper**

½ cup	all-purpose flour	125 mL
2 tbsp	quick-cooking rolled oats	30 mL
¼ tsp	baking soda	1 mL
Pinch	salt	Pinch
¼ cup	lard	60 mL
⅓ cup	packed dark brown sugar	75 mL
1	egg yolk	1
¼ tsp	pure vanilla extract	1 mL
¾ cup	semisweet chocolate chips (see Tips, left)	175 mL

1. In a small bowl, whisk together flour, oats, baking soda and salt. Set aside.
2. In a medium bowl, using a wooden spoon, beat together lard, brown sugar, egg yolk and vanilla, until creamy. Gradually add flour mixture, stirring well. Stir in chocolate chips.
3. Drop dough by tablespoonfuls (15 mL), spacing about 2 inches (5 cm) apart, on prepared baking sheet.
4. Bake in preheated oven for 8 to 12 minutes or until golden around the edges. Let cool for 10 minutes on sheet, then transfer to a wire rack and cool completely.

Make Ahead: Dough can be refrigerated in an airtight container for up to a week or frozen for up to 3 months. Thaw overnight in the refrigerator or for 1 hour at room temperature before baking.

Variations

Add ¼ cup (60 mL) chopped pecans to the dough with the chocolate chips.

Substitute 3 oz (90 g) chopped chocolate for the chocolate chips.

Peanut Fudgies

These cookies are like a chewy brownie that's loaded with chocolate chips and peanuts.

MAKES 8 MEDIUM OR 6 LARGE COOKIES (SEE TIPS, BELOW)

- Preparation: 15 minutes
- Baking: 13 minutes
- Freezing: excellent

Tips

I like to chop nuts on a cutting board, using a sharp chef's knife. You can do it in a food processor as well.

Store nuts in the freezer. They can go rancid quite quickly.

To make large cookies, drop dough by large spoonfuls (2 tbsp/30 mL). Bake for 10 to 14 minutes, as directed.

Cooled cookies will keep in an airtight container at room temperature for up to 1 week or can be frozen for up to 3 months. Thaw and bring to room temperature before serving.

- **Preheat oven to 350°F (180°C)**
- **Baking sheet, greased or lined with parchment paper**

9 tbsp	semisweet chocolate chips, divided	135 mL
2 tbsp	butter	30 mL
3 tbsp	all-purpose flour	45 mL
1/8 tsp	baking soda	0.5 mL
1	egg yolk	1
3 tbsp	packed brown sugar	45 mL
1/3 cup	chopped honey-roasted peanuts (see Tips, left)	75 mL
1/4 cup	peanut butter chips	60 mL

1. In a small microwave-safe bowl, combine 6 tbsp (90 mL) chocolate chips and butter. Microwave on Medium for 1 minute, stirring halfway through, until melted. Stir until smooth. Set aside to cool.
2. In a small bowl, whisk together flour and baking soda. Set aside.
3. In a medium bowl, using a wooden spoon, beat together egg yolk and brown sugar until smooth. Stir in cooled melted chocolate. Gradually add flour mixture, stirring well. Stir in peanuts, peanut butter chips and remaining 3 tbsp (45 mL) chocolate chips, until well combined.
4. Drop dough by heaping tablespoonfuls (22 mL), spacing about 2 inches (5 cm) apart, on prepared baking sheet.
5. Bake in preheated oven for 9 to 13 minutes or until set around the edges but slightly soft in the center. Let cool for 5 minutes on sheet, then transfer to a wire rack and cool completely.

Make Ahead: Dough can be refrigerated in an airtight container for up to a week or frozen for up to 3 months. Thaw overnight in the refrigerator or for 1 hour at room temperature before baking.

Variations

Use your favorite nut. Cashews, pecans, walnuts and hazelnuts all work great.

For a big hit of chocolate, substitute more semisweet chocolate chips for the peanut butter chips.

Soft and Chewy Chocolate Indulgence

These decadent cookies are loaded with chocolate flavor and are simply irresistible while still warm.

MAKES 8 MEDIUM OR 6 LARGE COOKIES (SEE TIPS, LEFT)

- Preparation: 20 minutes
- Baking: 14 minutes
- Freezing: excellent

Tips

Compared to some other drop cookie doughs, the dough for these cookies is quite stiff.

When you take them out of the oven, these cookies should be set around the edges but a little soft in the center. They'll continue to cook while cooling on the baking sheet.

To make large cookies, drop dough by large spoonfuls (2 tbsp/30 mL). Bake for 12 to 16 minutes, as directed.

Cooled cookies will keep in an airtight container at room temperature for up to 1 week or can be frozen for up to 3 months. Thaw and bring to room temperature before serving.

- **Preheat oven to 350°F (180°C)**
- **Baking sheet, greased or lined with parchment paper**

½ cup	all-purpose flour	125 mL
¼ cup	unsweetened cocoa powder, sifted	60 mL
¼ tsp	baking soda	1 mL
Pinch	salt	Pinch
⅓ cup	butter, softened	75 mL
⅓ cup	packed brown sugar	75 mL
3 tbsp	granulated sugar	45 mL
1	egg yolk	1
½ tsp	pure vanilla extract	2 mL
⅔ cup	semisweet chocolate chips	150 mL

1. In a small bowl, whisk together flour, cocoa powder, baking soda and salt. Set aside.
2. In a medium bowl, using a wooden spoon, beat together butter, brown and granulated sugars, egg yolk and vanilla. Stir in chocolate chips.
3. Drop dough by heaping tablespoonfuls (22 mL), spacing about 2 inches (5 cm) apart, on prepared baking sheet.
4. Bake in preheated oven for 10 to 14 minutes or until set around the edges but still soft in the center. Let cool for 5 minutes on sheet, then transfer to a wire rack and cool completely.

Make Ahead: Dough can be refrigerated in an airtight container for up to a week or frozen for up to 3 months. Thaw overnight in the refrigerator or for 1 hour at room temperature before baking.

Variations

Substitute white chocolate chips for the semisweet chocolate chips.

For a milder chocolate taste, use milk chocolate chips.

Chocolate-Dipped Brownie Mounds

◆

Bite-size brownies dipped in chocolate are easy to make from a roll of chocolate refrigerator cookie dough.

MAKES ABOUT 12 COOKIES

- Preparation: 25 minutes
- Chilling: 2½ hours
- Baking: 14 minutes
- Freezing: excellent

Tip

Sift cocoa powder before using, to remove any lumps that have formed during storage.

- **Baking sheet, greased or lined with parchment paper**

COOKIES

⅓ cup	all-purpose flour	75 mL
4 tsp	unsweetened cocoa powder, sifted	20 mL
⅛ tsp	baking powder	0.5 mL
⅛ tsp	baking soda	0.5 mL
Pinch	salt	Pinch
2 tbsp	butter, softened	30 mL
3 tbsp	granulated sugar	45 mL
1	egg yolk	1

CHOCOLATE DIP

1½ oz	semisweet chocolate, chopped	45 g
¼ tsp	vegetable oil	1 mL

1. *Cookies:* In a small bowl, whisk together flour, cocoa powder, baking powder, baking soda and salt. Set aside.
2. In a medium bowl, using a wooden spoon, beat together butter, sugar and egg yolk, until creamy. Gradually add flour mixture, beating well. Shape dough into a 12-inch (30 cm) cylinder. Wrap with plastic wrap and refrigerate until firm, at least 2 hours.
3. When ready to bake, preheat oven to 350°F (180°C).
4. Using a sharp knife, cut roll into ¾-inch (2 cm) slices. Place slices cut side down on prepared baking sheet, spacing about 1 inch (2.5 cm) apart.
5. Bake in preheated oven for 10 to 14 minutes or until set around the edges but still soft in the center. Let cool for 5 minutes on sheet, then transfer to a wire rack and cool completely.

6. *Chocolate Dip:* In a small microwave-safe bowl, combine chopped chocolate and oil. Microwave on Medium for about 1 minute, stirring halfway through, until melted and smooth. Dip one side of each cookie into melted chocolate, covering half the cookie. Set on a wire rack placed over a sheet of waxed paper. Refrigerate for 20 minutes to set the chocolate.

Make Ahead: Dough can be refrigerated in an airtight container for up to 3 weeks or frozen for up to 3 months. To freeze, prepare recipe up to the end of Step 5. To bake from frozen, thaw dough overnight in refrigerator before baking. Dip baked and cooled cookies in chocolate before serving (Step 6).

Variations

Dip some or all of the cookies in white chocolate.

Substitute semisweet chocolate chips for the chopped chocolate.

Fabulous Florentines

Florentines are chewy cookies with almonds and candied peel that are made more decadent when dipped in dark chocolate.

MAKES ABOUT 12 COOKIES

- Preparation: 25 minutes
- Baking: 11 minutes
- Standing: 1 hour
- Freezing: not recommended

Tips

Melt the chocolate in a small microwave-safe bowl on Medium for about 1 minute, stirring halfway through, until smooth.

These cookies are delicious served in, with or as a garnish for a scoop of orange sherbet or ice cream. They actually make great ice-cream sandwiches as well.

Bake only 6 cookies per sheet. The dough will spread considerably during baking, so be mindful of the amount of batter you use per cookie and leave ample space between them on the baking sheet.

Cooled cookies will keep in an airtight container at room temperature for up to 1 week.

- **Preheat oven to 350°F (180°C)**
- **Baking sheet, greased or lined with parchment paper**

1½ tbsp	butter	22 mL
1 tbsp	heavy or whipping (35%) cream or milk	15 mL
¾ tsp	corn syrup	3 mL
2 tbsp	granulated sugar	30 mL
1½ tsp	all-purpose flour	7 mL
¼ tsp	freshly grated orange zest	1 mL
¼ cup	slivered almonds, finely chopped	60 mL
2 tbsp	finely chopped candied orange peel	30 mL
2 oz	bittersweet chocolate, chopped, melted and cooled (see Tips, left)	60 g

1. In a small saucepan, combine butter, cream and corn syrup. Using a wooden spoon, stir in sugar, flour and orange zest. Mix until smooth. Over medium-high heat, bring mixture to a boil, stirring frequently. Remove from heat. Stir in almonds and candied orange peel. Let stand for 5 minutes.
2. Drop dough by 1½ teaspoonfuls (7 mL), spacing about 3 inches (7.5 cm) apart, on prepared baking sheet. Flatten slightly with the back of a spoon or an offset spatula.
3. Bake in preheated oven for 9 to 11 minutes or just until set and light golden. Let cool for 1 minute on sheet, then use a wide spatula to transfer cookies to a wire rack and cool completely.
4. Once cool, using a small offset spatula, spread melted chocolate over the flat bottom side of each cookie. Return to rack, chocolate side up, and leave until chocolate sets, about 1 hour.

Variations

Substitute mixed candied peel for the candied orange peel.

Try spreading white chocolate on some of the cookies. A mixture of cookies presented in a box or on a tray looks nice.

Chocolate Rum Balls

◆

These no-bake cookies improve with age, so plan to make them at least one day ahead.

MAKES 12 SMALL OR 8 MEDIUM COOKIES (SEE TIPS, BELOW)

- Preparation: 15 minutes
- Standing: 1 hour
- Freezing: not recommended

Tips

To make medium cookies, shape dough into 1½-inch (4 cm) balls.

Chocolate sprinkles are available in most bulk food stores or in the baking section of supermarkets.

Rum balls ripen with age, so make them at least 1 or 2 days before serving.

Store in an airtight container in the refrigerator for up to 3 weeks.

• **Baking sheet, lined with waxed paper**

¾ cup	chocolate wafer crumbs	175 mL
⅓ cup	confectioners' (icing) sugar, sifted	75 mL
¼ cup	finely chopped walnuts	60 mL
2 tsp	unsweetened cocoa powder, sifted	10 mL
1½ tbsp	butter, melted	22 mL
1½ tbsp	dark rum	22 mL
1 tbsp	corn syrup	15 mL
¼ cup	chocolate sprinkles (see Tips, left)	60 mL

1. In a medium bowl, using a wooden spoon, combine chocolate wafer crumbs, confectioners' sugar, walnuts and cocoa powder. Stir well. Set aside.

2. In a small bowl, using a wooden spoon, stir together melted butter, rum and corn syrup. Add to crumb mixture. Stir well, then use your hands to knead the mixture until it holds together.

3. Spread chocolate sprinkles over a small, shallow dish. Shape dough into 1-inch (2.5 cm) balls. Roll in chocolate sprinkles until thoroughly covered. Place on waxed paper. Set aside until dry, about 1 hour.

Variations

Substitute brandy for the rum.

Substitute 1 tsp (5 mL) pure rum extract for the rum.

Roll balls in toasted or plain medium flaked or shredded coconut or finely chopped nuts. It's nice to prepare a variety of coatings for one batch.

Fancy Pressed Shortbread

◆

These tiny, buttery, melt-in-your-mouth cookies were my mother's specialty. Use your favorite holiday disk in your cookie press—star, bell, tree, wreath—all work well.

MAKES 24 SMALL COOKIES (SEE TIPS, BELOW)

- Preparation: 15 minutes
- Baking: 10 minutes
- Freezing: excellent

Tips

Don't compromise: there is no substitute for butter in a shortbread recipe.

If you don't have a cookie press or don't have the time (they can be temperamental), you can shape these by hand. Roll (with floured hands) about 1 tsp (5 mL) dough into a ball, place on baking sheet and then flatten slightly. Decorate as desired.

Cooled cookies will keep in an airtight container at room temperature for up to 3 weeks or can be frozen for up to 3 months. Thaw and bring to room temperature before serving.

To bake only 12 cookies, divide dough in half. Bake one portion of dough as directed.

- **Preheat oven to 350°F (180°C)**
- **Cookie press with holiday-design disk (see Tips, left)**
- **Baking sheet, ungreased**

6 tbsp	butter, softened (see Tips, left)	90 mL
3 tbsp	confectioners' (icing) sugar, sifted	45 mL
¾ cup	all-purpose flour	175 mL
Pinch	salt	Pinch

1. In a small bowl, using a wooden spoon, beat butter and confectioners' sugar until light and creamy. Gradually add flour and salt, stirring well.
2. Fit press with desired disk, pack dough into press and press dough onto baking sheet, spacing cookies about 1 inch (2.5 cm) apart. Sprinkle with colored sugar and/or decorate with pieces of cherry, as desired.
3. Bake in preheated oven for 5 to 10 minutes or until light golden around the edges. Let cool for 5 minutes on sheet, then transfer to a wire rack and cool completely.

Make Ahead: Dough can be refrigerated in an airtight container for up to a week or frozen for up to 3 months. Thaw overnight in the refrigerator or for 1 hour at room temperature before baking.

Variations

Leave plain before baking and sprinkle with confectioners' sugar after.

Press a silver dragée into the center of each cookie before baking.

Oatmeal Pecan Shortbread

◆

Brown sugar gives this shortbread a nice caramel flavor and crisp texture.

MAKES ABOUT 12 COOKIES (SEE TIPS, BELOW)

- Preparation: 15 minutes
- Baking: 20 minutes
- Freezing: excellent

Tips

Use quick-cooking rolled oats (not large-flake rolled oats) so the cutters will cut through the dough easily.

Shortbread cookies can be fragile. Use an offset spatula to transfer them from the baking sheet to the wire rack.

Cooled cookies will keep in an airtight container at room temperature for up to 3 weeks or can be frozen for up to 3 months. Thaw and bring to room temperature before serving.

To bake only 6 cookies, divide dough in half. Bake one portion of dough as directed.

- **Preheat oven to 300°F (150°C)**
- **2-inch (5 cm) cookie cutters**
- **Baking sheet, ungreased**

6 tbsp	all-purpose flour	90 mL
2 tbsp	quick-cooking rolled oats (see Tips, left)	30 mL
2 tbsp	packed brown sugar	30 mL
1 tbsp	finely chopped pecans	15 mL
Pinch	ground cinnamon	Pinch
3 tbsp	butter, softened	45 mL

1. In a small bowl, using a wooden spoon, combine flour, oats, brown sugar, pecans and cinnamon. Stir well. Add butter and stir until mixture is crumbly. Using your hands, knead mixture until a soft, smooth dough forms. If necessary, cover and refrigerate for 30 minutes for easy rolling.
2. On a lightly floured surface, roll dough out to 1/4 inch (0.5 cm) thick. Dip cutters in flour and cut out desired shapes. Place on baking sheet, spacing about 1 inch (2.5 cm) apart.
3. Bake in preheated oven for 15 to 20 minutes or just until light golden around the edges. Let cool for 5 minutes on sheet, then transfer to a wire rack and cool completely (see Tips, left).

Make Ahead: Dough can be refrigerated in an airtight container for up to a week or frozen for up to 3 months. Thaw overnight in the refrigerator or for 1 hour at room temperature before baking.

Variations
Add 1/4 tsp (1 mL) ground ginger or nutmeg along with the cinnamon.

Cherry Pistachio Shortbread

◆

Although especially attractive during the holiday season, these cookies are delicious year-round.

MAKES ABOUT 8 COOKIES

- Preparation: 15 minutes
- Baking: 25 minutes
- Freezing: excellent

Tips

If you use unsalted butter for shortbread, add a pinch of salt along with the flour in Step 1.

Cooled cookies will keep in an airtight container at room temperature for up to 3 weeks or frozen for up to 3 months. Thaw and bring to room temperature before serving.

- **Preheat oven to 300°F (150°C)**
- **Baking sheet, ungreased**

⅓ cup	butter, softened (see Tips, left)	75 mL
3 tbsp	confectioners' (icing) sugar, sifted	45 mL
½ tsp	pure vanilla extract	2 mL
½ cup	all-purpose flour	125 mL
¼ cup	coarsely chopped unsalted pistachios	60 mL
3 tbsp	chopped dried cherries	45 mL
2 tsp	granulated sugar	10 mL

1. In a medium bowl, using a wooden spoon, beat together butter, confectioners' sugar and vanilla until smooth. Add flour, pistachios and cherries, stirring well.
2. Drop dough by heaping tablespoonfuls (22 mL), spacing about 1 inch (2.5 cm) apart, on baking sheet. Sprinkle evenly with granulated sugar.
3. Bake in preheated oven for 20 to 25 minutes or until golden around the edges. Let cool for 5 minutes on sheet, then transfer to a wire rack and cool completely.

Make Ahead: Dough can be refrigerated in an airtight container for up to a week or frozen for up to 3 months. Thaw overnight in the refrigerator or for 1 hour at room temperature before baking.

Variations

Substitute dried cranberries or apricots for the cherries.

Substitute pecans or almonds for the pistachios.

Mocha Java Shortbread Logs

◆

A great choice for coffee-lovers. Enjoy them with an espresso for a double dose of caffeine.

MAKES ABOUT 12 COOKIES

- Preparation: 15 minutes
- Baking: 20 minutes
- Freezing: excellent

Tips
. . . .

For a milder coffee flavor, decrease the amount of espresso to 1 tsp (5 mL).

Instant espresso coffee powder is available in most supermarkets and coffee houses where they sell ground coffee.

For a pretty finish, roll the warm cookies in confectioners' sugar.

Cooled cookies will keep in an airtight container at room temperature for up to 3 weeks or can be frozen for up to 3 months. Thaw and bring to room temperature before serving.

- **Preheat oven to 350°F (180°C)**
- **Baking sheet, ungreased**

½ cup	all-purpose flour	125 mL
1½ tsp	cornstarch	7 mL
1½ tsp	instant espresso coffee powder (see Tips, left)	7 mL
½ oz	semisweet chocolate, finely chopped	15 g
¼ cup	butter, softened	60 mL
2 tbsp	granulated sugar	30 mL

1. In a small bowl, whisk together flour, cornstarch, coffee powder and chocolate. Set aside.
2. In a medium bowl, using a wooden spoon, beat together butter and sugar until creamy. Gradually add flour mixture, stirring until well blended. Using your hands, knead until a smooth dough forms. Shape into small logs, each about ½ by 2 inches (1 by 5 cm). Place on baking sheet, spacing about 1 inch (2.5 cm) apart.
3. Bake in preheated oven for 15 to 20 minutes or until light golden around the edges. Let cool for 5 minutes on sheet, then transfer to a wire rack and cool completely.

Make Ahead: Dough can be refrigerated in an airtight container for up to a week or frozen for up to 3 months. Thaw overnight in the refrigerator or for 1 hour at room temperature before baking.

Variations

For a true coffee flavor, omit the chocolate.

Drizzle the logs with melted chocolate.

For an interesting crunch, substitute 3 tbsp (45 mL) finely crushed espresso or mocha java coffee beans for the instant espresso coffee powder.

Whipped Shortbread

◆

This cookie has the same tender, melt-in-your mouth texture and flavor as rolled shortbread, but with much less effort.

MAKES ABOUT 8 COOKIES

- Preparation: 15 minutes
- Baking: 20 minutes
- Freezing: excellent

Tips

You can use either unsalted or salted butter, but the sweet, delicate flavor of unsalted butter really comes through in shortbread, where butter is the main ingredient.

Bring butter to room temperature for easy blending.

If you don't have superfine sugar, whirl regular granulated sugar in a blender or food processor until fine.

White (colorless) vanilla is ideal for shortbread. You can find it in well-stocked supermarkets or baking supply stores.

Cooled cookies will keep in an airtight container at room temperature for up to 3 weeks or can be frozen for up to 3 months. Thaw and bring to room temperature before serving.

- **Preheat oven to 300°F (150°C)**
- **Baking sheet, ungreased**

½ cup	all-purpose flour	125 mL
1½ tbsp	cornstarch	22 mL
⅓ cup	butter, softened (see Tips, left)	75 mL
2½ tbsp	superfine granulated sugar (fruit sugar; see Tips, left)	37 mL
¼ tsp	pure vanilla extract (see Tips, left)	1 mL
	Candied cherries, halved, or pecan halves, optional	

1. In a small bowl, whisk together flour and cornstarch. Set aside.
2. In a medium bowl, using a wooden spoon, beat together butter, sugar and vanilla until very soft and creamy. Gradually add flour mixture, stirring well.
3. Drop dough by heaping tablespoonfuls (22 mL) on baking sheet, spacing about 1 inch (2.5 cm) apart. If desired, decorate tops of cookies with a cherry or pecan half.
4. Bake in preheated oven for 15 to 20 minutes or until light golden around the edges. Let cool for 5 minutes on sheet, then transfer to a wire rack and cool completely.

Make Ahead: Dough can be refrigerated in an airtight container for up to a week or frozen for up to 3 months. Thaw overnight in the refrigerator or for 1 hour at room temperature before baking.

Variations
Leave plain, decorate before baking or dust with confectioners' sugar after baking.

Chocolate Caramel Shortbread

◆

The best of both worlds: a melt-in-your mouth shortbread cookie combined with a favorite crunchy toffee chocolate bar.

MAKES ABOUT 8 COOKIES

- Preparation: 15 minutes
- Baking: 25 minutes
- Freezing: excellent

Tips

A common brand of chocolate toffee bar is Toblerone. Many generic-brand chocolate toffee bars are also available.

For a stronger chocolate flavor, use a dark chocolate toffee bar rather than a milk chocolate one.

Be sure to line your baking sheet with parchment paper, as the toffee is sticky.

Cooled cookies will keep in an airtight container at room temperature for up to 3 weeks or can be frozen for up to 3 months. Thaw and bring to room temperature before serving.

- **Preheat oven to 325°F (160°C)**
- **Baking sheet, lined with parchment paper**

⅓ cup	butter, softened	75 mL
3 tbsp	granulated sugar	45 mL
⅔ cup	all-purpose flour	150 mL
2 tsp	cornstarch	10 mL
2 oz	milk chocolate toffee bar, coarsely chopped (see Tips, left)	60 g

1. In a medium bowl, using a wooden spoon, beat together butter and sugar until light and creamy. Add flour and cornstarch, stirring well. Using your hands, knead until a smooth dough forms.
2. Reserve 8 larger pieces of the chocolate bar. Work the remainder into dough, using your hands or a wooden spoon.
3. Drop dough by heaping tablespoonsfuls (22 mL) on prepared baking sheet, spacing about 1 inch (2.5 cm) apart. Press a reserved chunk of chocolate on top of each cookie.
4. Bake in preheated oven for 20 to 25 minutes or until light golden around the edges. Let cool for 5 minutes on sheet, then transfer to a wire rack and cool completely.

Make Ahead: Dough can be refrigerated in an airtight container for up to a week or frozen for up to 3 months. Thaw overnight in the refrigerator or for 1 hour at room temperature before baking.

Variation
Dust cookies with confectioners' sugar just before serving.

Bars and Squares

Double Fudge Brownies

At first glance these brownies appear relatively plain, but don't be fooled. These are dense, moist and fudgy. An intensely flavored chocolate base is topped with a rich, creamy frosting.

MAKES 8 BROWNIES

- Preparation: 20 minutes
- Baking: 22 minutes
- Cooling: 15 minutes
- Freezing: excellent

Tip
. . . .

For a nicer frosting, substitute half and half (10%) cream for the milk.

- **Preheat oven to 325°F (160°C)**
- **8- by 4-inch (20 by 10 cm) loaf pan, greased and lined with parchment paper**

BROWNIES

¼ cup	butter	60 mL
1 oz	unsweetened chocolate, chopped	30 g
1	egg	1
½ cup	granulated sugar	125 mL
½ tsp	pure vanilla extract	2 mL
⅓ cup	all-purpose flour	75 mL
1 tbsp	unsweetened cocoa powder, sifted	15 mL
⅛ tsp	baking powder	0.5 mL
⅛ tsp	salt	0.5 mL

CHOCOLATE FROSTING

1 tbsp	butter	15 mL
½ oz	unsweetened chocolate, chopped	15 g
¾ cup	confectioners' (icing) sugar, sifted (see Quick Tip, right)	175 mL
1 tbsp	milk (see Tip, left)	15 mL
¼ tsp	pure vanilla extract	1 mL

1. *Brownies:* In a small microwave-safe bowl, combine butter and chocolate. Microwave on Medium for about 1 minute, stirring halfway through, until melted and smooth. Let cool until lukewarm, about 10 minutes.
2. In a medium bowl, whisk together egg, sugar and vanilla. Whisk in chocolate mixture.
3. In a small bowl, whisk together flour, cocoa powder, baking powder and salt. Add to chocolate mixture, whisking well. Spread batter evenly in prepared pan.
4. Bake in preheated oven for 18 to 22 minutes or until set. Let cool for 5 minutes in pan set on a wire rack.

Tip

. . . .

Cooled brownies will keep in an airtight container at room temperature for up to 1 week or can be frozen for up to 3 months. Thaw and bring to room temperature before serving.

5. *Chocolate Frosting:* In a small saucepan over low heat, melt butter and chocolate, stirring until smooth. Remove from heat. Let cool until lukewarm.

6. In alternating batches, using a wooden spoon, beat in confectioners' sugar, milk and vanilla, using just enough milk to reach a smooth, spreadable consistency.

7. Drop frosting by spoonfuls over warm brownie base. Spread to cover. Let cool completely in pan on wire rack. Remove from pan, using parchment liner, and cut into bars or squares.

Variation

For a mocha flavor, add 1 tsp (5 mL) instant espresso coffee powder along with the flour in Step 3.

QUICK TIP

Confectioners' (icing) sugar will clump during storage. Press through a fine-mesh sieve to remove any lumps so your frosting will be smooth.

Good and Gooey Caramel Brownies

◆

The name doesn't capture the amount of flavor packed in just one bite. Rich, chewy and loaded with gooey caramel, chocolate chips and crunchy pecans, these brownies are sensational.

MAKES 8 BROWNIES

- Preparation: 20 minutes
- Baking: 34 minutes
- Cooking: 5 minutes
- Freezing: excellent

Tips

Use fresh caramels. Stale ones will not melt smoothly.

Because oven temperatures vary, I recommend that you treat all recipe times as guidelines and begin checking what you're baking about 5 minutes before the minimum recommended cooking time.

- Preheat oven to 350°F (180°C)
- 8- by 4-inch (20 by 10 cm) loaf pan, greased and lined with parchment paper

6 tbsp	all-purpose flour	90 mL
¼ tsp	baking powder	1 mL
Pinch	salt	Pinch
½ cup	granulated sugar	125 mL
3 tbsp	unsweetened cocoa powder, sifted	45 mL
¼ cup	vegetable oil	60 mL
1	egg	1
1 tbsp	milk	15 mL
¼ cup	semisweet chocolate chips	60 mL
¼ cup	chopped pecans, divided	60 mL
3½ oz	soft caramels (about 13; see Tips, left)	105 g
⅓ cup	sweetened condensed milk	75 mL

1. In a small bowl, whisk together flour, baking powder and salt. Set aside.
2. In a medium bowl, whisk together sugar, cocoa powder, oil, egg and milk, until smooth. Gradually add flour mixture, whisking until smooth. Stir in chocolate chips and 2 tbsp (30 mL) pecans. Spread two-thirds of the batter evenly in prepared pan.
3. Bake in preheated oven for 10 to 12 minutes or until set.
4. Meanwhile, in a small, heavy saucepan over low heat, heat caramels and condensed milk, stirring often, until smooth. Pour over partially baked brownie base. Sprinkle remaining pecans overtop.
5. Drop tablespoonfuls (15 mL) of remaining chocolate batter evenly over caramel and pecans. Spread gently to cover. Using the tip of a knife, swirl the uncooked batter and caramel layers to marbleize.

Tips

Make sure the pan is well greased and lined with parchment paper, to prevent the caramel from sticking.

Cooled brownies will keep in an airtight container at room temperature for up to 1 week or can be frozen for up to 3 months. Thaw and bring to room temperature before serving.

6. Return pan to oven and bake for 18 to 22 minutes or just until set. Let cool completely in pan on a wire rack. Remove from pan, using parchment liner, and cut into bars or squares.

Variations

Substitute your favorite nut for the pecans.

Substitute milk chocolate chips for the semisweet chocolate chips.

QUICK TIP

A reliable kitchen scale is a good investment. You can purchase ingredients in bulk, then weigh out only what you need.

Cappuccino Brownies

These brownies are a coffee-lover's dream: rich, moist, dense and fudgy, topped with a creamy coffee frosting. Enjoy with a steaming cappuccino.

MAKES 8 BROWNIES

- Preparation: 25 minutes
- Baking: 22 minutes
- Chilling: 1½ hours
- Freezing: excellent

Tips

Instant espresso coffee is now available in most grocery stores as well as specialty coffee stores like Starbucks. If you can't find any, you can substitute double the amount of regular instant coffee powder.

When dissolving espresso powder in cold milk, first crush the granules with the back of a spoon. You can also warm the milk-coffee mixture in a microwave for 30 to 40 seconds.

- **Preheat oven to 350°F (180°C)**
- **8- by 4-inch (20 by 10 cm) loaf pan, greased and lined with parchment paper**

BROWNIES

½ cup	all-purpose flour	125 mL
1½ tsp	instant espresso coffee powder	7 mL
¼ tsp	baking powder	1 mL
¼ tsp	salt	1 mL
½ cup	semisweet chocolate chips	125 mL
¼ cup	butter	60 mL
½ cup	granulated sugar	125 mL
½ tsp	pure vanilla extract	2 mL
1	egg	1

FROSTING

¾ tsp	instant espresso coffee powder (see Tips, left)	3 mL
½ to 1 tbsp	milk	7 to 15 mL
1 cup	confectioners' (icing) sugar, sifted	250 mL
2 tbsp	butter, softened	30 mL

GLAZE (OPTIONAL)

½ cup	semisweet chocolate chips	125 mL
2½ tbsp	heavy or whipping (35%) cream	37 mL

1. *Brownies:* In a small bowl, whisk together flour, espresso powder, baking powder and salt. Set aside.
2. In a medium saucepan over low heat, melt chocolate chips and butter, stirring until smooth. Remove from heat. Whisk in sugar and vanilla. Add egg, whisking until smooth. Whisk in flour mixture until thoroughly combined. Spread batter evenly in prepared pan.
3. Bake in preheated oven for 18 to 22 minutes or just until set. Let cool completely in pan on a wire rack.

Tip

Cooled brownies will keep in an airtight container at room temperature for up to 1 week or can be frozen for up to 3 months. Thaw and bring to room temperature before serving.

4. *Frosting:* In a medium bowl, combine espresso powder and milk, stirring until dissolved (warm slightly in microwave if necessary to dissolve coffee). Add confectioners' sugar and butter. Beat with a wooden spoon until smooth. If necessary to reach a smooth spreading consistency, add a little more milk. Spread evenly over brownies. Refrigerate for about 1 hour to firm frosting.

5. *Glaze (optional):* In a small microwave-safe bowl, combine chocolate chips and cream. Microwave on Medium for about 1 minute, stirring halfway through, until chocolate is melted and smooth. Working quickly, spread evenly over frosting. Refrigerate until chocolate is set, about 30 minutes. Remove from pan and cut into bars or squares.

Variations

For a milder coffee flavor, reduce the amount of espresso powder by one-third in both the brownie batter and the frosting.

Instead of the glaze, drizzle 1 oz (30 g) melted semisweet chocolate over the frosting.

Chunky Chocolate Walnut Brownies

You can't go wrong with this: a deep, dark and delicious cakey chocolate brownie with lots of nuts. If you're feeling in the mood for a little excess, top with the yummy cocoa frosting. Either way, these are a winner.

MAKES 12 BROWNIES

- Preparation: 20 minutes
- Baking: 25 minutes
- Freezing: excellent

Tips

If frosting is too stiff to spread easily, beat in a little extra milk. If it seems too soft, add a bit more confectioners' sugar.

For a lighter brownie, omit the frosting.

The more you whisk the egg-sugar mixture, the lighter the texture will be. Less whisking yields a denser, firmer brownie.

Be careful not to overbake brownies; they can dry out quickly in the oven.

Cooled brownies will keep in an airtight container at room temperature for up to 1 week or can be frozen for up to 3 months. Thaw and bring to room temperature before serving

- Preheat oven to 350°F (180°C)
- 9- by 5-inch (23 by 12.5 cm) loaf pan, greased and lined with parchment paper

BROWNIES

2½ oz	unsweetened chocolate, chopped	75 g
⅓ cup	butter	75 mL
2	eggs	2
¾ cup	granulated sugar	175 mL
¾ tsp	pure vanilla extract	3 mL
½ cup	all-purpose flour	125 mL
½ cup	coarsely chopped walnuts	125 mL

COCOA FROSTING (OPTIONAL)

1 cup	confectioners' (icing) sugar, sifted	250 mL
2 tbsp	unsweetened cocoa powder	30 mL
1 tbsp	butter, softened	15 mL
2 tbsp	milk	30 mL

1. *Brownies:* In a small microwave-safe bowl, combine chocolate and butter. Microwave on Medium for about 1 minute, stirring halfway through, until melted and smooth. Set aside.
2. In a medium bowl, whisk eggs until light and frothy. Gradually add sugar, whisking until thick, about 1 minute. Whisk in chocolate mixture and vanilla. Add flour and walnuts and stir well. Spread batter evenly in prepared pan.
3. Bake in preheated oven for 20 to 25 minutes or just until set. Let cool completely in pan on a wire rack.
4. *Cocoa Frosting (optional):* In a small bowl, sift together confectioners' sugar and cocoa powder. In a medium bowl, using a wooden spoon, beat butter until creamy. In alternating batches, stir in confectioners' sugar mixture and milk, beating until smooth and spreadable.
5. Spread frosting over cooled brownie base. Remove from pan, using parchment liner, and cut into bars or squares.

Variation

Substitute coarsely chopped pecans for the walnuts.

White Chocolate Cranberry Hazelnut Brownies

♦

I'm sure this creamy white chocolate brownie, loaded with hazelnuts and cranberries, will become one of your favorites.

MAKES 8 BROWNIES

- Preparation: 15 minutes
- Baking: 30 minutes
- Freezing: excellent

Tips

If you can find orange-flavored dried cranberries, try them here. They taste particularly delicious in this brownie.

These make a nice holiday gift. Pack them in a small, airtight decorative cookie tin or box, tie with a festive ribbon and include the recipe with your gift tag.

Cooled brownies will keep in an airtight container at room temperature for up to 1 week or can be frozen for up to 3 months. Thaw and bring to room temperature before serving.

- Preheat oven to 375°F (190°C)
- 8- by 4-inch (20 by 10 cm) loaf pan, greased and lined with parchment paper

3 oz	white chocolate, chopped	90 g
1/3 cup	granulated sugar	75 mL
1	egg	1
3 tbsp	butter, melted	45 mL
1/2 tsp	pure vanilla extract	2 mL
2/3 cup	all-purpose flour	150 mL
1/4 tsp	baking powder	1 mL
1/3 cup	coarsely chopped hazelnuts	75 mL
1/4 cup	dried cranberries (se Tips, left)	60 mL

1. In a small saucepan over low heat, melt white chocolate, stirring constantly, until smooth. Remove pan from heat and set aside.
2. In a small bowl, whisk together sugar and egg. Whisk in melted butter and vanilla.
3. In another bowl, combine flour and baking powder. Add to egg mixture in alternating batches with melted chocolate, making two additions of each and stirring until smooth. Stir in hazelnuts and cranberries. Spread batter evenly in prepared pan.
4. Bake in preheated oven for 25 to 30 minutes, just until set and golden. Let cool completely in pan on a wire rack. Remove from pan, using parchment liner, and cut into bars or squares.

> ## Variations
> Substitute pecans or walnuts for the hazelnuts.
>
> Substitute dried cherries or apricots for the cranberries.

Apple Blondies with Brown Sugar Frosting

I'm not sure whether I like the frosting or the apple blondies the best. Both components are scrumptious. You'll have to decide for yourself.

MAKES 8 BLONDIES

- Preparation: 20 minutes
- Baking: 22 minutes
- Cooling: 15 minutes
- Freezing: excellent

Tips

Choose apples that are crisp, tart and not too moist. Granny Smith, Golden Delicious and Spartans are good choices for this recipe.

When first mixed, this frosting is very soft, making it very spreadable. It firms up when cool.

If you are counting calories, omit the frosting and sprinkle confectioners' sugar over the blondies just before serving.

- **Preheat oven to 350°F (180°C)**
- **8- by 4-inch (20 by 10 cm) loaf pan, greased and lined with parchment paper**

BLONDIES

½ cup	all-purpose flour	125 mL
½ tsp	baking powder	2 mL
Pinch	salt	Pinch
2½ tbsp	butter, softened	37 mL
½ cup	packed brown sugar	125 mL
1	egg	1
¼ tsp	pure vanilla extract	1 mL
½ cup	chopped peeled, cored apple (see Tips, left)	125 mL
¼ cup	chopped walnuts	60 mL

BROWN SUGAR FROSTING

2 tbsp	butter	30 mL
¼ cup	packed brown sugar	60 mL
1 tbsp	milk	15 mL
½ cup	confectioners' (icing) sugar, sifted	125 mL

1. *Blondies:* In a small bowl, whisk together flour, baking powder and salt. Set aside.
2. In a medium bowl, using a wooden spoon, beat together butter, brown sugar, egg and vanilla, until smooth and creamy. Whisk in flour mixture. Stir in apple and walnuts. Spread batter evenly in prepared pan.
3. Bake in preheated oven for 18 to 22 minutes or until set and golden. Let cool completely in pan on a wire rack.

Tip

Cooled blondies will keep in an airtight container at room temperature for up to 1 week or can be frozen for up to 3 months. Thaw and bring to room temperature before serving.

4. *Brown Sugar Frosting:* In a small saucepan over low heat, melt butter. Stir in brown sugar and milk. Bring mixture to just below a boil (don't boil), then remove pan from heat and let cool to lukewarm, about 15 minutes. Stir in confectioners' sugar, beating until smooth. Spread evenly over blondie base. Let stand until frosting is firm enough to cut. Remove from pan, using parchment liner, and cut into bars or squares.

Variations

For plain apple blondies, omit the frosting.

For a nut-free treat, omit the nuts.

Substitute pecans or almonds for the walnuts.

Two-Tone Dream Bars

◆

Although these look and sound quite decadent, they're actually fairly light in texture—the perfect solution for any midnight cravings.

MAKES 9 BARS

- Preparation: 20 minutes
- Baking: 30 minutes
- Chilling: 10 minutes
- Freezing: excellent

Tips

For a less sweet and lower-calorie bar, melt only 1 oz (30 g) white chocolate and 1 tsp (5 mL) butter, then drizzle it over the bars.

A small offset spatula makes spreading toppings over smaller surface areas easy. It's also good at getting into corners.

- **Preheat oven to 350°F (180°C)**
- **8- by 4-inch (20 by 10 cm) loaf pan, greased and lined with parchment paper**

CRUST

¼ cup	all-purpose flour	60 mL
1½ tbsp	granulated sugar	22 mL
1½ tbsp	butter, softened	22 mL

FILLING

¼ cup	graham wafer crumbs	60 mL
¼ cup	semisweet chocolate chips	60 mL
3 tbsp	chopped walnuts	45 mL
⅓ cup	sweetened condensed milk	75 mL

TOPPING

3 oz	white chocolate, chopped (see Tips, left)	90 g
1 tbsp	butter	15 mL

1. *Crust:* In a small bowl, combine flour and sugar. Using a wooden spoon, stir in butter, mixing until thoroughly blended and crumbly. Press mixture evenly into bottom of prepared pan.
2. Bake in preheated oven for 9 to 12 minutes or until golden around the edges.
3. *Filling:* In a small bowl, using a wooden spoon, stir together graham wafer crumbs, chocolate chips and walnuts. Add condensed milk, stirring until well blended.
4. Drop mixture by teaspoonfuls (5 mL) over warm crust. Spread evenly.
5. Return pan to oven and bake for 14 to 18 minutes longer or until top is lightly browned. Let cool completely in pan on a wire rack.

Bars will keep in an airtight container at room temperature for up to 1 week or can be frozen for up to 3 months (separate layers with waxed paper). Thaw and bring to room temperature before serving.

6. *Topping:* In a small microwave-safe bowl, combine white chocolate and butter. Microwave on High for about 1 minute, stirring halfway through, until melted and smooth. Spread evenly over bars. Refrigerate until topping sets, about 10 minutes. Remove from pan, using parchment liner, and cut into bars.

Variations

Substitute white or milk chocolate chips for the semisweet chocolate chips.

Substitute vanilla wafer crumbs for the graham wafer crumbs.

Chocolate Buttercrunch Bars

◆

These bars have everything. They're moist, chewy, crunchy and delicious all in one bite. You can tell from the batter (a bit of dough holding together lots of fabulous ingredients) that they'll be amazing.

MAKES 9 BARS

- Preparation: 20 minutes
- Baking: 22 minutes
- Freezing: excellent

Tips

To keep brown sugar soft, place an apple slice or piece of bread in a tightly sealed bag with the sugar.

Skor or Heath bars work well in this recipe.

Chill the candy bars before breaking them up. Put them in a heavy plastic bag and smash with a meat mallet. You'll end up with a nice mixture of large and small pieces.

Bars will keep in an airtight container at room temperature for up to 1 week or can be frozen for up to 3 months (separate layers with waxed paper). Thaw and bring to room temperature before serving.

- **Preheat oven to 350°F (180°C)**
- **9- by 5-inch (23 by 12.5 cm) loaf pan, greased and lined with parchment paper**

¼ cup	butter, melted	60 mL
⅓ cup	packed brown sugar	75 mL
2 tbsp	granulated sugar	30 mL
1	egg	1
¼ tsp	pure almond extract	1 mL
6 tbsp	all-purpose flour	90 mL
⅛ tsp	baking soda	0.5 mL
⅛ tsp	ground cinnamon	0.5 mL
2	crunchy chocolate-covered toffee bars (1.4 oz/39 g each), chopped (see Tips, left)	2
⅓ cup	chopped unblanched almonds, toasted	75 mL
⅓ cup	milk chocolate chips	75 mL

1. In a medium bowl, using a wooden spoon, stir together melted butter, brown and granulated sugars, egg and almond extract, until smooth. Stir in flour, baking soda and cinnamon, until well combined. Add chopped chocolate bar, almonds and chocolate chips; stir well. Spread batter evenly in prepared pan.

2. Bake in preheated oven for 18 to 22 minutes or until set and golden. Let cool completely in pan on a wire rack. Remove from pan, using parchment liner, and cut into bars.

Variation

For a stronger chocolate taste, use semisweet chocolate chips.

Chocolate Sandwich Squares

◆

This sandwich cookie is very easy to make. The filling bakes right in, so no last-minute filling is required.

MAKES 8 SQUARES

- Preparation: 20 minutes
- Cooking: 5 minutes
- Baking: 27 minutes
- Freezing: excellent

Tips

· ·

When measuring brown sugar, pack it firmly into a dry measuring cup. It should hold its shape when turned out.

For easy pouring, melt the butter in a measuring cup or bowl with a spout.

The filling can also be heated in a microwave on Medium for about 2 minutes, stirring often until smoothly melted.

Cooled squares will keep in an airtight container at room temperature for up to 1 week or can be frozen for up to 3 months (separate layers with waxed paper). Thaw and bring to room temperature before serving.

- **Preheat oven to 350°F (180°C)**
- **8- by 4-inch (20 by 10 cm) loaf pan, greased and lined with parchment paper**

FILLING

½ cup	semisweet chocolate chips	125 mL
⅓ cup	sweetened condensed milk	75 mL
1½ tsp	butter	7 mL

BASE AND TOPPING

½ cup	packed brown sugar (see Tips, left)	125 mL
1	egg	1
¼ cup	butter, melted (see Tips, left)	60 mL
¼ tsp	pure vanilla extract	1 mL
½ cup	all-purpose flour	125 mL
¼ cup	chopped unblanched almonds	60 mL

1. *Filling:* In a small saucepan over low heat, combine chocolate chips, condensed milk and butter. Heat, stirring constantly, until chocolate is melted and mixture is smooth. Remove from heat and set aside.
2. *Base and Topping:* In a medium bowl, whisk together brown sugar, egg, melted butter and vanilla. Stir in flour and almonds, until well combined. Spread half the mixture evenly in prepared pan. Spread filling evenly over base. Dot teaspoonfuls (5 mL) of remaining batter overtop and, using a knife, spread lightly over filling.
3. Bake in preheated oven for 23 to 27 minutes or until set and golden. Let cool completely in pan on a wire rack. Remove from pan, using parchment liner, and cut into squares.

> ## Variations
>
> For a blond bar, substitute butterscotch or peanut butter chips for the chocolate chips, and unsalted peanuts for the almonds.

White Chocolate Pecan Cranberry Squares

Fresh cranberries add a festive touch to these decadent squares. The thin crust emphasizes the filling.

MAKES 8 SQUARES

- Preparation: 20 minutes
- Baking: 37 minutes
- Freezing: excellent

Tips

If you prefer, prepare the crust in a food processor. Use cubed cold butter rather than softened. You can also prepare the crust in a bowl, cutting in cold butter with a pastry blender or two knives. Whichever method you use, the final mixture should resemble coarse crumbs.

For a pretty presentation, cut into triangles or diamonds instead of squares.

For a fancier presentation, melt 1 oz (30 g) white chocolate and drizzle over the bars.

Cooled squares will keep in an airtight container at room temperature for up to 1 week or can be frozen for up to 3 months (separate layers with waxed paper). Thaw and bring to room temperature before serving.

- **Preheat oven to 350°F (180°C)**
- **9- by 5-inch (23 by 12.5 cm) loaf pan, greased and lined with parchment paper**

CRUST

½ cup	all-purpose flour	125 mL
2 tbsp	granulated sugar	30 mL
3 tbsp	butter, softened	45 mL
1 tbsp	ground or finely chopped pecans	15 mL

TOPPING

1	egg	1
¼ cup	granulated sugar	60 mL
3 tbsp	corn syrup	45 mL
1 tbsp	butter, melted	15 mL
¼ cup	chopped pecans	60 mL
3 tbsp	chopped cranberries (fresh or frozen)	45 mL
3 tbsp	white chocolate chips	45 mL

1. *Crust:* In a small bowl, combine flour and sugar. Using a wooden spoon, stir in butter, mixing until thoroughly blended and crumbly. Stir in pecans. Press mixture evenly into bottom of prepared pan.
2. Bake in preheated oven for 10 to 12 minutes or until golden around the edges.
3. *Topping:* In a small bowl, whisk together egg, sugar, corn syrup and melted butter. Add pecans, cranberries and white chocolate chips; stir well. Pour over crust.
4. Return pan to oven and bake for 20 to 25 minutes longer or until set and golden. Let cool completely in pan on a wire rack. Remove from pan, using parchment liner, and cut into squares.

Variations

Substitute milk chocolate or semisweet chocolate chips for the white chocolate chips.

Substitute walnuts for the pecans.

Chocolate Caramel Peanut Bars

♦

These treats taste like a cookie and candy bar rolled into one.

MAKES 9 BARS

- Preparation: 20 minutes
- Baking: 32 minutes
- Freezing: excellent

Tips

Always assemble your ingredients before starting to bake. That way you'll be sure you have everything and not leave anything out.

Once opened, don't keep baking soda for longer than 6 months; it loses its potency. Invest in a new box and retire the old one to the refrigerator as a deodorizer.

Bars will keep in an airtight container at room temperature for up to 1 week or can be frozen for up to 3 months (separate layers with waxed paper). Thaw and bring to room temperature before serving.

- Preheat oven to 350°F (180°C)
- 8- by 4-inch (20 by 10 cm) loaf pan, greased and lined with parchment paper

BASE

½ cup	all-purpose flour	125 mL
½ cup	quick-cooking rolled oats	125 mL
⅓ cup	packed brown sugar	75 mL
¼ tsp	baking soda	1 mL
Pinch	salt	Pinch
¼ cup	butter, softened	60 mL
1	egg yolk, beaten	1

TOPPING

⅓ cup	semisweet chocolate chips	75 mL
¼ cup	chopped dry-roasted peanuts	60 mL
⅓ cup	dulce de leche	75 mL

1. *Base:* In a medium bowl, using a fork, combine flour, oats, brown sugar, baking soda and salt. Add butter and egg yolk, stirring until crumbly and uniform. Press half of the mixture evenly into bottom of prepared pan.
2. Bake in preheated oven for 10 minutes or until set.
3. *Topping:* Sprinkle chocolate chips and peanuts evenly over hot base. In a small microwave-safe bowl, microwave dulce de leche on Medium for 20 to 30 seconds, until warm and pourable. Drizzle evenly overtop, spreading lightly to cover chocolate chips. Sprinkle remaining oat mixture overtop.
4. Bake for 18 to 22 minutes or until top is golden. Let cool completely in pan on a wire rack. Remove from pan, using parchment liner, and cut into bars.

Variations

Substitute regular peanuts for the dry-roasted peanuts.

Substitute large-flake (old-fashioned) rolled oats for the quick-cooking rolled oats.

Chocolate Toffee Bars

◆

Super easy and super delicious, these taste just like a Skor or Heath candy bar.

MAKES 9 BARS

- Preparation: 15 minutes
- Baking: 15 minutes
- Freezing: excellent

Tips
. . . .

Toffee bits are available in bulk stores or the baking aisle of most supermarkets.

You can also crush crackers in a food processor fitted with the metal blade.

Bars will keep in an airtight container at room temperature for up to 1 week or can be frozen for up to 3 months (separate layers with waxed paper). Thaw and bring to room temperature before serving.

- **Preheat oven to 350°F (180°C)**
- **9- by 5-inch (23 by 12.5 cm) loaf pan, greased and lined with parchment paper**

4 oz	Ritz Crackers	125 g
⅔ cup	sweetened condensed milk	150 mL
⅔ cup	toffee bits (see Tips, left)	150 mL
⅔ cup	milk chocolate chips	150 mL

1. Place crackers in a thick plastic bag and, using a rolling pin, roll to crush them into fine crumbs (see Tips, left). Empty crumbs into a medium bowl. Add condensed milk and toffee bits. Stir well. Press mixture evenly into bottom of prepared pan.

2. Bake in preheated oven for 10 to 14 minutes or until set and golden. Sprinkle chocolate chips on top and return to oven for 1 minute to soften chocolate. Remove from oven and spread chocolate evenly over top. Let cool completely in pan on a wire rack. Remove from pan, using parchment liner, and cut into bars.

Variation

For a stronger chocolate taste, use semisweet chocolate chips.

Millionaire Squares

A woman who is always catering to several grandchildren gave me this recipe. It is one of those favorites you make over and over because it is so easy and tastes so good.

MAKES 8 SQUARES

- Preparation: 15 minutes
- Baking: 7 minutes
- Chilling: 30 minutes
- Freezing: excellent

Tips

You should get about 1 cup (250 mL) cookie crumbs from 12 cookies.

Since, like a candy bar, these are quite rich, you may want to cut them into small bars.

Squares will keep in an airtight container at room temperature for up to 1 week or can be frozen for up to 3 months (separate layers with waxed paper). Thaw and bring to room temperature before serving.

- **Preheat oven to 350°F (180°C)**
- **Food processor**
- **8- by 4-inch (20 by 10 cm) loaf pan, greased and lined with parchment paper**

BASE

12	packaged crisp oatmeal cookies	12
3 tbsp	butter, melted	45 mL

TOPPING

3 tbsp	butter	45 mL
⅓ cup	semisweet chocolate chips	75 mL
1	egg yolk	1
1 cup	confectioners' (icing) sugar, sifted	250 mL

1. *Base:* Using a food processor fitted with the metal blade, process cookies into fine crumbs (see Tips, left).
2. In a small bowl, combine cookie crumbs and melted butter. Reserve 2 tbsp (30 mL) for topping. Press remaining buttered crumbs evenly into bottom of prepared pan.
3. Bake in preheated oven for 5 to 7 minutes or until firm. Let cool completely in pan on a wire rack.
4. *Topping:* In a small saucepan, heat butter and chocolate chips over low heat, stirring constantly until melted. Remove from heat and let cool for 10 minutes, until lukewarm. Whisk in egg yolk. Stir in confectioners' sugar until smooth. Spread evenly over cooled base. Sprinkle with reserved crumbs, pressing in lightly. Cover and refrigerate before serving. Remove from pan, using parchment liner, and cut into squares.

Variation

For a milder chocolate flavor, use milk chocolate chips.

Chocolate Cheesecake Squares

These bars are scrumptious. Creamy chocolate cheesecake filling on a chocolate crumb crust doubles the chocolate delight.

MAKES 8 SQUARES

- Preparation: 20 minutes
- Baking: 32 minutes
- Standing: 30 minutes
- Freezing: excellent

Tips

For a fancy presentation, drizzle a little melted chocolate over the squares.

Cut into bite-size pieces for a cookie tray or larger for a dessert portion.

Cooled squares will keep in an airtight container at room temperature for up to 1 week or can be frozen for up to 3 months (separate layers with waxed paper). Thaw and bring to room temperature before serving.

- Preheat oven to 300°F (150°C)
- Electric hand mixer
- 8- by 4-inch (20 by 10 cm) loaf pan, greased and lined with parchment paper

CRUST

$2/3$ cup	chocolate wafer crumbs	150 mL
2 tbsp	butter, melted	30 mL
1 tbsp	granulated sugar	15 mL

FILLING

8 oz	cream cheese, softened	250 g
$1/3$ cup	granulated sugar	75 mL
1	egg	1
$1/4$ tsp	pure almond extract	1 mL
$2\frac{1}{2}$ oz	semisweet chocolate, chopped	75 g
2 tbsp	butter, softened	30 mL

1. *Crust:* In a small bowl, combine chocolate wafer crumbs, butter and sugar. Stir well. Press mixture evenly into bottom of prepared pan. Cover and refrigerate while preparing filling.
2. *Filling:* In a small bowl, using an electric mixer at high speed, beat cream cheese until smooth. Add sugar, egg and almond extract, beating well.
3. In a small microwave-safe bowl, combine chocolate and butter. Microwave on High for about 1 minute, stirring halfway through, until melted and smooth. Set aside until lukewarm. Add to cream cheese mixture, beating at low speed just until combined. Spread evenly over chocolate crust.
4. Bake in preheated oven for 28 to 32 minutes or just until softly set. Turn oven off and leave cheesecake inside for 30 minutes. Let cool completely in pan on a wire rack. Cover and refrigerate until ready to serve. Remove from pan, using parchment liner, and cut into squares.

> ## Variation
> Substitute pure peppermint extract for the almond extract.

Raspberry Coconut Pinwheels (page 22)

Black Forest Cookies (page 24)

Key Lime Coconut Macaroons (page 26)

Oatmeal Candy Cookies (page 35)

Apricot Fig Pinwheels (page 38)

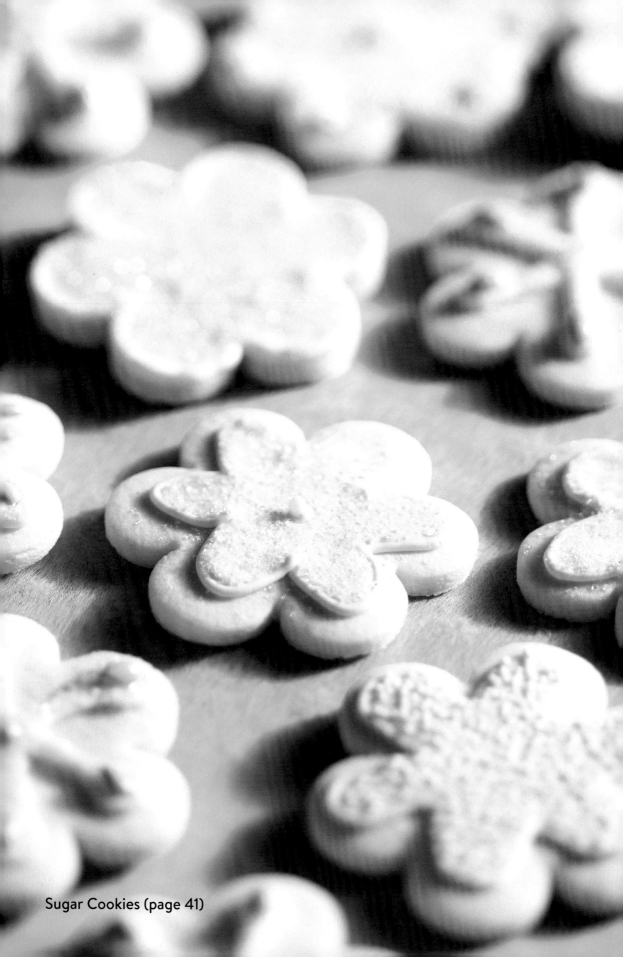

Sugar Cookies (page 41)

Viennese Fingers (page 42)

Crunchy Almond Crescents (page 48)

Chocolate-Wrapped Ginger Biscotti (page 52)

Peanut Fudgies (page 64)

Chocolate-Dipped Brownie Mounds (page 66)

Cherry Pistachio Shortbread (page 72)

Caramel Apple Bars

These bars bring back fond memories of the caramel apples I enjoyed as a kid at fall fairs, exhibitions and Halloween.

MAKES 9 BARS

- Preparation: 15 minutes
- Baking: 22 minutes
- Freezing: excellent

Tips

To avoid a soggy crust, use a firm, crisp apple such as Granny Smith or Spartan.

If you're using a glass baking dish, reduce the oven temperature to 325°F (160°C).

Bars will keep in an airtight container at room temperature for up to 1 week or can be frozen for up to 3 months (separate layers with waxed paper). Thaw and bring to room temperature before serving.

- **Preheat oven to 350°F (180°C)**
- **8- by 4-inch (20 by 10 cm) loaf pan, greased and lined with parchment paper**

3 tbsp	butter, softened	45 mL
3 tbsp	packed brown sugar	45 mL
½ cup	quick-cooking rolled oats	125 mL
6 tbsp	all-purpose flour	90 mL
½ tsp	ground cinnamon	2 mL
½ cup	coarsely grated peeled, cored apple	125 mL
2 tbsp	caramel sundae sauce	30 mL
3 tbsp	chopped peanuts	45 mL

1. In a medium bowl, using a wooden spoon, beat together butter and brown sugar. Gradually stir in oats, flour and cinnamon, mixing until crumbly. Set aside ⅓ cup (75 mL) for topping. Press remaining mixture evenly into bottom of prepared pan. Scatter apples evenly overtop. Sprinkle with reserved oat mixture. Drizzle with caramel sauce. Sprinkle peanuts overtop.

2. Bake in preheated oven for 18 to 22 minutes or until set and golden. Let cool completely in pan on a wire rack. Remove from pan, using parchment liner. Cut into bars.

Variations

Use a combination of half pears and half apples.

Substitute cashews for the peanuts.

Festive Fruit Squares

This is an attractive candied fruit and almond Florentine cookie on a shortbread crust, with a drizzle of chocolate to top it off. Tasty and elegant.

MAKES 8 SQUARES

- Preparation: 20 minutes
- Baking: 16 minutes
- Cooling: 30 minutes
- Freezing: excellent

Tips

If the candied fruit is packed in a thick syrup, wipe off excess syrup with paper towels before chopping.

Squares will keep in an airtight container at room temperature for up to 1 week or can be frozen for up to 3 months (separate layers with waxed paper). Thaw and bring to room temperature before serving.

You can also cut the squares into triangles for an attractive presentation.

If you prefer, use ¼ cup (60 mL) of one color of candied cherries.

You can omit chocolate drizzle. Instead dip one side of square in melted chocolate and cool as directed.

- **Preheat oven to 375°F (190°C)**
- **9- by 5-inch (23 by 12.5 cm) loaf pan, greased and lined with parchment paper**

CRUST

6 tbsp	all-purpose flour	90 mL
2 tbsp	confectioners' (icing) sugar, sifted	30 mL
2 tbsp	butter, softened	30 mL
1	egg yolk, beaten	1
¼ tsp	pure vanilla extract	1 mL

TOPPING

3 tbsp	butter	45 mL
2 tbsp	granulated sugar	30 mL
1 tbsp	milk	15 mL
¼ cup	sliced blanched almonds	60 mL
3 tbsp	chopped red candied (glacé) cherries (see Tips, left)	45 mL
3 tbsp	chopped candied (glacé) pineapple	45 mL
1 tbsp	chopped green candied (glacé) cherries	15 mL
½ oz	semisweet chocolate, melted	15 g

1. *Crust:* In a medium bowl, whisk together flour and confectioners' sugar. Using a fork, mix in butter, egg yolk and vanilla to make a moist, crumbly mixture. Using your hands, work dough until it comes together. Press evenly into bottom of prepared pan. Cover and refrigerate while preparing topping.
2. *Topping:* In a small saucepan over medium heat, combine butter, sugar and milk. Bring to a boil, stirring often with a wooden spoon. Boil, stirring constantly, until thickened, 1 to 2 minutes. Remove from heat. Add almonds, red cherries, pineapple and green cherries; stir well. Spread evenly over crust.
3. Bake in preheated oven for 12 to 16 minutes or until golden. Let cool completely in pan on a wire rack. Drizzle evenly with melted chocolate. Let cool for about 30 minutes to set chocolate. Remove from pan, using parchment liner. Cut into 8 squares.

Blueberry Cheesecake Bars

◆

These bars are really just small cheesecakes with a double dose of blueberries—yum!

MAKES 9 BARS

- Preparation: 20 minutes
- Baking: 45 minutes
- Freezing: excellent

Tips

You can beat the cheesecake mixture with a wooden spoon, but the texture will not be as light.

Bring eggs and cream cheese to room temperature before using, for easy blending.

If you have to soften cream cheese in a hurry, the microwave works well. Microwave on High for 15 to 20 seconds.

Bars will keep in an airtight container at room temperature for up to 1 week or can be frozen for up to 3 months (separate layers with waxed paper). Thaw and bring to room temperature before serving.

- **Preheat oven to 350°F (180°C)**
- **8- by 4-inch (20 by 10 cm) loaf pan, greased and lined with parchment paper**

CRUST

½ cup	all-purpose flour	125 mL
2 tbsp	granulated sugar	30 mL
2½ tbsp	cold butter, cubed	37 mL

TOPPING

4 oz	cream cheese, softened (see Tips, left)	125 g
3 tbsp	granulated sugar	45 mL
1	egg (see Tips, left)	1
1 tsp	freshly grated lemon zest	5 mL
1 tsp	freshly squeezed lemon juice	5 mL
¼ cup	blueberry jam	60 mL
¼ cup	fresh blueberries	60 mL

1. *Crust:* In a small bowl, combine flour and sugar. Using a pastry blender or two knives, cut in butter until mixture resembles coarse crumbs. Press evenly into bottom of prepared pan.
2. Bake in preheated oven for 12 to 15 minutes or until golden around the edges. Let cool in pan on a wire rack while preparing topping.
3. *Topping:* In a small bowl, using an electric mixer at medium speed, beat cream cheese and sugar until smooth. Add egg, lemon zest and lemon juice, beating until smooth.
4. Spread jam over cooled crust. Sprinkle blueberries on top. Pour cheese mixture over blueberries, spreading with a spoon to cover berries.
5. Return pan to oven and bake for 25 to 30 minutes or just until set. Let cool completely in pan on a wire rack. Remove from pan, using parchment liner. Cut into bars.

Variations

Replace the blueberry jam and fresh blueberries with strawberry or raspberry jam and sliced fresh strawberries or raspberries.

Lemony Lemon Squares

◆

This is one of my favorite lemon squares to make, as well as to eat. It's very easy to prepare and has a super-tart lemon taste.

MAKES 8 SQUARES

- Preparation: 15 minutes
- Baking: 30 minutes
- Freezing: excellent

Tips

For less pucker-up tartness, decrease the amount of lemon juice to 3 tbsp (45 mL).

One fresh lemon will give you 3 to 4 tbsp (45 to 60 mL) lemon juice.

Just before serving, dust these squares lightly with confectioners' sugar, if desired. Don't do it too far ahead, as it will eventually soak into the topping.

Cooled squares will keep in an airtight container at room temperature for up to 1 week or can be frozen for up to 3 months (separate layers with waxed paper). Thaw and bring to room temperature before serving.

- **Preheat oven to 350°F (180°C)**
- **8- by 4-inch (20 by 10 cm) loaf pan, greased and lined with parchment paper**

CRUST

½ cup	all-purpose flour	125 mL
2 tbsp	granulated sugar	30 mL
¼ cup	cold butter, cubed	60 mL

TOPPING

2	eggs	2
½ cup	granulated sugar	125 mL
1 tsp	freshly grated lemon zest	5 mL
¼ cup	freshly squeezed lemon juice (see Tips, left)	60 mL

1. *Crust:* In a small bowl, combine flour and sugar. Using a pastry blender or two knives, cut in butter until mixture resembles coarse crumbs. Press evenly into bottom of prepared pan.
2. Bake in preheated oven for 10 to 12 minutes or until golden around the edges.
3. *Topping:* In a small bowl, whisk together eggs, sugar, lemon zest and lemon juice, until well blended. Pour over crust.
4. Return pan to oven and bake for 15 to 18 minutes longer or until set. Let cool completely in pan on a wire rack. Remove from pan, using parchment liner, and cut into squares.

Variation

You can easily transform these into lime squares by substituting an equal quantity of lime juice and zest for half of the lemon juice and zest.

Cranberry Orange Apricot Bars

◆

This not-too-sweet bar is great with a cup of coffee or a glass of milk.

MAKES 9 BARS

- Preparation: 20 minutes
- Baking: 40 minutes
- Standing: 30 minutes
- Freezing: excellent

Tips

Spices don't last forever. Their flavor comes from volatile oils that lose their punch over time. Buy in small amounts that will be used fairly quickly. To ensure optimum flavor, keep spices in airtight containers in a cool, dry place. Label the container with the date of purchase.

Even though the fruits here are dried, they should still be soft and chewy when purchased.

Bars will keep in an airtight container at room temperature for up to 1 week or can be frozen for up to 3 months (separate layers with waxed paper). Thaw and bring to room temperature before serving.

Substitute chopped pitted dates or dried figs for the raisins.

Substitute apple juice, brandy or water for the orange juice.

- **Preheat oven to 350°F (180°C)**
- **9- by 5-inch (23 by 12.5 cm) loaf pan, greased and lined with parchment paper**

CRUST

½ cup	all-purpose flour	125 mL
2 tbsp	packed brown sugar	30 mL
¼ cup	cold butter, cubed	60 mL

TOPPING

¼ cup	golden raisins	60 mL
¼ cup	dried cranberries	60 mL
¼ cup	chopped dried apricots	60 mL
3 tbsp	freshly squeezed orange juice	45 mL
1	egg	1
½ cup	packed brown sugar	125 mL
2 tbsp	all-purpose flour	30 mL
¼ tsp	ground cinnamon	1 mL
3 tbsp	chopped pecans	45 mL

1. *Crust:* In a small bowl, combine flour and brown sugar. Using a pastry blender or two knives, cut in butter until mixture resembles coarse crumbs. Press evenly into bottom of prepared pan.
2. Bake in preheated oven for 12 to 15 minutes or until golden around the edges.
3. *Topping:* In a small saucepan, using a wooden spoon, combine raisins, cranberries, apricots and orange juice. Bring to a boil over medium heat, them remove from heat and let stand for 15 minutes. The liquid should be absorbed by the dried fruit. If necessary, drain off any excess. Set aside.
4. In a medium bowl, whisk together egg, brown sugar, flour and cinnamon. Stir in pecans and reserved fruits. Spread evenly over crust.
5. Return to oven and bake for 22 to 25 minutes or until set and golden. Let cool completely in pan on a wire rack. Remove from pan, using parchment liner. Cut into bars.

Raspberry Almond Bars

These bars are a colorful addition to cookie trays, and they taste as great as they look.

MAKES 9 BARS

- Preparation: 20 minutes
- Baking: 45 minutes
- Freezing: excellent

Tips

Although the filling has a tender but dense, cake-like texture, it doesn't contain any leavening agents such as baking soda or baking powder. Beating the egg into the batter provides the lightness.

Add a sprinkling of toasted, sliced almonds after the bars have been frosted.

- Preheat oven to 350°F (180°C)
- 8- by 4-inch (20 by 10 cm) loaf pan, greased and lined with parchment paper

CRUST

½ cup	all-purpose flour	125 mL
2 tbsp	granulated sugar	30 mL
¼ cup	cold butter, cubed	60 mL

FILLING

¼ cup	raspberry jam	60 mL
¼ cup	butter, softened	60 mL
⅓ cup	granulated sugar	75 mL
1	egg	1
⅓ cup	all-purpose flour	75 mL
⅛ tsp	salt	0.5 mL
	Red and green food coloring	

FROSTING

1 tbsp	butter, softened	15 mL
¾ cup	confectioners' (icing) sugar, sifted	175 mL
1 to 1½ tbsp	milk	15 to 22 mL
¼ to ½ tsp	pure almond extract	1 to 2 mL

1. *Crust:* In a small bowl, combine flour and sugar. Using a pastry blender or two knives, cut in butter until mixture resembles coarse crumbs. Press evenly into bottom of prepared pan.
2. Bake in preheated oven for 10 to 15 minutes or until golden around edges.

· · · · · · · · · · · · · · · · · ·

Bars will keep in an airtight container at room temperature for up to 1 week or can be frozen for up to 3 months (separate layers with waxed paper). Thaw and bring to room temperature before serving.

3. *Filling:* Spread jam over crust. Set aside.

4. In a small bowl, using a wooden spoon, beat together butter, sugar and egg, until smooth. Gradually add flour and salt. Stir well.

5. Divide batter evenly between two bowls. To one of the bowls, add red food coloring a few drops at a time, stirring, to make a pastel pink. Using green food coloring, repeat with the other bowl to make a pastel green.

6. In an alternating pattern, drop teaspoonfuls (5 mL) of each color over jam. Tap pan gently on counter to level batter.

7. Return to oven and bake for 25 to 30 minutes or until set and golden. Let cool completely in pan on a wire rack. Remove from pan, using parchment liner.

8. *Frosting:* In a small bowl, using a wooden spoon, beat butter until smooth. In alternating batches, gradually add confectioners' sugar and milk, using just enough milk to reach a smooth, spreadable consistency. Stir in almond extract. Spread evenly over cooled filling. Cut into bars.

Variation

For a plain bar, omit the food coloring—it'll still taste great.

Pink Coconut Squares

This soft, creamy frosting is a perfect match for a moist coconut filling and graham wafer crust.

MAKES 8 SQUARES

- Preparation: 20 minutes
- Baking: 37 minutes
- Cooling: 40 minutes
- Freezing: excellent

Tips

Half a 10-ounce (300 mL) can of sweetened condensed milk is about $\frac{2}{3}$ cup (150 mL).

The crust is fragile, so be careful when spreading filling over it. Drop the filling by teaspoonfuls (5 mL) evenly over the surface, then spread where needed.

- **Preheat oven to 350°F (180°C)**
- **9- by 5-inch (23 by 12.5 cm) loaf pan, greased and lined with parchment paper**

CRUST

¾ cup	graham wafer crumbs	175 mL
2 tbsp	packed brown sugar	30 mL
1½ tbsp	all-purpose flour	22 mL
¼ cup	butter, melted	60 mL

FILLING

⅔ cup	sweetened condensed milk (see Tips, left)	150 mL
1 cup	sweetened medium coconut	250 mL

FROSTING

¼ cup	butter, softened	60 mL
1 cup	confectioners' (icing) sugar, sifted	250 mL
1 tsp	milk	5 mL
1 to 2	drops red food coloring	1 to 2

1. *Crust:* In a medium bowl, using a wooden spoon, stir together graham wafer crumbs, brown sugar, flour and melted butter, mixing until all ingredients are moistened. Press mixture evenly into bottom of prepared pan.
2. Bake in preheated oven for 9 to 12 minutes or until firm. Let cool in pan on a wire rack for 10 minutes.
3. *Filling:* In a medium bowl, stir together condensed milk and coconut until thoroughly moistened. Spread evenly over crust (see Tips, left).
4. Return to oven and bake for 20 to 25 minutes longer or until light golden. Let cool completely in pan on a wire rack.

Squares will keep in an airtight container at room temperature for up to 1 week or can be frozen for up to 3 months (separate layers with waxed paper). Thaw and bring to room temperature before serving.

5. *Frosting:* In a medium bowl, using a wooden spoon, beat butter until smooth. In alternating batches, gradually add confectioners' sugar and milk, stirring until smooth and spreadable. Stir in coloring to make a pretty pink frosting. Spread evenly over filling. Refrigerate until frosting is firm, about 30 minutes. Remove from pan, using parchment liner. Cut into squares.

Variations
Add $1/2$ tsp (2 mL) pure almond extract to the filling.

Omit the red coloring for white coconut squares.

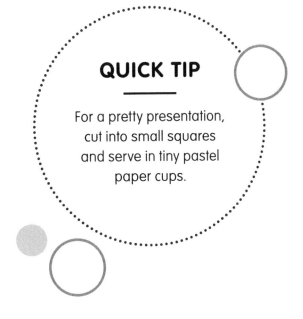

QUICK TIP

For a pretty presentation, cut into small squares and serve in tiny pastel paper cups.

Fabulous Fig Bars

◆

These bars are a childhood favorite. I'm not sure whether I love making these for the taste of the moist fig filling in a buttery crust or just for the memories.

MAKES 9 BARS

- Preparation: 25 minutes
- Cooking: 10 minutes
- Cooling: 10 minutes
- Baking: 23 minutes

Tips

Be sure to cut the stems off the dried figs before chopping.

Lightly oil your knife blade to prevent the figs from sticking when chopping.

- **Preheat oven to 350°F (180°C)**
- **8- by 4-inch (20 by 10 cm) loaf pan, greased and lined with parchment paper**

FILLING

1 cup	chopped dried figs (5 oz/150 g; see Tips, left)	250 mL
½ cup	water	125 mL
1½ tsp	freshly squeezed lemon juice	7 mL

CRUST

6 tbsp	all-purpose flour	90 mL
¼ cup	whole wheat flour	60 mL
½ tsp	baking powder	2 mL
½ tsp	ground cinnamon	2 mL
Pinch	salt	Pinch
3 tbsp	butter, softened	45 mL
¼ cup	granulated sugar	60 mL
1	egg yolk	1

1. *Filling:* In a small saucepan, combine figs, water and lemon juice. Bring to a boil over medium heat. Reduce heat to low and simmer, uncovered, until liquid is absorbed, about 10 minutes. Remove from heat and let cool until lukewarm. Transfer to a food processor fitted with the metal blade and purée. Set aside until cool, about 10 minutes.

2. *Crust:* In a medium bowl, whisk together all-purpose and whole wheat flours, baking powder, cinnamon and salt.

3. In a medium bowl, using a wooden spoon, beat together butter, sugar and egg yolk, until smooth. Gradually add flour mixture, stirring until thoroughly blended. With floured hands, knead dough to form a smooth ball.

4. Between two sheets of waxed paper, roll out dough into an 8-inch (20 cm) square. Remove top sheet of waxed paper. Cut dough in half. Transfer one half to prepared pan. Using moistened fingers or the back of a spoon, spread filling over dough. Place remaining half of dough on top.

5. Bake in preheated oven for 18 to 23 minutes or until golden. Let cool completely in pan on a wire rack. Remove from pan, using parchment liner. Cut into bars.

Variations

Substitute chopped pitted dates for the figs.

For a more fruity taste, substitute orange or apple juice for the water.

QUICK TIP

There is no need for an electric mixer when making small batches of squares. You can get the butter-sugar mixture to a light, creamy consistency by beating it with a wooden spoon.

Apricot Seed Bars

◆

Packed full of dried fruits and seeds, these bars make a great snack when you're hiking or biking.

MAKES 9 BARS

- Preparation: 15 minutes
- Baking: 25 minutes
- Freezing: excellent

Tips

Store seeds in an airtight container in the freezer to prevent rancidity.

These make great lunch-box treats. Individually wrap them in plastic wrap so you can grab and go.

Bulk food stores are a great alternative for purchasing small amounts of ingredients. By purchasing only what you need, you can be sure your ingredients are fresh.

Bars will keep in an airtight container at room temperature for up to 1 week or can be frozen for up to 3 months (separate layers with waxed paper). Thaw and bring to room temperature before serving.

- **Preheat oven to 350°F (180°C)**
- **8- by 4-inch (20 by 10 cm) loaf pan, greased and lined with parchment paper**

3 tbsp	butter, softened	45 mL
3 tbsp	packed brown sugar	45 mL
1	egg	1
¼ cup	whole wheat flour	60 mL
⅛ tsp	baking soda	0.5 mL
Pinch	salt	Pinch
¼ tsp	ground cinnamon	1 mL
⅓ cup	quick-cooking rolled oats	75 mL
¼ cup	finely chopped dried apricots	60 mL
3 tbsp	dried cranberries	45 mL
1 tbsp	raw sesame seeds	15 mL
1 tbsp	flax seeds	15 mL
1 tbsp	unsalted sunflower seeds	15 mL

1. In a medium bowl, using a wooden spoon, beat together butter, brown sugar and egg until creamy.
2. In a small bowl, whisk together flour, baking soda, salt and cinnamon. Stir in butter mixture until well combined. Add oats, apricots, cranberries, sesame seeds, flax seeds and sunflower seeds; stir well. Spread evenly in prepared pan.
3. Bake in preheated oven for 20 to 25 minutes or until set and golden. Let cool completely in pan on a wire rack. Remove from pan, using parchment liner. Cut into bars.

Variations

Substitute chopped dried figs or raisins for the cranberries.

Add ⅓ cup (75 mL) chopped almonds along with the seeds in Step 2.

Substitute pumpkin seeds or chia seeds for the sunflower seeds.

Substitute all-purpose flour for the whole wheat flour.

Cherry Lime Squares

Here's a square for all seasons. I love these flavors during the holiday season, but the refreshing combination of fruit is great in the summer as well.

MAKES 8 SQUARES

- Preparation: 15 minutes
- Baking: 35 minutes
- Freezing: excellent

Tips

For the best flavor, always use freshly squeezed lime juice.

To yield the most juice, warm limes for about 10 seconds on High in the microwave. Just remember to grate the zest first.

Cooled squares will keep in an airtight container at room temperature for up to 1 week or can be frozen for up to 3 months (separate layers with waxed paper). Thaw and bring to room temperature before serving.

- Preheat oven to 350°F (180°C)
- 8- by 4-inch (20 by 10 cm) loaf pan, greased and lined with parchment paper

CRUST

½ cup	all-purpose flour	125 mL
2 tbsp	confectioners' (icing) sugar, sifted	30 mL
1 tsp	freshly grated lime zest	5 mL
¼ cup	cold butter, cubed	60 mL

TOPPING

1	egg	1
½ cup	granulated sugar	125 mL
1 tsp	freshly grated lime zest	5 mL
1½ tbsp	freshly squeezed lime juice (see Tips, left)	22 mL
1 tbsp	all-purpose flour	15 mL
¼ tsp	baking powder	1 mL
¼ cup	chopped dried cherries	60 mL
	Confectioners' (icing) sugar, optional	

1. *Crust:* In a medium bowl, whisk flour, confectioners' sugar and lemon zest. Using a pastry blender or two knives, cut in butter until mixture resembles coarse crumbs. Press evenly into bottom of pan.
2. Bake in preheated oven for 12 to 15 minutes or until golden around the edges.
3. *Topping:* In a medium bowl, whisk together egg, sugar, lime zest and juice. Add flour and baking powder, whisking until smooth. Stir in cherries. Pour over crust.
4. Return pan to oven and bake for 15 to 20 minutes longer or until topping is set and light golden. Let cool completely in pan on a wire rack. Remove from pan, using parchment liner. Cut into squares. Sprinkle with confectioners' sugar just before serving, if desired.

Variations

Substitute equal quantities of lemon juice and zest for the lime.

Add ⅓ cup (75 mL) ground almonds to the crust, along with the flour.

Oatmeal Date Squares

◆

Also known as "matrimonial squares," these are old-fashioned favorites that never go out of style.

MAKES 8 SQUARES

- Preparation: 15 minutes
- Cooking: 15 minutes
- Baking: 25 minutes
- Freezing: excellent

Tips

Dates are very sweet. Balancing them with a little lemon or orange juice cuts the sweetness while adding flavor.

Dried fruits such as dates, raisins, figs and apricots are packed with vitamins and fiber.

Loaded with dates and oats, these tasty squares are a great choice for a healthy snack. For even more fiber, use whole wheat flour instead of all-purpose.

Cooled squares will keep in an airtight container at room temperature for up to 1 week or can be frozen for up to 3 months (separate layers with waxed paper). Thaw and bring to room temperature before serving.

- **Preheat oven to 350°F (180°C)**
- **8- by 4-inch (20 by 10 cm) loaf pan, greased and lined with parchment paper**

FILLING

1 cup	chopped pitted dates	250 mL
1 tsp	freshly grated orange zest	5 mL
½ cup	freshly squeezed orange juice	125 mL
2 tbsp	granulated sugar	30 mL

BASE AND TOPPING

½ cup	large-flake (old-fashioned) rolled oats	125 mL
⅓ cup	all-purpose flour	75 mL
⅓ cup	packed brown sugar	75 mL
¼ tsp	baking soda	1 mL
3 tbsp	cold butter, cubed	45 mL

1. *Filling:* In a small saucepan, combine dates, orange zest, orange juice and sugar. Cook over medium heat, stirring often, until thick and smooth, about 15 minutes. Set aside.

2. *Base and Topping:* In a large bowl, combine oats, flour, brown sugar and baking soda. Using two knives or a pastry blender, cut in butter until mixture resembles coarse crumbs. Press half of the mixture (⅔ cup/150 mL) evenly into bottom of prepared pan. Spread prepared filling over base. Sprinkle with remaining oat mixture. Pat down lightly.

3. Bake in preheated oven for 20 to 25 minutes or until light golden. Let cool completely in pan on a wire rack, then cut into squares.

Variation

Replace the orange zest with lemon zest, and the orange juice with 2 tbsp (30 mL) freshly squeezed lemon juice plus enough water to make ½ cup (125 mL).

Butterscotch Peanut Squares

A crisp crust and a chewy caramel topping with lots of peanuts in the middle make these squares the perfect partner for a cold glass of milk.

MAKES 8 SQUARES

- Preparation: 15 minutes
- Baking: 22 minutes
- Freezing: excellent

Tips

Like all nuts, peanuts become rancid quickly because they're high in fat. Keep them in your freezer in airtight containers to retain freshness, or buy them as you need them. Taste nuts before using to make sure they're fresh.

When butterscotch chips are old, they taste stale and do not melt properly. Be sure to always use fresh chips.

Cooled squares will keep in an airtight container at room temperature for up to 1 week or can be frozen for up to 3 months (separate layers with waxed paper). Thaw and bring to room temperature before serving.

- Preheat oven to 350°F (180°C)
- 8- by 4-inch (20 by 10 cm) loaf pan, greased and lined with parchment paper

CRUST

6 tbsp	all-purpose flour	90 mL
3 tbsp	packed brown sugar	45 mL
2 tbsp	butter, softened	30 mL

TOPPING

2/3 cup	salted peanuts (see Tips, left)	150 mL
3 tbsp	corn syrup	45 mL
1 tbsp	butter	15 mL
2 tbsp	water	30 mL
1/3 cup	butterscotch chips (see Tips, left)	75 mL

1. *Crust:* In a small bowl, using a fork, mix together flour, brown sugar and butter, until crumbly. Press mixture evenly into bottom of prepared pan.
2. Bake in preheated oven for 8 to 10 minutes or until golden around the edges.
3. *Topping:* Sprinkle peanuts over crust. In a small saucepan over low heat, combine corn syrup, butter, water and butterscotch chips. Cook, stirring often, until chips are melted and mixture is smooth. Pour evenly over peanuts.
4. Return pan to oven and bake for 8 to 12 minutes or until set. Let cool in pan on a wire rack. Remove from pan, using parchment liner, and cut into squares.

Variations

Substitute peanut butter chips or semisweet chocolate chips for the butterscotch chips.

Use dry-roasted peanuts instead of salted.

Substitute cashews for the peanuts.

Maple Nut Bars

Real maple syrup makes anything special, but especially these crunchy nut bars.

MAKES 9 BARS

- Preparation: 20 minutes
- Baking: 29 minutes
- Freezing: excellent

Tips

In all your baking, you can replace all-purpose flour with unbleached all-purpose flour if you prefer. They are interchangeable.

Always use pure maple syrup for baking. Pancake syrup doesn't have enough maple flavor and can react differently in baking.

Buy California walnuts for baking—they're usually fresher and of a higher quality. If you have the time, buy walnut halves and chop them rather than using pieces.

Bars will keep in an airtight container at room temperature for up to 1 week or can be frozen for up to 3 months (separate layers with waxed paper). Thaw and bring to room temperature before serving.

- **Preheat oven to 350°F (180°C)**
- **9- by 5-inch (23 by 12.5 cm) loaf pan, greased and lined with parchment paper**

CRUST

¼ cup	butter, softened	60 mL
2 tbsp	packed brown sugar	30 mL
½ cup	all-purpose flour (see Tips, left)	125 mL

TOPPING

1	egg	1
¼ cup	packed brown sugar	60 mL
1 tbsp	pure maple syrup (see Tips, left)	15 mL
1½ tsp	butter, melted	7 mL
1 tbsp	all-purpose flour	15 mL
⅛ tsp	baking powder	0.5 mL
¼ cup	coarsely chopped pecans	60 mL
3 tbsp	sliced hazelnuts	45 mL
3 tbsp	coarsely chopped walnuts (see Tips, left)	45 mL

1. *Crust:* In a small bowl, using a wooden spoon, cream butter and brown sugar until smooth. Gradually add flour and stir until thoroughly blended and crumbly. Press mixture evenly into bottom of prepared pan.
2. Bake in preheated oven for 9 to 11 minutes or until golden around the edges.
3. *Topping:* In a small bowl, whisk together egg, brown sugar, maple syrup and melted butter, until smooth. Whisk in flour and baking powder. Stir in pecans, hazelnuts and walnuts. Spread evenly over warm crust.
4. Return to oven and bake for 13 to 18 minutes or until topping is set. Let cool completely in pan on a wire rack. Remove from pan, using parchment liner, and cut into bars.

Variations

Substitute your favorite combination of nuts. To make the texture more interesting, use a combination of sliced and chopped nuts.

Chewy Toffee Almond Squares

These squares have a delicate candy-like base and a crunchy layer of sliced almonds covered by a thin, chewy caramel coating. It's a mouth-watering combination.

MAKES 8 SQUARES

- Preparation: 20 minutes
- Baking: 28 minutes
- Cooking: 10 minutes
- Freezing: excellent

Tips

Toffee bits are available in bulk food stores or the baking aisle of well-stocked grocers.

I have specified sweetened coconut because it seems to be more readily available than the unsweetened variety. But sweetened and unsweetened coconut can be used interchangeably in any recipe to suit your preference.

Cooled squares will keep in an airtight container at room temperature for up to 1 week or can be frozen for up to 3 months (separate layers with waxed paper). Thaw and bring to room temperature before serving.

- **Preheat oven to 350°F (180°C)**
- **8- by 4-inch (20 by 10 cm) loaf pan, greased and lined with parchment paper**

CRUST

¼ cup	butter, softened	60 mL
2 tbsp	granulated sugar	30 mL
½ cup	all-purpose flour	125 mL

TOPPING

⅓ cup	toffee bits (see Tips, left)	75 mL
3 tbsp	corn syrup	45 mL
¼ cup	slivered almonds, divided	60 mL
3 tbsp	sweetened flaked coconut, divided (see Tips, left)	45 mL

1. *Crust:* In a small bowl, using a wooden spoon, beat butter and sugar until smooth. Gradually add flour, stirring until thoroughly blended and crumbly. Press mixture evenly into bottom of prepared pan.
2. Bake in preheated oven for 12 to 14 minutes or until golden around the edges.
3. *Topping:* In a small saucepan over medium heat, combine toffee bits and corn syrup. Heat, whisking constantly, until toffee is melted and smooth, about 10 minutes. Stir in 2 tbsp (30 mL) almonds and 2 tbsp (30 mL) coconut. Spread evenly over crust, leaving a ¼-inch (5 mm) border clear. Sprinkle with remaining almonds and coconut.
4. Return pan to oven and bake for 10 to 14 minutes or until bubbly and golden around the edges. Let cool completely in pan on a wire rack. Remove from pan, using parchment liner, and cut into squares.

Variations

Substitute hazelnuts for the almonds.

For an attractive topping, use sliced unblanched almonds. The taste is the same as for the blanched variety, but the contrasting colors are pleasing.

For an attractive presentation, cut the squares into triangles.

Chocolate-Glazed Almond Squares

◆

These squares combine two favorites: cookies and candy. It's no wonder they are so popular.

MAKES 8 SQUARES

- Preparation: 20 minutes
- Baking: 22 minutes
- Cooking: 3 minutes
- Cooling: 30 minutes
- Freezing: excellent

Tip

You can also line the pan with aluminum foil, which fits nicely into the corners. Once the pan is lined, spray the foil with vegetable cooking oil to prevent sticking.

- **Preheat oven to 350°F (180°C)**
- **8- by 4-inch (20 by 10 cm) loaf pan, greased and lined with parchment paper (see Tip, left)**

CRUST

2 tbsp	butter, softened	30 mL
1/3 cup	confectioners' (icing) sugar, sifted	75 mL
1/4 cup	ground almonds	60 mL
2 tbsp	all-purpose flour	30 mL

TOPPING

3 tbsp	butter	45 mL
1/4 cup	packed brown sugar	60 mL
1/4 cup	corn syrup (see Quick Tip, right)	60 mL
1 1/2 tsp	water	7 mL
1 1/2 tsp	freshly squeezed lemon juice	7 mL
1/2 cup	sliced almonds	125 mL
1/4 tsp	pure almond extract	1 mL

GLAZE

1/2 oz	semisweet chocolate, chopped	15 g
1 1/2 tsp	butter	7 mL

1. *Crust:* In a small bowl, using a wooden spoon, beat together butter and confectioners' sugar until smooth. Gradually add ground almonds and flour, stirring until thoroughly blended and crumbly. Press mixture evenly into bottom of prepared pan.
2. Bake in preheated oven for 8 to 10 minutes. Let pan cool on a wire rack for 10 minutes.
3. *Topping:* In a small saucepan over medium heat, melt butter. Add brown sugar, corn syrup, water and lemon juice, whisking until smooth. Bring to a boil over medium-high heat and boil for 3 minutes, stirring constantly, until thickened. Remove from heat. Stir in almonds and almond extract. Spread evenly over crust.

Tip

Squares will keep in an airtight container at room temperature for up to 1 week or can be frozen for up to 3 months (separate layers with waxed paper). Thaw and bring to room temperature before serving.

4. Return pan to oven and bake until topping is set and golden, about 12 minutes. Let cool completely in pan on a wire rack.

5. *Glaze:* In a small microwave-safe bowl, combine chocolate and butter. Microwave on High for about 1 minute, stirring halfway through, until melted and smooth. Drizzle over topping. Let cool until chocolate is set, about 30 minutes. Remove from pan, using parchment liner, and cut into squares.

Variations

Although the chocolate drizzle is attractive, the bars store better and taste equally good without it.

Substitute hazelnuts for the almonds.

QUICK TIP

Corn syrup comes in white and golden versions. The white is used mainly for candy making, while the golden is used for baking.

Frosted Carrot Nut Bars

This is my bite-size version of an all-time favorite cake. Once you try it, you'll be hard-pressed to stop at just one!

MAKES 9 BARS

- Preparation: 20 minutes
- Baking: 18 minutes
- Freezing: excellent

Tips

Using spreadable cream cheese makes mixing easier. If you want to use regular block cream cheese, bring it to room temperature before using.

For an added touch, sprinkle some finely chopped walnuts over the frosting.

Bars will keep in an airtight container at room temperature for up to 1 week or can be frozen for up to 3 months (separate layers with waxed paper). Thaw and bring to room temperature before serving.

Substitute raisins, pecans or dried cranberries for the walnuts.

- **Preheat oven to 350°F (180°C)**
- **9- by 5-inch (23 by 12.5 cm) loaf pan, greased and lined with parchment paper**

BARS

½ cup	all-purpose flour	125 mL
½ tsp	baking soda	2 mL
½ tsp	ground cinnamon	2 mL
¼ tsp	ground nutmeg	1 mL
2 tbsp	butter, softened	30 mL
⅓ cup	packed brown sugar	75 mL
1	egg	1
½ tsp	pure vanilla extract	2 mL
¾ cup	peeled, shredded carrots	175 mL
¼ cup	chopped walnuts	60 mL

FROSTING

2 tbsp	spreadable cream cheese (see Tips, left)	30 mL
1 tbsp	butter, softened	15 mL
⅔ cup	confectioners' (icing) sugar, sifted	150 mL
⅛ tsp	ground cinnamon	0.5 mL

1. *Bars:* In a small bowl, whisk together flour, baking soda, cinnamon and nutmeg. Set aside.
2. In a medium bowl, using a wooden spoon, beat together butter, brown sugar, egg and vanilla, until creamy. Gradually add flour mixture, stirring until thoroughly blended. Add carrots and walnuts and stir well. Spread evenly into prepared pan.
3. Bake in preheated oven for 13 to 18 minutes or until a toothpick inserted in the center comes out clean. Let cool completely in pan on a wire rack. Remove from pan, using parchment liner.
4. *Frosting:* In a medium bowl, using a wooden spoon, beat together cream cheese and butter until smooth. Gradually add confectioners' sugar and cinnamon, beating until smooth and spreadable. Spread evenly over cooled bars. Cut into bars.

Caramel Honey Pecan Bars

◆

There's nothing I'd want to change about these bars, which are a favorite in my family. The honey adds a lovely flavor.

MAKES 9 BARS

- Preparation: 15 minutes
- Baking: 24 minutes
- Cooking: 5 minutes
- Freezing: excellent

Tips

For a plain crust, omit the pecans and increase the amount of flour by 1 tbsp (15 mL).

It takes a little extra time, but if you place the pecans right side up before adding the syrup, your bars will be more visually appealing.

Always taste your nuts before using. They go rancid quickly.

If you don't have heavy cream you can use an equal amount of evaporated milk.

Bars will keep in an airtight container at room temperature for up to 1 week or can be frozen for up to 3 months (separate layers with waxed paper). Thaw and bring to room temperature before serving.

- Preheat oven to 350°F (180°C)
- Food processor
- 9- by 5-inch (23 by 12.5 cm) loaf pan, greased and lined with parchment paper

CRUST

¾ cup	all-purpose flour	175 mL
2 tbsp	pecan halves	30 mL
1 tbsp	packed brown sugar	15 mL
1	egg yolk	1
¼ cup	cold butter, cubed	60 mL

TOPPING

1 cup	pecan halves	250 mL
3 tbsp	butter	45 mL
2 tbsp	liquid honey	30 mL
3 tbsp	packed brown sugar	45 mL
¼ tsp	ground cinnamon	1 mL
1 tbsp	heavy or whipping (35%) cream (see Tips, left)	15 mL

1. *Crust:* In a food processor fitted with the metal blade, combine flour, pecans and brown sugar; process until mixture resembles fine crumbs. Add egg yolk and butter and process into coarse moist crumbs. Press mixture evenly into bottom of prepared pan.
2. Bake in preheated oven for 10 to 12 minutes or until golden around the edges. Set aside.
3. *Topping:* Sprinkle pecans over crust (see Tips, left). In a medium saucepan over medium-high heat, melt butter and honey. Using a wooden spoon, stir in brown sugar and cinnamon. Bring to a boil, stirring constantly until mixture is a rich caramel color, 4 to 5 minutes. Remove from heat. Add cream and stir well. Pour evenly over pecans.
4. Return pan to oven and bake for 8 to 12 minutes or until topping is bubbly. Let cool completely on a wire rack. Remove from pan, using parchment liner. Cut into bars.

Crunchy Caramel Almond Squares

◆

These squares are one of the simplest recipes in this book. They're also one of my favorites. With a recipe like this, there's no excuse for not making homemade treats anytime.

MAKES 8 SQUARES

- Preparation: 10 minutes
- Cooking: 2 minutes
- Baking: 12 minutes
- Freezing: excellent

Tips

Be sure not to boil the sugar mixture, or sugar crystals may form and the mixture may become too thick.

Instead of cutting this into neat squares, break it into irregular pieces after it has cooled.

For a decadent treat, use these squares to make ice-cream sandwiches.

Cooled squares will keep in an airtight container at room temperature for up to 1 week or can be frozen for up to 3 months (separate layers with waxed paper). Thaw and bring to room temperature before serving.

- Preheat oven to 375°F (190°C)
- 8- by 4-inch (20 by 10 cm) loaf pan, greased and lined with parchment paper

4½	graham crackers square	4 ½
¼ cup	butter	60 mL
¼ cup	packed brown sugar	60 mL
6 tbsp	sliced almonds	90 mL

1. In prepared pan, arrange graham crackers in a single layer. Cut if necessary to cover pan bottom. Set aside.
2. In a small saucepan over medium heat, melt butter. Whisk in brown sugar. Bring to a boil, then reduce heat to low and simmer for 2 minutes (don't boil). Remove from heat. Stir in almonds. Quickly pour over crackers and spread evenly to cover.
3. Bake in preheated oven for 8 to 12 minutes or until bubbly and golden. Let cool completely in pan on a wire rack. Remove from pan, using parchment liner, and cut into squares.

Variations

Substitute hazelnuts for the almonds.

For a more intense caramel taste, use dark brown sugar.

For an attractive finish, drizzle the squares with melted white or dark chocolate.

Mom's Dream Cake

◆

For as long as I can remember, my mother, who was very fond of nuts of any kind, loved making and eating these delicious squares.

MAKES 8 SQUARES

- Preparation: 15 minutes
- Baking: 30 minutes
- Freezing: excellent

Tips

Toasting walnuts before using brings out their wonderful flavor and provides a pleasing crunch. Spread walnuts in an even layer on a baking sheet and bake in a preheated 350°F (180°C) oven for about 5 minutes, stirring often for even toasting, until light golden and fragrant.

In this recipe, sweetened or unsweetened coconut can be used since the amount called for is so small.

Cooled squares will keep in an airtight container at room temperature for up to 1 week or can be frozen for up to 3 months (separate layers with waxed paper). Thaw and bring to room temperature before serving.

- **Preheat oven to 350°F (180°C)**
- **9- by 5-inch (23 by 12.5 cm) loaf pan, greased and lined with parchment paper**

CRUST

½ cup	all-purpose flour	125 mL
2 tbsp	granulated sugar	30 mL
¼ cup	cold butter, cubed	60 mL

TOPPING

1	egg	1
⅔ cup	packed brown sugar	150 mL
½ tsp	pure vanilla extract	2 mL
1 tbsp	all-purpose flour	15 mL
½ tsp	baking powder	2 mL
½ cup	chopped walnuts (see Tips, left)	125 mL
¼ cup	sweetened flaked coconut (see Tips, left)	60 mL

1. *Crust:* In a small bowl, whisk together flour and sugar. Using a pastry blender or two knives, cut in butter until mixture resembles coarse crumbs. Press evenly into bottom of prepared pan.
2. Bake in preheated oven for 10 to 12 minutes or until golden around the edges.
3. *Topping:* In a medium bowl, whisk together egg, brown sugar and vanilla. Whisk in flour and baking powder. Stir in walnuts and coconut. Spread evenly over warm crust.
4. Return to oven and bake for 15 to 18 minutes or until set and golden. Cool completely in pan on a wire rack. Remove from pan, using parchment liner. Cut into 8 squares.

Variations

Substitute pecans for the walnuts.

For a more intense caramel taste, use dark brown sugar.

Chunky Chocolate Shortbread Bars

◆

These crisp chocolate shortbread bars have lots of crunch from the nuts.

MAKES 9 BARS

- Preparation: 15 minutes
- Baking: 20 minutes
- Freezing: excellent

Tips

Chocolate used to be sold in 1 oz (30 g) squares. However, they aren't always that weight anymore. Using a scale to weigh them will give you an accurate measure.

Toasting nuts before using gives them a pleasant fresh, nutty flavor and crunch. Arrange them in a single layer on a baking sheet and toast in a preheated 350°F (180°C) oven for about 5 minutes, stirring occasionally.

Cooled bars will keep in an airtight container at room temperature for up to 1 week or can be frozen for up to 3 months. Thaw and bring to room temperature before serving.

- **Preheat oven to 350°F (180°C)**
- **8- by 4-inch (20 by 10 cm) loaf pan, lined with parchment paper**

7 tbsp	all-purpose flour	105 mL
1 tbsp	cornstarch	15 mL
¼ cup	butter, softened	60 mL
2 tbsp	superfine granulated sugar (see Tips, page 123)	30 mL
1 oz	bittersweet chocolate, chopped (see Tips, left)	30 g
3 tbsp	coarsely chopped pecans, toasted (see Tips, left)	45 mL

1. In a small bowl, whisk together flour and cornstarch. Set aside.
2. In a medium bowl, using a wooden spoon, beat together butter and sugar until creamy. Gradually stir in flour mixture, stirring until well blended. Stir in chopped chocolate and pecans. Press mixture evenly into bottom of prepared pan.
3. Bake in preheated oven for 15 to 20 minutes or until lightly browned around the edges. Let cool completely in pan on a wire rack. Remove from pan, using parchment liner, and cut into bars.

Variations

Substitute cashews or hazelnuts for the pecans.

Substitute semisweet chocolate for the bittersweet chocolate.

Lemon Poppy Seed Shortbread Bars

The poppy seeds give these rich, buttery bars an interesting crunch and attractive appearance.

MAKES 9 BARS

- Preparation: 15 minutes
- Baking: 35 minutes
- Freezing: excellent

Tips

Butter is a must for making shortbread. You just don't get the same rich, buttery flavor using margarine.

Sift confectioners' sugar to eliminate any lumps that may have formed during storage.

For neat edges, cut shortbread while it is warm.

Cooled bars will keep in an airtight container at room temperature for up to 3 weeks or can be frozen for up to 3 months. Thaw and bring to room temperature before serving.

- **Preheat oven to 300°F (150°C)**
- **9- by 5-inch (23 by 12.5 cm) loaf pan, lined with parchment paper**

½ cup	butter, softened (see Tips, left)	125 mL
½ cup	confectioners' (icing) sugar, sifted (see Tips, left)	125 mL
1 cup	all-purpose flour	250 mL
1 tbsp	poppy seeds	15 mL
1 tbsp	freshly grated lemon zest	15 mL
1½ tsp	freshly squeezed lemon juice	7 mL
1 tbsp	granulated sugar	15 mL

1. In a medium bowl, using a wooden spoon, beat together butter and confectioners' sugar until light and creamy. Gradually stir in flour, poppy seeds, lemon zest and lemon juice until well combined. Using your hands, knead until a smooth dough forms. Press evenly into bottom of prepared pan. Sprinkle granulated sugar evenly overtop.
2. Bake in preheated oven for 30 to 35 minutes or until lightly browned around the edges. Let cool in pan on a wire rack. Remove from pan, using parchment liner. Cut into bars.

Variations

Substitute lime or orange zest and juice for the lemon.

For a plain citrus shortbread, omit the poppy seeds.

Cherry Pecan Shortbread Bars

◆

These bars have a soft shortbread dough base. They're enhanced with favorite holiday ingredients: candied cherries and pecans.

MAKES 9 BARS

- Preparation: 15 minutes
- Baking: 20 minutes
- Freezing: excellent

Tips

When shortbread is plain, you can cut it while the dough is warm, for neat edges. When shortbread contains chunky ingredients such as nuts and fruit, however, cutting it while warm isn't necessary.

Cooled bars will keep in an airtight container at room temperature for up to 3 weeks or can be frozen for up to 3 months. Thaw and bring to room temperature before serving.

- Preheat oven to 325°F (160°C)
- 8- by 4-inch (20 by 10 cm) loaf pan, lined with parchment paper

¼ cup	butter, softened	60 mL
3 tbsp	granulated sugar	45 mL
1	egg yolk	1
⅔ cup	all-purpose flour	150 mL
1 tsp	freshly grated lemon zest	5 mL
3 tbsp	chopped pecans	45 mL
3 tbsp	chopped red candied (glacé) cherries	45 mL

1. In a medium bowl, using a wooden spoon, beat together butter, sugar and egg yolk until light and creamy. Gradually add flour and lemon zest; stir until well combined. Stir in pecans and cherries. Using your hands, knead until a smooth dough forms. Press evenly into bottom of prepared pan.
2. Bake in preheated oven for 15 to 20 minutes or until lightly browned around the edges. Let cool completely in pan on a wire rack. Remove from pan, using parchment liner, and cut into bars.

Variations

Substitute walnuts or almonds for the pecans.

If desired, use green candied cherries instead of red.

Substitute an equal amount of pure vanilla extract for the lemon zest.

Add 1 oz (30 g) chopped semisweet or white chocolate to the dough along with the pecans and cherries.

Chocolate Ginger Shortbread Bars

◆

Filled with bits of sweet, tangy crystallized ginger, these buttery bars are a hit with ginger fans. They're perfect with a cup of tea.

MAKES 9 BARS

- Preparation: 15 minutes
- Baking: 40 minutes
- Freezing: excellent

Tips

Superfine sugar is also called fruit sugar or instant-dissolving sugar.

Although crystallized ginger is dried, make sure it is fresh when you buy it. It should have a slightly soft texture and smell like ginger. It can get very hard and lose its flavor with age.

Cooled bars will keep in an airtight container at room temperature for up to 3 weeks or can be frozen for up to 3 months. Thaw and bring to room temperature before serving.

- Preheat oven to 350°F (180°C)
- 9- by 5-inch (23 by 12.5 cm) loaf pan, lined with parchment paper

½ cup	butter, softened	125 mL
¼ cup	superfine granulated sugar (see Tips, left)	60 mL
1 cup	all-purpose flour	250 mL
¼ cup	finely chopped crystallized ginger (see Tips, left)	60 mL
¼ cup	chopped milk chocolate (1½ oz/45 g)	60 mL

1. In a medium bowl, using a wooden spoon, beat together butter and sugar until light and creamy. Gradually add flour, ginger and chocolate, stirring well after each addition. Using your hands, knead until a smooth dough forms. Press evenly into bottom of prepared pan.
2. Bake in preheated oven for 35 to 40 minutes or until lightly browned around the edges. Let cool completely in pan on a wire rack. Remove from pan, using parchment liner, and cut into bars.

Variation

For a stronger chocolate flavor, use semisweet chocolate.

Chocolate-Dipped Peanut Butter Shortbread Bars

◆

The great thing about making shortbread bars is that with a minimal amount of work you can make several types of shortbread in one pan. They taste every bit as good as the kind you roll out and cut individually.

MAKES 9 BARS

- Preparation: 20 minutes
- Baking: 15 minutes
- Standing: 1 hour
- Freezing: excellent

Tips

For an attractive presentation, cut the shortbread into triangles, dip the bottoms in chocolate and sprinkle with finely chopped peanuts.

These bars are quite thin and delicate. If you prefer a thicker bar, use an 8- by 4-inch (22 by 11 cm) loaf pan and bake for about 5 minutes longer.

- **Preheat oven to 350°F (180°C)**
- **9- by 5-inch (23 by 12.5 cm) loaf pan, lined with parchment paper**

SHORTBREAD

3 tbsp	butter, softened	45 mL
2 tbsp	creamy peanut butter	30 mL
1 tbsp	granulated sugar	15 mL
1 tbsp	packed brown sugar	15 mL
½ cup	all-purpose flour	125 mL
3 tbsp	miniature semisweet chocolate chips	45 mL

CHOCOLATE DIP

⅓ cup	semisweet chocolate chips	75 mL
1½ tsp	vegetable oil	7 mL

1. *Shortbread:* In a medium bowl, using a wooden spoon, beat together butter, peanut butter and granulated and brown sugars, until light and creamy. Gradually stir in flour. Using your hands, knead until a smooth dough forms. Knead in chocolate chips. Press evenly into bottom of prepared pan.
2. Bake in preheated oven for 12 to 15 minutes or until lightly browned around the edges. Let cool completely in pan on a wire rack. Remove from pan, using parchment liner, and cut into bars.

Bars will keep in an airtight container at room temperature for up to 3 weeks or can be frozen for up to 3 months (separate layers with waxed paper). Thaw and bring to room temperature before serving.

3. *Chocolate Dip:* In a medium microwave-safe bowl, combine chocolate chips and oil. Microwave on Medium for about 1 minute, stirring halfway through, until chocolate is melted and smooth. Dip one or both ends of shortbread bars into melted chocolate. Place on a wire rack over waxed paper. Let stand until chocolate is set, about 1 hour.

Variations

Instead of dipping the ends in melted chocolate, you can drizzle the chocolate overtop. You'll only need half the quantity of dip.

Knead in 2 tbsp (30 mL) finely chopped peanuts along with the chocolate chips in Step 1.

QUICK TIP

Coating or molding chocolate is ideal for dipping. It hardens quickly and, unlike pure chocolate, doesn't melt again once it's on the product. It tastes great, too. You can find it sold as small coins in bulk food and cake supply stores.

Rice Flour Shortbread Bars

This melt-in-your mouth shortbread is similar to the Scottish version, which is usually baked in rounds or decorative molds and cut into wedges.

MAKES 9 BARS

- Preparation: 15 minutes
- Baking: 30 minutes
- Freezing: excellent

Tips

Superfine sugar is also called fruit sugar or instant-dissolving sugar. It yields a smooth, melt-in-your-mouth shortbread that isn't grainy.

Use salted or unsalted butter. The choice is yours.

To ease mixing, bring the butter to room temperature before using.

Cooled bars will keep in an airtight container at room temperature for up to 3 weeks or can be frozen for up to 3 months. Thaw and bring to room temperature before serving.

- Preheat oven to 300°F (150°C)
- 9- by 5-inch (23 by 12.5 cm) loaf pan, lined with parchment paper

¾ cup	all-purpose flour	175 mL
6 tbsp	superfine granulated sugar (see Tips, left)	90 mL
¼ cup	rice flour	60 mL
Pinch	salt	Pinch
½ cup	butter, softened (see Tips, left)	125 mL

1. In a small bowl, whisk together all-purpose flour, sugar, rice flour and salt. Set aside.
2. In a medium bowl, using a wooden spoon, beat butter until light and creamy. Gradually add flour mixture, stirring thoroughly. Using your hands, knead until a smooth dough forms. Press evenly into bottom of prepared pan. Use the tines of a fork to prick the surface all over.
3. Bake in preheated oven for 25 to 30 minutes or until light golden around the edges. Let cool completely in pan on a wire rack. Remove from pan, using parchment liner, and cut into bars.

Variation

For a nice finish, sprinkle the surface with a little sugar before baking.

Cool Cranberry Pistachio Squares

◆

These tasty squares, with red and green layers on a dark chocolate base, look particularly festive on Christmas cookie trays. Cut them into triangles for a different look.

MAKES 8 SQUARES

- Preparation: 15 minutes
- Cooking: 5 minutes
- Chilling: 2 hours 20 minutes
- Freezing: excellent

Tips

The butter, chocolate and corn syrup mixture can also be melted in the microwave on Medium for about 1 minute, stirring halfway through.

Use either regular or miniature white chocolate chips. The miniatures will take less time to melt.

Dried fruits like cranberries, cherries and apricots are soft and chewy when fresh. Avoid fruits that are overly dry and hard.

Squares will keep in an airtight container at room temperature for up to 1 week or can be frozen for up to 3 months (separate layers with waxed paper). Thaw and bring to room temperature before serving.

- **9- by 5-inch (23 by 12.5 cm) loaf pan, lined with parchment paper**

BASE

3 tbsp	butter	45 mL
4 oz	semisweet chocolate, chopped	120 g
2 tbsp	corn syrup	30 mL
1¼ cups	chocolate wafer crumbs	300 mL

TOPPING

¾ cup	white chocolate chips (see Tips, left)	175 mL
⅓ cup	chopped dried cranberries (see Tips, left)	75 mL
2 tbsp	chopped pistachios	30 mL

1. *Base:* In a small saucepan over low heat, using a wooden spoon, combine butter, chocolate and corn syrup (see Tips, left). Heat, stirring constantly, until chocolate is melted and mixture is smooth. Remove from heat. Stir in chocolate wafer crumbs until well combined. Spread mixture evenly in prepared pan. Refrigerate for 20 minutes, until set.

2. *Topping:* In a small saucepan over low heat, melt white chocolate chips, stirring constantly until smooth. Stir in cranberries. Spread evenly over base. Sprinkle evenly with pistachios. Refrigerate until chocolate is firm, about 2 hours. Remove from pan, using parchment liner, and cut into squares.

Variations

For an all-chocolate treat, use semisweet chocolate chips instead of white.

Substitute finely chopped candied pineapple for the dried cranberries.

Triple-Layer Chocolate Peanut Butter Bars

◆

Peanut butter and chocolate are an all-time favorite combination. To make a peanut-free version, you can substitute almond or hazelnut butter.

MAKES 9 BARS

- Preparation: 20 minutes
- Cooking: 2 minutes
- Chilling: 2 hours
- Freezing: excellent

Tips

In these bars, fine or medium coconut works better than flaked or shredded. They also make the bars easier to cut.

Confectioners' sugar tends to clump during storage, so sift before using.

- **8- by 4-inch (20 by 10 cm) loaf pan, lined with parchment paper**

BASE

¼ cup	butter	60 mL
4 tsp	granulated sugar	20 mL
4 tsp	unsweetened cocoa powder, sifted	20 mL
1	egg, beaten	1
⅔ cup	graham wafer crumbs	150 mL
3 tbsp	sweetened fine or medium coconut (see Tips, left)	45 mL
3 tbsp	finely chopped pecans	45 mL

FILLING

¼ cup	creamy peanut butter	60 mL
2 tbsp	butter, softened	30 mL
¾ cup	confectioners' (icing) sugar, sifted (see Tips, left)	175 mL
1 tbsp	milk	15 mL

TOPPING

2 oz	semisweet chocolate, chopped	60 g
1 tbsp	butter	15 mL
2 tbsp	finely chopped peanuts	30 mL

1. *Base:* In a medium saucepan over low heat, melt butter. Using a wooden spoon, stir in sugar, cocoa powder and egg. Cook, stirring constantly, until mixture starts to thicken, about 2 minutes. Remove from heat. Add graham wafer crumbs, coconut and pecans; stir well. Press evenly into bottom of prepared pan. Refrigerate until cold, about 30 minutes.

2. *Filling:* Meanwhile, in a small bowl, using a wooden spoon, beat together peanut butter and butter. In alternating batches, gradually add confectioners' sugar and milk, beating until smooth and creamy. Spread evenly over chilled base. Refrigerate until firm, about 1 hour.

3. *Topping:* In a small microwave-safe bowl, combine chocolate and butter. Microwave on High for 1 minute, stirring halfway through, until melted and smooth. Pour over filling and, working quickly, spread to cover evenly. Sprinkle peanuts evenly overtop. Refrigerate until chocolate is set, about 30 minutes. Remove from pan, using parchment liner, and cut into bars.

Variations

Use almond butter and almonds, hazelnut butter and hazelnuts or cashew butter and cashews in place of the peanut butter and peanuts.

Crispy Cereal Bars

◆

These no-bake bars put a different spin on breakfast cereal—kids are sure to love them.

MAKES 9 BARS

- Preparation: 15 minutes
- Cooking: 5 minutes
- Cooling: 1 hour
- Freezing: excellent

Tips
....

Keep nuts and seeds fresh by storing them in airtight containers in the freezer.

To keep the mixture from sticking, lightly butter a spoon or offset spatula to press the cereal mixture into the pan.

Bars will keep in an airtight container at room temperature for up to 1 week or can be frozen for up to 3 months (separate layers with waxed paper). Thaw and bring to room temperature before serving.

- **9- by 5-inch (23 by 12.5 cm) loaf pan, lined with parchment paper**

¼ cup	quick-cooking rolled oats	60 mL
1 tbsp	butter	15 mL
2 oz	regular marshmallows (about 10)	60 g
1¼ cups	crisp rice cereal	300 mL
2 tbsp	raisins	30 mL
2 tbsp	sunflower seeds	30 mL
2 tbsp	chopped dried apricots	30 mL
1 tbsp	chopped unblanched almonds	15 mL

1. In a dry frying pan over medium heat, lightly toast oats, stirring often, until light golden brown, about 5 minutes. Transfer to a bowl and let cool completely.
2. In a small saucepan over low heat, combine butter and marshmallows. Heat, stirring often with a wooden spoon, until melted and smooth. Remove from heat. Add raisins, sunflower seeds, apricots and almonds; stir well. Press mixture evenly into bottom of prepared pan. Let cool completely, about 1 hour. Remove from pan, using parchment liner, and cut into bars.

Variations

Simply omit the almonds for a nut-free bar.

Vary the dried fruit, seeds and nuts to suit your tastes. Dried cranberries and cherries are great, as are pumpkin seeds and chai seeds.

Rocky Road Chocolate Bars

Rocky road, a mixture of chocolate, nuts and marshmallows, is a favorite of kids young and old. These make a great after-school snack.

MAKES 9 BARS

- Preparation: 15 minutes
- Cooking: 3 minutes
- Chilling: 1 hour
- Freezing: excellent

Tips

Sift confectioners' sugar before using to remove any lumps that have formed during storage.

If chocolate chips have developed a whitish coating, don't worry. It will disappear when they melt.

Bars will keep in an airtight container at room temperature for up to 1 week or can be frozen for up to 3 months (separate layers with waxed paper). Thaw and bring to room temperature before serving.

- **9- by 5-inch (23 by 12.5 cm) loaf pan, lined with parchment paper**

CRUMB MIX

¾ cup	graham wafer crumbs	175 mL
¾ cup	miniature marshmallows	175 mL
¼ cup	chopped pecans	60 mL
¼ cup	confectioners' (icing) sugar, sifted (see Tips, left)	60 mL
1 tbsp	milk	15 mL

CHOCOLATE MIX

1 cup	semisweet chocolate chips (see Tips, left)	250 mL
¼ cup	milk	60 mL
2 tbsp	butter	30 mL
2 tbsp	confectioners' (icing) sugar, sifted	30 mL

1. *Crumb Mix:* In a small bowl, using a wooden spoon, stir together graham wafer crumbs, marshmallows, pecans, confectioners' sugar and milk, until all ingredients are moistened but crumbly. Set aside.
2. *Chocolate Mix:* In a small saucepan over low heat, combine chocolate chips, milk and butter. Heat for about 3 minutes, stirring often, until chocolate is melted and smooth. Pour half of the mixture, about ½ cup (125 mL), over crumb mix. Stir well. Spread mixture evenly in prepared pan.
3. Add confectioners' sugar to remaining chocolate mix and stir until smooth. Spread evenly over crumb mix. Refrigerate until set, about 1 hour. Remove from pan, using parchment liner. Cut into bars.

Variations

Substitute walnuts or almonds for the pecans.

For a fun treat for kids, use colored marshmallows.

Crispy Peanut Butter Cereal Bars

♦

This no-bake bar is great for summer, as no oven is required.

MAKES 9 BARS

- Preparation: 15 minutes
- Cooking: 3 minutes
- Chilling: 2 hours
- Freezing: excellent

Tips

Honey and corn syrup may seem similar, but each add something special to the super flavor of these bars.

Bars will keep in an airtight container at room temperature for up to 1 week or can be frozen for up to 3 months (separate layers with waxed paper). Thaw and bring to room temperature before serving.

- **9- by 5-inch (23 by 12.5 cm) loaf pan, lined with parchment paper**

BASE

¼ cup	creamy peanut butter	60 mL
3 tbsp	corn syrup (see Tips, left)	45 mL
2 tbsp	honey	30 mL
¼ cup	unsweetened cocoa powder, sifted	60 mL
2 tbsp	packed brown sugar	30 mL
1½ cups	miniature marshmallows	375 mL
1½ cups	crisp rice cereal	375 mL
¾ cup	semisweet chocolate chips	175 mL
½ cup	peanuts	125 mL

GLAZE

¾ cup	semisweet chocolate chips	175 mL
2 tbsp	butter	30 mL

1. *Base:* In a medium saucepan over low heat, combine peanut butter, corn syrup, honey, cocoa powder and brown sugar. Cook, stirring with a wooden spoon, until smooth, about 3 minutes. Reduce heat to low. Add marshmallows and cook, stirring often, until marshmallows are melted and mixture is smooth. Remove from heat. Add cereal, chocolate chips and peanuts; stir well. Press mixture firmly into bottom of prepared pan. Refrigerate for about 1 hour, until set.
2. *Glaze:* In a small microwave-safe bowl, melt chocolate chips and butter on High for about 1 minute, stirring halfway through. Stir until smooth. Spread evenly over chilled base. Refrigerate until set, about 1 hour. Remove from pan, using parchment liner, and cut into bars.

Variations

Replace the peanut butter and peanuts with almond, hazelnut or cashew butter and their corresponding nuts.

Crispy Chocolate Peanut Butter Bars

◆

This no-bake snack bar is akin to a soft yet crunchy granola bar. It's a perfect after-school treat.

MAKES 9 BARS

- Preparation: 15 minutes
- Chilling: 1 hour
- Freezing: excellent

Tips

Replace the peanut butter and peanuts with almond or cashew butter and their corresponding nuts.

When mixing, be sure you stir until all the dry ingredients are moistened.

Bars will keep in an airtight container at room temperature for up to 1 week or can be frozen for up to 3 months (separate layers with waxed paper). Thaw and bring to room temperature before serving.

- **8- by 4-inch (20 by 10 cm) loaf pan, lined with parchment paper**

⅔ cup	crisp rice cereal	150 mL
⅓ cup	quick-cooking rolled oats	75 mL
¼ cup	chopped mixed dried fruit (apricots, dates, raisins, apples, cranberries)	60 mL
¼ cup	chopped peanuts	60 mL
3 tbsp	packed brown sugar	45 mL
3 tbsp	creamy peanut butter (see Tips, left)	45 mL
3 tbsp	liquid honey	45 mL
2 tbsp	unsweetened cocoa powder, sifted	30 mL

1. In a medium bowl, stir together cereal, oats, dried fruit and peanuts. Set aside.
2. In a small saucepan over low heat, combine brown sugar, peanut butter and honey. Heat, stirring often, until brown sugar is melted and mixture is smooth. Stir in cocoa powder. Pour over cereal mixture and stir well. Press firmly into prepared pan.
3. Refrigerate until set, about 1 hour. Remove from pan, using parchment liner, and cut into bars.

Variations

Use your favorite dried fruits. A combination is nice, but using just a single type of fruit is fine, too.

Cappuccino Nanaimo Bars

Nanaimo bars, which originated in Nanaimo, British Columbia, have become a favorite around the world. This coffee variation is superb.

MAKES 9 BARS

- Preparation: 25 minutes
- Cooking: 4 minutes
- Chilling: 3 hours
- Freezing: excellent

Tips

I have specified sweetened coconut because it seems to be more readily available than the unsweetened variety. However, sweetened and unsweetened coconut can be used interchangeably in any recipe, to suit your preference.

Replace the espresso powder with double the amount of instant coffee granules. Look for finely ground coffee granules so they will dissolve easily, or crush them with the back of a spoon before using.

- 8- by 4-inch (20 by 10 cm) loaf pan, lined with parchment paper

BASE

⅓ cup	butter	75 mL
3 tbsp	unsweetened cocoa powder, sifted	45 mL
2 tbsp	granulated sugar	30 mL
1½ tsp	instant espresso powder (see Tips, left)	7 mL
1	egg, beaten	1
¾ cup	graham wafer crumbs	175 mL
½ cup	sweetened flaked coconut	125 mL
⅓ cup	chopped almonds	75 mL

FILLING

2 tbsp	butter, softened	30 mL
1½ tsp	instant espresso powder	7 mL
1 cup	confectioners' (icing) sugar, sifted	250 mL
1 tbsp	warm brewed coffee or water	15 mL

TOPPING

2 oz	semisweet chocolate, chopped	60 g
1 tbsp	butter	15 mL
1½ tsp	instant espresso powder	7 mL

1. *Base:* In a small saucepan over low heat, using a wooden spoon, combine butter, cocoa powder, sugar, espresso powder and egg. Cook, stirring constantly, until mixture starts to thicken, about 3 minutes. Remove from heat. Stir in graham wafer crumbs, coconut and almonds. Stir well. Press mixture firmly into bottom of prepared pan. Refrigerate until cold, about 30 minutes.

2. *Filling:* In a small bowl, using a wooden spoon, beat together butter and espresso powder until smooth and creamy. In alternating batches, gradually add confectioners' sugar and warm coffee, stirring until smooth. Spread evenly over base. Refrigerate until firm, about 2 hours.

Bars will keep in an airtight container at room temperature for up to 2 weeks or can be frozen for up to 3 months (separate layers with waxed paper). Thaw and bring to room temperature before serving.

3. *Topping:* In a small microwave-safe bowl, combine chocolate, butter and espresso powder. Microwave on Medium for about 1 minute, stirring halfway through, until chocolate is melted and smooth. Pour over filling and, working quickly, spread evenly. Refrigerate until chocolate is set, about 30 minutes. Remove from pan, using parchment liner, and cut into bars.

Variations

Substitute walnuts or pecans for the almonds.

For a nut-free bar, substitute additional coconut for the nuts.

Quick Breads

MUFFINS

LOAVES AND BISCUITS

Banana Cranberry Muffins

Once you've tried these delicious muffins you'll always want to have ripe bananas on hand so you can whip up a batch anytime.

MAKES 6 MUFFINS

- Preparation: 15 minutes
- Baking: 25 minutes
- Freezing: excellent

Tips

The riper the bananas, the better the flavor.

The large quantity of banana in proportion to the flour makes these muffins very moist and flavorful.

To measure flour and other dry ingredients, spoon into a dry measuring cup and level off with a spatula or the back of a knife (do not pack down).

Cooled muffins will keep in an airtight container at room temperature for up to 3 days or can be frozen for up to 3 months. Thaw and bring to room temperature before serving.

- **Preheat oven to 375°F (190°C)**
- **6-cup muffin pan, greased or lined with paper liners**

¾ cup	all-purpose flour	175 mL
⅓ cup	granulated sugar	75 mL
½ tsp	baking powder	2 mL
½ tsp	baking soda	2 mL
¼ tsp	salt	1 mL
3 tbsp	butter	45 mL
¾ cup	mashed ripe bananas (2 small; see Tips, left)	175 mL
1	egg	1
½ cup	cranberries (fresh or frozen)	125 mL

1. In a small bowl, whisk together flour, sugar, baking powder, baking soda and salt. Set aside.
2. In a medium microwave-safe bowl, heat butter on High for 30 to 45 seconds, until melted. Add banana and egg, stirring well.
3. Add flour mixture, stirring to blend. Fold in cranberries. Divide batter evenly among prepared muffin cups.
4. Bake in preheated oven for 20 to 25 minutes or until tops spring back when lightly touched. Let cool in pan on a wire rack for at least 10 minutes, then remove from pan.

Variations

Substitute blueberries, chopped nuts or chocolate chips for the cranberries. You can also omit the berries and make just 5 muffins or 6 smaller ones.

Try substituting whole wheat flour for the all-purpose flour.

Apple Streusel Muffins

◆

These muffins are like apple crisp in muffin form. The streusel topping adds a pleasant crunch and flavor.

MAKES 4 MUFFINS

- Preparation: 20 minutes
- Baking: 25 minutes
- Freezing: excellent

Tips
· · · · · · · · · · · · · · · ·

To ensure even baking and to prevent the pan from burning, fill the two empty muffin cups with water.

For evenly shaped muffins, use a large ice-cream scoop (about ¼ cup/60 mL) to spoon batter into the prepared muffin pan.

Cooled muffins will keep in an airtight container at room temperature for up to 3 days or can be frozen for up to 3 months. Thaw and bring to room temperature before serving.

- **Preheat oven to 350°F (180°C)**
- **6-cup muffin pan, 4 cups greased or lined with paper liners**

STREUSEL

2 tbsp	all-purpose flour	30 mL
2 tbsp	packed brown sugar	30 mL
¼ tsp	ground cinnamon	1 mL
1 tbsp	butter, melted	15 mL

MUFFINS

⅔ cup	all-purpose flour	150 mL
¼ tsp	baking soda	1 mL
¼ tsp	ground cinnamon	1 mL
Pinch	salt	Pinch
½ cup	diced peeled, cored apple	125 mL
1	egg	1
6 tbsp	packed brown sugar	90 mL
¼ cup	plain yogurt	60 mL
2 tbsp	vegetable oil	30 mL

1. *Streusel:* In a small bowl, stir together flour, brown sugar, cinnamon and melted butter, until crumbly. Set aside.
2. *Muffins:* In a small bowl, whisk together flour, baking soda, cinnamon and salt. Stir in apple. Set aside.
3. In a medium bowl, whisk together egg, brown sugar, yogurt and oil. Add flour mixture, stirring just until combined. Divide batter evenly among prepared muffin cups.
4. Bake in preheated oven for 20 to 25 minutes or until tops spring back when lightly touched. Let cool in pan on a wire rack for at least 10 minutes, then remove from pan.

Variation
Add 2 tbsp (30 mL) chopped nuts to the streusel topping.

Blueberry Cornmeal Muffins

The combination of blueberries and cornmeal in these muffins is unusual, but awesome.

MAKES 4 MUFFINS

- Preparation: 15 minutes
- Baking: 20 minutes
- Freezing: excellent

Tips

Yellow cornmeal gives muffins and cornbread a nicer appearance.

Do not thaw frozen blueberries before using. This keeps the juices from bleeding into the batter.

Cooled muffins will keep in an airtight container at room temperature for up to 3 days or can be frozen for up to 3 months. Thaw and bring to room temperature before serving.

- **Preheat oven to 375°F (190°C)**
- **6-cup muffin pan, 4 cups greased or lined with paper liners**

¼ cup	all-purpose flour	60 mL
¼ cup	cornmeal (fine grind; see Tips, left)	60 mL
1 tbsp	granulated sugar	15 mL
½ tsp	baking powder	2 mL
¼ tsp	baking soda	1 mL
Pinch	salt	Pinch
⅓ cup	plain Greek yogurt	75 mL
1 tbsp	vegetable oil	15 mL
1	egg	1
½ cup	blueberries (fresh or frozen; see Tips, left)	125 mL

1. In a small bowl, whisk together flour, cornmeal, sugar, baking powder, baking soda and salt. Set aside.
2. In a large bowl, whisk together yogurt, oil and egg. Add flour mixture, stirring just until combined. Gently fold in blueberries. Divide batter evenly among prepared muffin cups.
3. Bake in preheated oven for 16 to 20 minutes or until tops spring back when lightly touched. Let cool in pan on a wire rack for at least 10 minutes, then remove from pan.

Variations

Substitute cranberries for the blueberries.

Omit the blueberries for a plain cornmeal muffin.

Substitute whole wheat flour for the all-purpose flour.

Honey Orange Cranberry Muffins

Tart lemon and cranberries with a hint of honey make a pleasant combination.

MAKES 6 MUFFINS

- Preparation: 20 minutes
- Baking: 23 minutes
- Freezing: excellent

Tips

Do not thaw frozen cranberries before using. This keeps the juices from bleeding into the batter.

If desired, cut down on calories by omitting the glaze.

Cooled muffins will keep in an airtight container at room temperature for up to 3 days or can be frozen for up to 3 months. Thaw and bring to room temperature before serving.

- **Preheat oven to 400°F (200°C)**
- **6-cup muffin pan, greased or lined with paper liners**

MUFFINS

1¼ cups	all-purpose flour	300 mL
1½ tsp	baking powder	7 mL
¼ tsp	salt	1 mL
¼ tsp	ground cinnamon	1 mL
1	egg	1
⅔ cup	milk	150 mL
2 tbsp	vegetable oil	30 mL
2 tbsp	liquid honey	30 mL
1 tsp	grated orange zest	5 mL
¾ cup	cranberries (fresh or frozen; see Tips, left)	175 mL

GLAZE (OPTIONAL)

⅓ cup	confectioners' (icing) sugar, sifted	75 mL
½ tsp	freshly grated orange zest	2 mL
1½ to 2 tsp	freshly squeezed orange juice	7 to 10 mL

1. *Muffins:* In a small bowl, whisk together flour, baking powder, salt and cinnamon. Set aside.
2. In a medium bowl, whisk together egg, milk, oil, honey and orange zest. Add flour mixture, stirring just until combined. Fold in cranberries. Divide batter evenly among prepared muffin cups.
3. Bake in preheated oven for 18 to 23 minutes or until tops spring back when lightly touched.
4. *Glaze (optional):* In a bowl, combine confectioners' sugar, orange zest and orange juice, stirring until smooth and spreadable. Spread on warm muffins. Let cool in pan on a wire rack for at least 10 minutes, then remove from pan.

Variations

Substitute lemon zest for the orange.

Substitute blueberries for the cranberries.

Carrot Spice Muffins

Not only are these muffins full of flavor, they are nutritious as well—a great way to start the day.

MAKES 4 MUFFINS

- Preparation: 20 minutes
- Baking: 23 minutes
- Freezing: excellent

Tips

For more fiber, use whole wheat flour.

Cooled muffins will keep in an airtight container at room temperature for up to 3 days or can be frozen for up to 3 months. Thaw and bring to room temperature before serving.

- **Preheat oven to 350°F (180°C)**
- **6-cup muffin pan, 4 cups greased or lined with paper liners**

⅔ cup	all-purpose flour (see Tips, left)	150 mL
½ cup	granulated sugar	125 mL
¼ cup	raisins	60 mL
3 tbsp	chopped walnuts	45 mL
¾ tsp	baking soda	3 mL
¾ tsp	ground cinnamon	3 mL
¼ tsp	ground nutmeg	1 mL
⅛ tsp	salt	0.5 mL
¾ cup	grated peeled carrots	175 mL
1	egg	1
¼ cup	vegetable oil	60 mL

1. In a large bowl, whisk together flour, sugar, raisins, walnuts, baking soda, cinnamon, nutmeg and salt. Set aside.
2. In a small bowl, combine carrots, egg and oil. Add to flour mixture all at once, stirring just until moistened. Divide batter evenly among prepared muffin cups.
3. Bake in preheated oven for 18 to 23 minutes or until tops spring back when lightly touched. Let cool in pan on a wire rack for at least 10 minutes, then remove from pan.

Variations

Substitute an equal amount of grated zucchini (unpeeled) for the carrots.

Substitute dried cranberries for the raisins.

Omit the nuts if desired.

Apple Bran Muffins

These bran muffins are especially moist, thanks to the inclusion of apple. Nutritious and delicious.

MAKES 4 MUFFINS

- Preparation: 20 minutes
- Baking: 18 minutes
- Freezing: excellent

Tips

Be sure to use natural bran, not bran cereal. Natural bran has a dry, flaky texture; it is not a hard, ready-to-eat cereal.

Measure bran as you would flour. Spoon it into a dry measuring cup and level off the top with a spatula or knife.

Cooled muffins will keep in an airtight container at room temperature for up to 3 days or can be frozen for up to 3 months. Thaw and bring to room temperature before serving.

- Preheat oven to 400°F (200°C)
- 6-cup muffin pan, 4 cups greased or lined with paper liners

½ cup	whole wheat flour	125 mL
½ cup	natural wheat bran (see Tips, left)	125 mL
½ tsp	baking soda	2 mL
⅛ tsp	baking powder	0.5 mL
⅛ tsp	salt	0.5 mL
¼ cup	packed brown sugar	60 mL
1	egg	1
⅓ cup	plain yogurt	75 mL
2 tbsp	vegetable oil	30 mL
1 tbsp	molasses	15 mL
⅓ cup	finely chopped peeled, cored apple	75 mL
¼ cup	raisins	60 mL

1. In a medium bowl, whisk together flour, bran, baking soda, baking powder and salt. Set aside.
2. In a medium bowl, using a wooden spoon, stir together brown sugar, egg, yogurt, oil and molasses. Add flour mixture all at once, stirring well. Add apple and raisins and stir well. Divide batter evenly among prepared muffin cups.
3. Bake in preheated oven for 13 to 18 minutes or until tops spring back when lightly touched. Let cool in pan on a wire rack for at least 10 minutes, then remove from pan.

Variations

Substitute an equal amount of chopped pitted dates or figs for the raisins.

If you prefer, substitute an equal amount of all-purpose flour for the whole wheat flour.

Carrot Orange Pineapple Loaf

This pretty golden loaf cake is oh so moist and topped with a crowd-pleasing cream cheese icing.

MAKES 2 MINI LOAVES

- Preparation: 25 minutes
- Baking: 25 minutes
- Freezing: excellent

Tip

Enjoy one loaf right away and freeze the other (it will keep for up to 4 months tightly wrapped in plastic in the freezer). If freezing, do not add the icing. To thaw, let stand at room temperature for about 2 hours. Add icing before serving.

- **Preheat oven to 350°F (180°C)**
- **Two 5½- by 2¾-inch (14 by 7 cm) mini loaf pans, greased**

LOAVES

½ cup	all-purpose flour	125 mL
½ tsp	baking powder	2 mL
¼ tsp	baking soda	1 mL
Pinch	salt	Pinch
1	egg	1
2 tbsp	vegetable oil	30 mL
¼ cup	granulated sugar	60 mL
1 tsp	freshly grated orange zest	5 mL
½ cup	grated peeled carrot (see Quick Tip, right)	125 mL
¼ cup	drained crushed pineapple	60 mL
2 tbsp	chopped walnuts	30 mL

CREAM CHEESE ICING (OPTIONAL)

1 tbsp	cream cheese, softened	15 mL
1 tbsp	butter, softened	15 mL
¼ tsp	freshly grated orange zest	1 mL
6 tbsp	confectioners' (icing) sugar, sifted	90 mL

1. *Loaves:* In a small bowl, whisk together flour, baking powder, baking soda and salt. Set aside.
2. In a medium bowl, whisk together egg, oil, sugar, orange zest, carrot, pineapple and nuts. Add flour mixture, stirring to blend. Divide batter evenly between prepared pans.
3. Bake in preheated oven for 20 to 25 minutes or until a toothpick inserted in the center comes out clean. Let cool for 15 minutes in pans, then transfer loaves to a wire rack to cool completely.

Loaves will keep in an airtight container at room temperature for up to 3 days or can be frozen for up to 3 months. Thaw and bring to room temperature before serving.

4. *Cream Cheese Icing (optional):* In a small bowl, using a wooden spoon, beat together cream cheese, butter and orange zest, until smooth. Gradually beat in confectioners' sugar until light and creamy. Divide into 2 equal portions and spread evenly over loaves.

Variations

Substitute an equal amount of pure vanilla extract for the orange zest.

Substitute an equal amount of grated zucchini for the carrot.

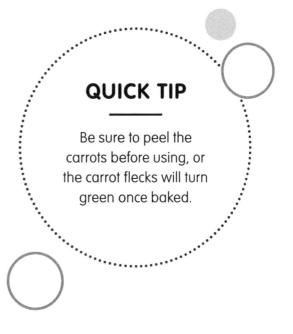

QUICK TIP

Be sure to peel the carrots before using, or the carrot flecks will turn green once baked.

Mini Banana Loaf

◆

These mini loaves are great for gifting.

MAKES 2 MINI LOAVES

- Preparation: 20 minutes
- Baking: 28 minutes
- Freezing: excellent

Tips

The riper the banana, the better the flavor.

Frozen mashed banana is too wet to be substituted for the fresh mashed banana in this recipe.

Loaves will keep in an airtight container at room temperature for up to 3 days or can be frozen for up to 3 months. Thaw and bring to room temperature before serving.

- **Preheat oven to 350°F (180°C)**
- **Two 5½- by 2¾-inch (14 by 7 cm) mini loaf pans, greased**

¾ cup	all-purpose flour	175 mL
½ tsp	baking soda	2 mL
¼ tsp	baking powder	1 mL
Pinch	salt	Pinch
Pinch	ground nutmeg	Pinch
½ cup	mashed ripe banana (1 large; see Tips, left)	125 mL
1 tbsp	freshly squeezed lemon juice	15 mL
2 tbsp	butter, softened	30 mL
3 tbsp	granulated sugar	45 mL
1	egg	1

1. In a small bowl, whisk together flour, baking soda, baking powder, salt and nutmeg. Set aside.
2. In another small bowl, whisk together mashed banana and lemon juice. Set aside.
3. In a medium bowl, using a wooden spoon, beat together butter, sugar and egg, until light and smooth. Add banana mixture. Gradually add flour mixture, stirring well. Divide batter evenly between prepared pans.
4. Bake in preheated oven for 23 to 28 minutes or until a toothpick inserted in the center comes out clean. Let cool for 15 minutes in pans, then transfer loaves to a wire rack to cool completely.

Variations

Stir ¼ cup (60 mL) chopped nuts or chocolate chips into the batter.

Zucchini Loaf

◆

This loaf is a great way to sneak additional vegetables into your kids.

MAKES 2 MINI LOAVES

- Preparation: 20 minutes
- Baking: 40 minutes
- Freezing: excellent

Tips

Add fiber by replacing all or half the quantity of all-purpose flour with whole wheat flour.

This may seem like a lot of zucchini, but it disappears in the baking.

You can peel the zucchini if you prefer not to see green flecks in the finished loaves.

Foil loaf pans work well and are especially nice for gift-giving.

Loaves will keep in an airtight container at room temperature for up to 3 days or can be frozen for up to 3 months. Thaw and bring to room temperature before serving.

- **Preheat oven to 325°F (160°C)**
- **Two 5$\frac{1}{2}$- by 3$\frac{1}{4}$-inch (14 by 8 cm) mini loaf pans, greased**

1 cup	all-purpose flour (see Tips, left)	250 mL
1$\frac{1}{2}$ tsp	ground cinnamon	7 mL
$\frac{1}{2}$ tsp	baking powder	2 mL
$\frac{1}{2}$ tsp	baking soda	2 mL
$\frac{1}{4}$ tsp	salt	1 mL
$\frac{1}{4}$ tsp	ground nutmeg	1 mL
1	egg	1
$\frac{1}{2}$ cup	packed brown sugar	125 mL
2 tbsp	vegetable oil	30 mL
2 cups	grated zucchini (unpeeled; see Tips, left)	500 mL
$\frac{1}{3}$ cup	chopped walnuts	75 mL

1. In a small bowl, whisk together flour, cinnamon, baking powder, baking soda, salt and nutmeg. Set aside.
2. In a medium bowl, whisk together egg, brown sugar and oil, until smooth. Stir in zucchini and nuts. Add flour mixture, stirring to blend. Divide batter evenly between prepared pans.
3. Bake in preheated oven for 35 to 40 minutes or until a toothpick inserted in the center comes out clean. Let cool for 15 minutes in pans, then transfer loaves to a wire rack to cool completely.

Variations

Use your favorite nuts, or omit for a nut-free loaf.

Add $\frac{1}{3}$ cup (75 mL) raisins or dried cranberries along with the nuts in Step 2.

Glazed Lemon Poppy Seed Loaf

Lemon poppy seed loaves are an old-fashioned favorite.

MAKES 1 MINI LOAF

- Preparation: 20 minutes
- Baking: 35 minutes
- Freezing: excellent

Tips

When zesting lemons, use only the outer yellow rind. The inner white pith is bitter.

Warm lemons slightly in a microwave for 5 seconds before squeezing, to obtain the most juice.

Loaf will keep in an airtight container at room temperature for up to 3 days or can be frozen for up to 3 months. Thaw and bring to room temperature before serving.

- Preheat oven to 350°F (180°C)
- 5½- by 2¾-inch (14 by 7 cm) mini loaf pan, greased

LOAF

¾ cup	all-purpose flour	175 mL
1 tbsp	poppy seeds	15 mL
1 tsp	freshly grated lemon zest (see Tips, left)	5 mL
¾ tsp	baking powder	3 mL
¼ tsp	salt	1 mL
3 tbsp	butter, softened	45 mL
½ cup	granulated sugar	125 mL
1	egg	1
¼ cup	milk	60 mL

LEMON GLAZE

2 tbsp	confectioners' (icing) sugar, sifted	30 mL
1 tbsp	freshly squeezed lemon juice	15 mL

1. *Loaf:* In a small bowl, whisk together flour, poppy seeds, lemon zest, baking powder and salt. Set aside.
2. In a medium bowl, using a wooden spoon, beat together butter, sugar and egg, until light and creamy. In alternating batches (3 dry and 2 liquid additions), add flour mixture and milk, stirring well after each addition. Pour batter into prepared pan.
3. Bake in preheated oven for 30 to 35 minutes or until a toothpick inserted in the center comes out clean. Using a toothpick or fork, prick top of loaf all over.
4. *Lemon Glaze:* In a small bowl, combine confectioners' sugar and lemon juice, stirring until sugar is dissolved. Brush on warm loaf. Let cool for 15 minutes in pan, then transfer loaf to a wire rack to cool completely.

Variations

Substitute an equal amount of chopped nuts for the poppy seeds.

Omit the poppy seeds, if desired.

Easy, Cheesy Drop Biscuits

These drop biscuits taste like moist tea biscuits but are much easier to make—no kneading, rolling or cutting required.

MAKES 4 BISCUITS

- Preparation: 15 minutes
- Baking: 22 minutes
- Freezing: excellent

Tips

The sharper the cheese, the more cheese flavor in the biscuits.

For the best results, always use fresh ingredients.

These biscuits are best served warm from the oven. Prepare and bake just before you want to eat them.

These are free-form biscuits, but if you keep them uniform in size they will bake evenly.

Cooled biscuits will keep in an airtight container at room temperature for up to 3 days or can be frozen for up to 3 months. Thaw and bring to room temperature before serving.

- **Preheat oven to 400°F (200°C)**
- **Baking sheet, lined with parchment paper**

¾ cup	all-purpose flour	175 mL
1 tsp	baking powder	5 mL
¼ tsp	salt	1 mL
2 tbsp	cold butter	30 mL
½ cup	shredded sharp Cheddar cheese (see Tips, left)	125 mL
½ cup	milk	125 mL

1. In a medium bowl, whisk together flour, baking powder and salt. Using a pastry blender or two knives, cut in butter until mixture resembles coarse crumbs. Stir in cheese, tossing to coat cheese with flour.
2. Add milk all at once. Using a wooden spoon, stir until a soft, sticky dough forms.
3. Drop 4 mounds of dough, about ½ cup (115 mL) each, onto prepared baking sheet. Bake in preheated oven for 18 to 22 minutes or until set and golden. Serve warm or at room temperature.

Variations

Add 1 tbsp (15 mL) each green onion or chives and diced cooked bacon to the flour mixture along with the cheese.

Try Swiss cheese in place of Cheddar, and add some diced ham.

Chocolate Almond Scones

◆

These are best enjoyed warm from the oven.

MAKES 4 SCONES

- Preparation: 10 minutes
- Baking: 15 minutes
- Freezing: excellent

Tip
. . . .
For real indulgence, top the cooled scones with ready-to-serve chocolate frosting.

- **Preheat oven to 400°F (200°C)**
- **Baking sheet, lined with parchment paper**

⅔ cup	all-purpose flour	150 mL
2½ tbsp	unsweetened cocoa powder, sifted	37 mL
2 tbsp	granulated sugar	30 mL
1 tsp	baking powder	5 mL
¼ tsp	baking soda	1 mL
¼ tsp	salt	1 mL
3 tbsp	cold butter	45 mL
1	egg	1
3 tbsp	plain yogurt	45 mL
¼ cup	chopped unblanched almonds	60 mL
¼ cup	semisweet chocolate chips (see Quick Tip, right)	60 mL

1. In a medium bowl, whisk together flour, cocoa powder, sugar, baking powder, baking soda and salt. Using a pastry blender or two knives, cut in butter until mixture resembles coarse crumbs.
2. In a small bowl, whisk together egg and yogurt. Add to flour mixture along with almonds and chocolate chips. Using a fork, stir until ingredients are moistened and form a soft, rough dough. With floured hands, shape dough into a ball, then knead on a lightly floured surface about 10 times. Pat into a 7- by 3½-inch (18 by 9 cm) rectangle. Cut in half, then cut each half diagonally into two triangles. Transfer to prepared baking sheet.

Tip

Cooled scones will keep in an airtight container at room temperature for up to 3 days or can be frozen for up to 3 months. Thaw and bring to room temperature before serving.

3. Bake in preheated oven for 12 to 15 minutes or until firm. Let cool for 5 minutes on a wire rack, then serve warm or at room temperature.

Variations

Omit the nuts or chocolate chips if desired, but it's nice to keep one.

Drizzle cooled scones with melted chocolate or sprinkle with confectioners' (icing) sugar for a nice presentation.

QUICK TIP

Mini chocolate chips distribute well throughout the batter, while regular chocolate chips provide a nice crunch in every bite.

Fabulous Fruit Scones

♦

These make a great breakfast, brunch or afternoon treat.

MAKES 4 SCONES

- Preparation: 15 minutes
- Baking: 15 minutes
- Freezing: excellent

Tips
· · · · · · · · · · · · · · · · · · · ·

The butter can also be frozen, then grated coarsely into the flour mixture.

A drizzle of chocolate over the scones adds a bit of sweetness. Try melted white or semisweet chocolate.

Cooled scones will keep in an airtight container at room temperature for up to 3 days or can be frozen for up to 3 months. Thaw and bring to room temperature before serving.

- **Preheat oven to 400°F (200°C)**
- **Baking sheet, lined with parchment paper**

1 cup	all-purpose flour	250 mL
3 tbsp	granulated sugar	45 mL
½ tsp	baking powder	2 mL
¼ tsp	salt	1 mL
⅛ tsp	baking soda	0.5 mL
¼ cup	cold butter (see Tips, left)	60 mL
¼ cup	dried cranberries	60 mL
1	egg	1
3 tbsp	sour cream	45 mL
1 tsp	freshly grated orange zest	5 mL

1. In a medium bowl, whisk together flour, sugar, baking powder, salt and baking soda.
2. Using a pastry blender or two knives, cut in butter until mixture resembles coarse crumbs. Stir in cranberries. Set aside.
3. In a small bowl, whisk together egg, sour cream and orange zest. Using a fork, stir into flour mixture until a soft dough forms. With floured fingers, shape dough into a ball, then knead on a lightly floured surface about 10 times. Pat into a 5-inch (12.5 cm) circle. Using a sharp knife, cut into 4 even wedges. Transfer to prepared baking sheet.
4. Bake in preheated oven for 12 to 15 minutes or until golden. Let cool for 5 minutes on a wire rack, then serve warm or at room temperature.

Variations

Substitute dried cherries, blueberries or apricots for the cranberries.

Substitute lemon zest for the orange zest.

Southern Cornbread

◆

The addition of cheese, corn and peppers takes this cornbread to a new level.

MAKES 1 LOAF (4 TO 6 SERVINGS)

- Preparation: 15 minutes
- Baking: 25 minutes
- Freezing: excellent

Tips

Substitute plain yogurt for the buttermilk. You can also make your own buttermilk by adding 1 tsp (5 mL) lemon juice to ½ cup (125 mL) milk; let stand for 5 minutes, then stir before using.

Fresh, frozen or canned corn all works well.

Try other cheeses. Swiss and Monterey Jack are good options.

This recipe also makes 6 great muffins. Decrease the baking time to 15 to 18 minutes.

Cooled cornbread will keep in an airtight container at room temperature for up to 3 days or can be frozen for up to 3 months. Thaw and bring to room temperature before serving.

- **Preheat oven to 400°F (200°C)**
- **8- by 4-inch (20 by 10 cm) loaf pan, greased**

½ cup	all-purpose flour	125 mL
½ cup	yellow cornmeal (fine grind)	125 mL
1½ tbsp	granulated sugar	22 mL
1½ tsp	baking powder	7 mL
¼ tsp	baking soda	1 mL
¼ tsp	salt	1 mL
1	egg	1
½ cup	buttermilk (see Tips, left)	125 mL
2 tbsp	butter, melted	30 mL
½ cup	corn kernels (see Tips, left)	125 mL
½ cup	shredded sharp Cheddar cheese (see Tips, left)	125 mL
2 tbsp	chopped red or green bell pepper	30 mL

1. In a small bowl, whisk together flour, cornmeal, sugar, baking powder, baking soda and salt. Set aside.
2. In a medium bowl, whisk together egg, buttermilk and melted butter. Stir in corn, cheese and bell pepper. Add dry ingredients all at once, stirring just until moistened. Spread batter evenly in prepared pan.
3. Bake in preheated oven for 20 to 25 minutes or until a toothpick inserted in the center comes out clean. Let cool for 15 minutes in pan on a wire rack. Using a sharp knife, cut into 4 or 6 servings. Enjoy warm or at room temperature.

Variations

Try an equal amount of chopped pitted olives in place of the bell pepper.

Spice it up with a little finely diced chile pepper, to taste.

Cakes

Bumbleberry Shortcake

This cake-like version of shortcake is easy to prepare, lighter and more tender than the biscuit type.

MAKES 3 SERVINGS

- Preparation: 20 minutes
- Baking: 22 minutes
- Freezing: excellent

Tips

Frozen fruits are juicier but work well, as the cake soaks up the juice and the flavor.

To make a quick buttermilk, combine 2 tsp (10 mL) fresh lemon juice and ½ cup (125 mL) milk in a small bowl. Let stand 5 minutes, then stir before using.

- **Preheat oven to 375°F (190°C)**
- **8- by 4-inch (20 by 10 cm) loaf pan, greased**

CAKE

1 cup	all-purpose flour	250 mL
¼ cup	granulated sugar	60 mL
1½ tsp	baking powder	7 mL
¼ tsp	baking soda	1 mL
¼ tsp	salt	1 mL
¼ cup	cold butter, cubed	60 mL
½ cup	buttermilk (see Tips, left)	125 mL

FILLING

1½ cups	mixed fresh berries (raspberries, strawberries, blackberries, blueberries)	375 mL
1 tbsp	granulated sugar	15 mL
	Sweetened whipped cream (see Tips, right)	

1. *Cake:* In a medium bowl, whisk together flour, sugar, baking powder, baking soda and salt. With a pastry blender or two knives, cut in butter until mixture resembles coarse crumbs. Gradually add buttermilk, stirring with a wooden spoon just until moistened. Spread batter evenly in prepared pan.
2. Bake in preheated oven for 17 to 22 minutes or until a toothpick inserted in the center comes out clean. Let cool in pan on a wire rack for 15 minutes, then remove from pan and cool completely.

Tips

To sweeten whipped cream, beat together about 1 cup (250 mL) heavy or whipping (35%) cream and 1 to 2 tbsp (15 to 30 mL) confectioners' sugar, until stiff peaks form.

Shortcake (unfilled) will keep in an airtight container at room temperature for up to 3 days or can be frozen for up to 3 months. Thaw and bring to room temperature before filling.

3. *Filling:* In a small bowl, combine berries and sugar. Let stand for 10 minutes, until sugar is dissolved.

4. To serve, cut cake horizontally in half, then cut into three equal portions. Arrange half the fruit equally over the bottom halves and top with a spoonful of whipped cream. Cover with top halves and finish with remaining berries and whipped cream.

Variations

Feel free to use your favorite berry or combination of berries.

Instead of the mixed berries, combine peach slices and blueberries.

Serve with vanilla ice cream instead of whipped cream.

Strawberry Shortcake

◆

Strawberry season would not be complete without shortcake biscuits, whipped cream and fresh berries.

MAKES
4 SHORTCAKES

- Preparation: 20 minutes
- Baking: 17 minutes
- Freezing: excellent

Tips

If your berries are tart, toss them in a bowl with a bit of sugar or maple syrup to taste and let stand for about 10 minutes. The amount of berries is up to you, but a general guide for 4 shortcakes is 2 cups (500 mL) sliced strawberries mixed with 1 tbsp (15 mL) sugar or maple syrup.

To make sweetened whipped cream, beat together 1 cup (250 mL) heavy or whipping (35%) cream and 1 to 2 tbsp (15 to 30 mL) confectioners' sugar, until stiff peaks form.

Cooled biscuits will keep in an airtight container at room temperature for up to 3 days or can be frozen for up to 3 months. Thaw and bring to room temperature before filling.

- **Preheat oven to 400°F (200°C)**
- **Baking sheet, lined with parchment paper**
- **2½-inch (6 cm) round pastry cutter**

1¼ cups	all-purpose flour	300 mL
2 tbsp	granulated sugar	30 mL
1½ tsp	baking powder	7 mL
¼ tsp	salt	1 mL
1 tsp	freshly grated lemon zest	5 mL
2 tbsp	cold butter	30 mL
½ cup	heavy or whipping (35%) cream	125 mL
⅓ cup	milk	75 mL
	Sliced strawberries (see Tips, left)	
	Sweetened whipped cream (see Tips, left)	

1. In a medium bowl, whisk together flour, sugar, baking powder, salt and lemon zest. Using a pastry blender or two knives, cut in butter until mixture resembles coarse crumbs. Gradually add milk, stirring with a fork until a soft dough forms.
2. Turn dough out onto a floured work surface. Using your hands, flatten until about ¾ inch (2 cm) thick. Using pastry cutter, cut into four rounds. Transfer to prepared baking sheet.
3. Bake in preheated oven for 12 to 17 minutes or until lightly browned. Let cool on a wire rack.
4. To serve, split biscuits. Pile some berries on the bottom half. Replace top half of biscuit, then add more berries and whipped cream.

Variations
You can serve these with almost any berry. Try whatever is in season. Sliced peaches also work great.

Apple Pinwheel Cake

◆

A year-round coffee cake that looks as good as it tastes.

MAKES ONE 6-INCH (15 CM) CAKE (4 TO 6 SERVINGS)

- Preparation: 25 minutes
- Baking: 55 minutes
- Freezing: excellent

Tips

Use firm apples such as Golden Delicious, Granny Smith or Fuji. They'll retain their shape while baking.

Brushing lemon juice onto any cut or peeled fruit helps keep it from browning.

For easy spreading, press the jam through a fine-mesh sieve with the back of a spoon, to remove any lumps of fruit.

Cooled cake will keep in an airtight container in the refrigerator for up to 3 days or can be frozen for up to 3 months. Thaw and bring to room temperature before serving.

- **Preheat oven to 350°F (180°C)**
- **6-inch (15 cm) springform pan, greased and floured**

2	small apples (see Tips, left)	2
1½ tsp	freshly squeezed lemon juice	7 mL
1 cup	all-purpose flour	250 mL
¾ tsp	baking powder	3 mL
¼ tsp	salt	1 mL
¼ cup	butter, softened	60 mL
6 tbsp	granulated sugar	90 mL
1	egg	1
½ tsp	pure lemon extract	2 mL
⅓ cup	milk	75 mL
¼ cup	strained apricot jam (see Tips, left)	60 mL

1. Peel and core apples. Cut lengthwise into quarters, then make several diagonal slashes in each quarter (just score the surface; do not cut right through). Brush with lemon juice (see Tips, left). Set aside.

2. In a small bowl, whisk together flour, baking powder and salt. Set aside.

3. In a medium bowl, using a wooden spoon, beat together butter, sugar, egg and lemon extract, until light and creamy. In alternating batches (3 dry and 2 liquid additions), add flour mixture and milk, stirring well after each addition until smooth. Spread batter evenly in prepared pan. Arrange apple pieces, slashed sides up, evenly on top.

4. Bake in preheated oven for 50 to 55 minutes or until a toothpick inserted in the center comes out clean. Let cool completely in pan on a wire rack. To unmold cake, run a knife around edge of pan and remove ring. Brush apricot jam over top of cake.

Variations

Substitute pears for the apples.

Substitute pure vanilla or almond extract for the lemon extract.

Plum Kuchen

Take advantage of fresh plums while they are in season to make this light, fruity cake.

MAKES 4 SERVINGS

- Preparation: 20 minutes
- Baking: 40 minutes
- Freezing: excellent

Tips
. . . .

Regular red or black plums and prune plums all taste great. Prune plums are smaller, so you will likely need 4 if using.

If you prefer to use unsalted butter, increase the salt in the batter by a pinch.

Serve kuchen warm or at room temperature (not cold) for optimum flavor.

For a finger-food treat, cut the cake into thin strips or small rectangles.

Sprinkling the cake with confectioners' (icing) sugar instead of spreading it with jam is an attractive alternative. Sprinkle just before serving, as it will eventually soak into the plums.

Cooled cake will keep in an airtight container in the refrigerator for up to 3 days or can be frozen for up to 3 months. Thaw and bring to room temperature before serving.

- Preheat oven to 350°F (180°C)
- 9- by 5-inch (23 by 12.5 cm) loaf pan, greased and floured

2	large plums (5 oz/150 g; see Tips, left)	2
¾ cup	all-purpose flour	175 mL
½ tsp	baking powder	2 mL
¼ tsp	baking soda	1 mL
Pinch	salt	Pinch
3 tbsp	butter, softened (see Tips, left)	45 mL
½ cup	granulated sugar	125 mL
1	egg	1
1 tsp	freshly grated orange zest	5 mL
½ cup	sour cream	125 mL
2 tbsp	vegetable oil	30 mL
1 tbsp	granulated sugar	15 mL
¼ tsp	ground cinnamon	1 mL
¼ cup	strained apricot jam, optional	60 mL

1. Pit plums and cut into ¼-inch (5 mm) slices. Set aside.
2. In a small bowl, whisk together flour, baking powder, baking soda and salt. Set aside.
3. In a medium bowl, using a wooden spoon, beat together butter, ½ cup (125 mL) sugar, egg and orange zest, until light and creamy.
4. In a small bowl, whisk together sour cream and oil. In alternating batches (3 dry and 2 liquid additions), add flour mixture and sour cream mixture, stirring well after each addition until smooth. Spread batter evenly in prepared pan. Arrange plums on top of batter, down the length of the pan in two rows.
5. In a small bowl, combine 1 tbsp (15 mL) sugar and cinnamon. Sprinkle overtop plums.
6. Bake in preheated oven for 35 to 40 minutes or until a toothpick inserted in the center comes out clean. Let cool in pan on a wire rack for 20 minutes. If desired, brush apricot jam over top of warm cake.

Variation

Although not as colorful, apricots work well, too.

Two-Tone Dream Bars (page 88)

Chocolate Buttercrunch Bars (page 90)

Caramel Apple Bars (page 97)

Blueberry Cheesecake Bars (page 99)

Pink Coconut Squares (page 104)

Chewy Toffee Almond Squares (page 113)

Frosted Carrot Nut Bars (page 116)

Cool Cranberry Pistachio Squares (page 127)

Rocky Road Chocolate Bars (page 131)

Chocolate Toffee Candy Bar Cupcakes (page 168)

Strawberry Rhubarb Crisp (page 226)

Mixed Berry Meringue Nests (page 234)

Rhubarb Crumble Cake

◆

Even those who claim to not like rhubarb love this cake.

MAKES 4 SERVINGS

- Preparation: 20 minutes
- Baking: 40 minutes
- Freezing: excellent

Tips

Substitute Greek yogurt for the sour cream.

If you are using frozen rhubarb, there is no need to thaw it first.

The pinker the rhubarb, the sweeter it tastes. It looks better when baked, too.

Cooled cake will keep in an airtight container in the refrigerator for up to 3 days or can be frozen for up to 3 months. Thaw and bring to room temperature before serving.

- **Preheat oven to 350°F (180°C)**
- **9- by 5-inch (23 by 12.5 cm) loaf pan, greased and floured**

TOPPING

½ cup	all-purpose flour	125 mL
¼ cup	packed brown sugar	60 mL
½ tsp	ground cinnamon	2 mL
3 tbsp	butter, softened	45 mL

CAKE

¾ cup	all-purpose flour	175 mL
½ tsp	baking powder	2 mL
¼ tsp	baking soda	1 mL
⅛ tsp	salt	0.5 mL
3 tbsp	butter, softened	45 mL
¼ cup	granulated sugar	60 mL
1	egg	1
½ tsp	pure vanilla extract	2 mL
¼ cup	sour cream (see Tips, left)	60 mL
1½ cups	chopped rhubarb (½-inch/1 cm; see Tips, left)	375 mL

1. *Topping:* In a small bowl, using a fork, stir together flour, brown sugar, cinnamon and butter, until crumbly. Set aside.
2. *Cake:* In a small bowl, whisk together flour, baking powder, baking soda and salt. Set aside.
3. In a medium bowl, using a wooden spoon, beat together butter, sugar, egg and vanilla, until light and creamy. In alternating batches (3 dry and 2 liquid additions), add flour mixture and sour cream, stirring well after each addition. Spread batter evenly in prepared pan. Sprinkle with half the topping mixture. Cover with rhubarb. Sprinkle remaining topping over rhubarb.
4. Bake in preheated oven for 35 to 40 minutes or until a toothpick inserted in the center comes out clean.

Variation

A combination of strawberries and rhubarb is also nice.

Blueberry Brunch Cake

◆

Don't limit this to brunch. It's ideal for breakfast and dessert, too.

MAKES ONE 6-INCH (15 CM) CAKE (4 TO 6 SERVINGS)

- Preparation: 25 minutes
- Baking: 40 minutes
- Freezing: excellent

Tips

Don't use frozen berries. They are too wet.

Sprinkle with confectioners' sugar just before serving.

Mix 3 tbsp (45 mL) confectioners' sugar and about 2 tsp (10 mL) milk and drizzle over the cake for another attractive finish.

Cooled cake will keep in an airtight container in the refrigerator for up to 3 days or can be frozen for up to 3 months. Thaw and bring to room temperature before serving.

- **Preheat oven to 350°F (180°C)**
- **6-inch (15 cm) springform pan, greased and floured**

CAKE

¾ cup	all-purpose flour	175 mL
1 tbsp	poppy seeds	15 mL
¼ tsp	baking soda	1 mL
⅛ tsp	salt	0.5 mL
¼ cup	butter, softened	60 mL
⅓ cup	granulated sugar	75 mL
1	egg yolk	1
1 tsp	freshly grated lemon zest	5 mL
¼ cup	sour cream	60 mL

FILLING

1 cup	fresh blueberries (see Tips, left)	250 mL
2 tbsp	granulated sugar	30 mL
1 tsp	all-purpose flour	5 mL

1. *Cake:* In a small bowl, whisk together flour, poppy seeds, baking soda and salt. Set aside.
2. In a medium bowl, using a wooden spoon, beat together butter, sugar, egg yolk and lemon zest, until light and creamy. In alternating batches (3 dry and 2 liquid additions), add flour mixture and sour cream, stirring well after each addition. Spread batter evenly over bottom and 1 inch (2.5 cm) up sides of prepared pan (batter should be ¼ inch/0.5 cm thick).
3. *Filling:* In a small bowl, stir together blueberries, sugar and flour. Spoon evenly over base.
4. Bake in preheated oven for 35 to 40 minutes or until crust is golden. Let cool in pan on a wire rack for about 15 minutes, then release ring from pan.

> ## Variation
> Omit the poppy seeds if you don't like crunch.

Raspberry Coffee Cake

◆

This is one of my favorite coffee cakes. Fresh raspberries and moist cake make it irresistible.

MAKES ONE 6-INCH (15 CM) CAKE (4 TO 6 SERVINGS)

- Preparation: 20 minutes
- Baking: 40 minutes
- Freezing: excellent

Tips

. . . .

To keep brown sugar moist, store in an airtight container with a slice of bread or apple.

Cooled cake will keep in an airtight container in the refrigerator for up to 3 days or can be frozen for up to 3 months. Thaw and bring to room temperature before serving.

Replace the raspberries with blueberries, or try a mixture of berries.

- Preheat oven to 375°F (190°C)
- 6-inch (15 cm) square cake pan, greased and floured or lined with parchment paper

STREUSEL

¼ cup	all-purpose flour	60 mL
3 tbsp	packed brown sugar	45 mL
2 tbsp	butter, softened	30 mL
½ tsp	ground cinnamon	2 mL

CAKE

1 cup	all-purpose flour	250 mL
1½ tsp	baking powder	7 mL
¼ tsp	salt	1 mL
2 tbsp	butter, softened	30 mL
⅓ cup	granulated sugar	75 mL
1	egg	1
½ tsp	pure vanilla extract	2 mL
¼ cup	milk	60 mL
1 cup	fresh raspberries	250 mL

1. *Streusel:* In a small bowl, using a fork, stir together flour, brown sugar, butter and cinnamon, until crumbly. Set aside.
2. *Cake:* In a small bowl, whisk together flour, baking powder and salt. Set aside.
3. In a medium bowl, using a wooden spoon, beat together butter, sugar, egg and vanilla, until light and creamy. In alternating batches (3 dry and 2 liquid additions), add flour mixture and milk, stirring well after each addition. Spread half the batter evenly in prepared pan. Sprinkle with raspberries. Spread remaining batter evenly over berries. Sprinkle topping evenly over batter.
4. Bake in preheated oven for 35 to 40 minutes or until a toothpick inserted in the center comes out clean. Let cool in pan on a wire rack for 15 minutes, then remove from pan. Serve warm or at room temperature.

Cinnamon Streusel Coffee Cake

◆

Plain and simple—this cake is one of the best.

MAKES ONE 6-INCH (15 CM) CAKE (4 TO 6 SERVINGS)

- Preparation: 20 minutes
- Baking: 30 minutes
- Freezing: excellent

Tips

. . . .

I prefer to use golden brown sugar, but dark brown sugar, which has a slight molasses flavor, also works well. Use whichever you prefer.

Check expiry dates on leavenings such as baking powder. If they are old, your cake will not rise properly and will be tough rather than tender.

Substitute Greek yogurt for the sour cream.

Cooled cake will keep in an airtight container at room temperature for up to 1 week or can be frozen for up to 3 months. Thaw and bring to room temperature before serving.

- **Preheat oven to 350°F (180 C)**
- **6-inch (15 cm) square cake pan, greased and floured**

STREUSEL

⅓ cup	all-purpose flour	75 mL
¼ cup	packed brown sugar (see Tips, left)	60 mL
½ tsp	ground cinnamon	2 mL
2 tbsp	butter, melted	30 mL

CAKE

⅔ cup	all-purpose flour	150 mL
½ tsp	baking powder (see Tips, left)	2 mL
⅛ tsp	baking soda	0.5 mL
⅛ tsp	salt	0.5 mL
¼ cup	butter, softened	60 mL
⅓ cup	granulated sugar	75 mL
1	egg	1
½ tsp	pure vanilla extract	2 mL
¼ cup	sour cream (see Tips, left)	60 mL

1. *Streusel:* In a small bowl, combine flour, brown sugar, cinnamon and melted butter. Stir well. Set aside.
2. *Cake:* In a small bowl, whisk together flour, baking powder, baking soda and salt. Set aside.
3. In a medium bowl, using a wooden spoon, beat together butter, sugar, egg and vanilla, until light and creamy. In alternating batches, add flour mixture and sour cream, stirring well after each addition. Spread half the batter evenly in prepared pan. Sprinkle half the streusel overtop. Repeat with remaining batter and streusel.
4. Bake in preheated oven for 25 to 30 minutes or until a toothpick inserted in the center comes out clean. Let cool completely in pan on a wire rack, then cut into squares to serve.

> ## Variations
>
> Add 3 tbsp (45 mL) chopped pecans or walnuts to the streusel.

Vanilla Cupcakes

◆

This is a great basic white cupcake recipe to have in your repertoire. You can change the frosting to suit the occasion.

MAKES 6 CUPCAKES

- Preparation: 15 minutes
- Baking: 20 minutes
- Freezing: excellent

Tips

To ease blending, bring butter to room temperature before using.

To make buttermilk, combine 1 tsp (5 mL) fresh lemon juice and ⅓ cup (75 mL) milk in a small bowl. Let stand 5 minutes, then stir before using.

Frosted cupcakes will keep in an airtight container at room temperature for up to 3 days or can be frozen for up to 3 months. Thaw and bring to room temperature before serving.

- **Preheat oven to 350°F (180°C)**
- **6-cup muffin pan, lined with paper liners**

⅔ cup	all-purpose flour	150 mL
¼ tsp	baking powder	1 mL
⅛ tsp	baking soda	0.5 mL
Pinch	salt	Pinch
2 tbsp	unsalted butter, softened	30 mL
⅓ cup	granulated sugar	75 mL
½ tsp	pure vanilla extract	2 mL
⅓ cup	buttermilk (see Tips, left) or plain yogurt	75 mL

Frosting (optional; pick one)
    Cream Cheese Frosting (page 185)
    Milk Chocolate Frosting (page 188)
    Basic Vanilla Frosting (page 184)

1. In a small bowl, whisk together flour, baking powder, baking soda and salt. Set aside.
2. In a medium bowl, using a wooden spoon, beat together butter, sugar and vanilla, until light and creamy. Add buttermilk and stir well. Add flour mixture, stirring until smooth. Divide batter evenly among prepared muffin cups.
3. Bake in preheated oven for 15 to 20 minutes or until tops spring back when lightly touched. Let cool in pan on a wire rack for 10 minutes, then remove from pan and cool completely on rack.
4. Once cupcakes are completely cooled, top with frosting of choice.

Variations

Substitute 1 tsp (5 mL) freshly grated lemon zest for the vanilla.

Substitute ¼ tsp (1 mL) pure almond extract for the vanilla.

Chocolate Cupcakes

♦

Who doesn't love a great chocolate cupcake? It's so versatile. You can simply change the frosting and decorations to suit your mood or event.

MAKES 4 CUPCAKES

- Preparation: 15 minutes
- Baking: 22 minutes
- Freezing: excellent

Tips

To ensure even baking and to prevent the pan from burning, fill the two empty muffin cups with water.

Frosted cupcakes will keep in an airtight container at room temperature for up to 3 days or can be frozen for up to 3 months. Thaw and bring to room temperature before serving.

- **Preheat oven to 350°F (180°C)**
- **6-cup muffin pan, 4 cups lined with paper liners**

⅓ cup	all-purpose flour	75 mL
2 tbsp	unsweetened cocoa powder, sifted	30 mL
¼ tsp	baking soda	1 mL
Pinch	salt	Pinch
3 tbsp	granulated sugar	45 mL
3 tbsp	plain yogurt or buttermilk	45 mL
2 tbsp	vegetable oil	30 mL
1	egg	1
¼ tsp	pure vanilla extract	1 mL
2 tbsp	mini semisweet chocolate chips	30 mL

Frosting (optional; pick one)
  Cream Cheese Frosting (page 185)
  Milk Chocolate Frosting (page 188)
  Basic Vanilla Frosting (page 184)

1. In a small bowl, whisk together flour, cocoa powder, baking soda and salt. Set aside.
2. In a medium bowl, whisk together sugar, yogurt, oil, egg and vanilla. Using a wooden spoon, stir in dry ingredients. Mix until smooth. Divide batter evenly among prepared muffin cups.
3. Bake in preheated oven for 18 to 22 minutes or until tops spring back when lightly touched. Let cool in pan on a wire rack for 10 minutes, then remove from pan and cool completely on rack.
4. Once cupcakes are completely cooled, top with frosting of choice.

Variations

Use regular chocolate chips instead of minis.

If desired, omit the chocolate chips.

Substitute white chocolate chips for the semisweet.

White Chocolate Macadamia Cupcakes

◆

The combination of white chocolate and macadamia nuts is a hit in almost any baked treat.

MAKES 4 CUPCAKES

- Preparation: 15 minutes
- Baking: 26 minutes
- Freezing: excellent

Tips

Toast nuts to bring out their flavor. Place the nuts in a dry frying pan over medium heat and toast, stirring constantly, for about 5 minutes. Alternatively, you can toast them in the microwave. Place on a microwave-safe plate and heat on High for for 1 to 3 minutes, stirring every 30 seconds.

There is no need for an electric mixer when making small batches of cupcakes. You can get the butter-sugar mixture to a light, creamy consistency by beating it with a wooden spoon.

Cooled cupcakes will keep in an airtight container at room temperature for up to 3 days or can be frozen for up to 3 months. Thaw and bring to room temperature before serving.

- **Preheat oven to 350°F (180°C)**
- **6-cup muffin pan, 4 cups lined with paper liners**

½ cup	all-purpose flour	125 mL
¼ cup	chopped macadamia nuts (see Tips, left)	60 mL
½ tsp	baking powder	2 mL
Pinch	salt	Pinch
⅓ cup	granulated sugar	75 mL
3 tbsp	vegetable oil	45 mL
1	egg	1
2 tbsp	milk	30 mL
3 tbsp	white chocolate chips	45 mL

1. In a small bowl, whisk together flour, nuts, baking powder and salt. Set aside.
2. In a medium bowl, whisk together sugar, oil and egg. In alternating batches (3 dry and 2 liquid additions), add flour mixture and milk, stirring well after each addition. Stir in white chocolate chips. Divide batter evenly among prepared muffin cups.
3. Bake in preheated oven for 22 to 26 minutes or until tops spring back when lightly touched. Let cool in pan on a wire rack for 10 minutes, then remove from pan and cool completely on rack.

Variation

Substitute semisweet chocolate chips for the white chocolate chips, and pecans for the macadamia nuts.

These are great topped with Cream Cheese Frosting (page 185) and a sprinkling of toasted nuts.

Chocolate Toffee Candy Bar Cupcakes

Crispy toffee chocolate bars add texture and flavor to these decadent cupcakes.

MAKES 4 CUPCAKES

- Preparation: 25 minutes
- Baking: 22 minutes
- Freezing: excellent

Tip

My favorite candy bar for these is a Skor bar, but other chocolate toffee bars, such as Crispy Crunch or Heath, will also work.

- **Preheat oven to 375°F (190°C)**
- **6-cup muffin pan, 4 cups lined with paper liners**
- **Piping bag fitted with large star tip**

CUPCAKES

⅔ cup	all-purpose flour	150 mL
½ tsp	baking powder	2 mL
Pinch	salt	Pinch
¼ cup	butter, softened	60 mL
⅓ cup	granulated sugar	75 mL
1	egg	1
¼ cup	milk	60 mL
¼ tsp	pure vanilla extract	1 mL
3 tbsp	toffee bits (see Tips, right)	45 mL

CHOCOLATE DIP

½ cup	light chocolate molding wafers, melted (see Quick Tip, right)	125 mL
¼ cup	toffee bits	60 mL

FROSTING

¼ cup	butter, softened	60 mL
1 tbsp	melted light chocolate molding wafers	15 mL
1½ cups	confectioners' (icing) sugar, sifted	375 mL
1½ to 2 tbsp	milk	22 to 30 mL
4	broken pieces chocolate toffee bar (see Tips, left)	4

1. *Cupcakes:* In a small bowl, whisk together flour, baking powder and salt. Set aside.
2. In a medium bowl, using a wooden spoon, beat together butter and sugar. Add egg, milk and vanilla, beating until light and creamy. Add flour mixture and toffee bits and stir well. Divide batter evenly among prepared muffin cups.

Tips

Toffee bits are available in bulk food stores or in the baking aisle of well-stocked supermarkets.

Frosted cupcakes will keep in an airtight container at room temperature for up to 3 days or can be frozen for up to 3 months. Thaw and bring to room temperature before serving.

3. Bake in preheated oven for 18 to 22 minutes or until tops spring back when lightly touched. Let cool in pan on a wire rack for 10 minutes, then remove from pan and cool completely on rack.

4. *Chocolate Dip:* Dip tops of cupcakes in melted chocolate and roll top edges in toffee bits, pressing firmly so they stick. Set aside until chocolate is set.

5. *Frosting:* In a medium bowl, using a wooden spoon, beat together butter and melted chocolate until light and creamy. In alternating batches, add confectioners' sugar and milk, using just enough milk to achieve a smooth piping consistency. Transfer frosting to piping bag and pipe onto center of each cupcake. Garnish each with a piece of candy bar.

Variation

Substitute an equal amount of dark chocolate molding wafers for the light chocolate.

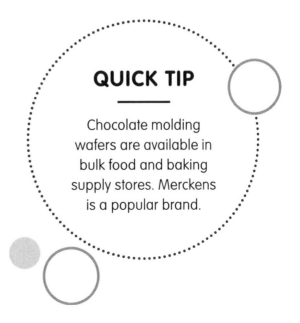

QUICK TIP

Chocolate molding wafers are available in bulk food and baking supply stores. Merckens is a popular brand.

Lemon Yogurt Cupcakes

◆

A lemon loaf in cupcake form, these will appeal to anyone who loves lemon.

MAKES 4 CUPCAKES

- Preparation: 15 minutes
- Baking: 22 minutes
- Freezing: excellent

Tips
. . . .

Freeze any excess lemon zest for another use. Spread out on a baking sheet and freeze; once frozen, transfer to an airtight container.

These cupcakes have flat tops, making them ideal for frosting.

For special occasions, add a lemon frosting and garnish with sugared walnuts.

Frosted cupcakes will keep in an airtight container at room temperature for up to 3 days or can be frozen for up to 3 months. Thaw and bring to room temperature before serving.

- **Preheat oven to 350°F (180°C)**
- **6-cup muffin pan, 4 cups lined with paper liners**

6 tbsp	all-purpose flour	90 mL
½ tsp	baking powder	2 mL
Pinch	salt	Pinch
⅓ cup	granulated sugar	75 mL
3 tbsp	butter, melted and cooled	45 mL
1	egg	1
2 tbsp	plain yogurt	30 mL
¾ tsp	freshly grated lemon zest (see Tips, left)	3 mL
1 tbsp	freshly squeezed lemon juice	15 mL
	Frosting (optional; pick one)	
	Lemon Frosting (Variation, page 184)	
	Basic Vanilla Frosting (page 184)	

1. In a small bowl, whisk together flour, baking powder and salt. Set aside.
2. In a medium bowl, whisk together sugar, melted butter, egg, yogurt, lemon zest and lemon juice. Using a wooden spoon, stir in flour mixture, beating until smooth. Divide batter evenly among prepared muffin cups.
3. Bake in preheated oven for 18 to 22 minutes or until tops spring back when lightly touched. Let cool in pan on a wire rack for 10 minutes, then remove from pan and cool completely on rack.
4. Once cupcakes are completely cooled, top with frosting of choice.

Variations

Substitute lime zest and juice for the lemon.

For an extra hit of flavor, add ¼ tsp (1 mL) pure lemon extract.

Apple Crumble Cupcakes

◆

The famous comfort-food dessert is just as good in a cupcake.

MAKES 4 CUPCAKES

- Preparation: 20 minutes
- Baking: 25 minutes
- Freezing: excellent

Tips

Prepare the apple just before using, to prevent browning.

To ensure uniform cupcakes, use a large ice-cream scoop (about ¼ cup/60 mL) to evenly portion out batter.

For a decadent dessert cupcake, add a swirl of Cream Cheese Frosting (page 185) on top of the streusel.

Cooled cupcakes will keep in an airtight container at room temperature for up to 3 days or can be frozen for up to 3 months. Thaw and bring to room temperature before serving.

- **Preheat oven to 350°F (180°C)**
- **6-cup muffin pan, 4 cups lined with paper liners**

STREUSEL

2 tbsp	packed brown sugar	30 mL
2 tsp	butter, softened	10 mL
¼ tsp	ground cinnamon	1 mL

CUPCAKES

½ cup	all-purpose flour	125 mL
½ tsp	baking powder	2 mL
Pinch	salt	Pinch
3 tbsp	butter, melted and cooled	45 mL
3 tbsp	granulated sugar	45 mL
1	egg	1
¼ tsp	pure vanilla extract	1 mL
½ cup	diced peeled, cored apple (see Tips, left)	125 mL

1. *Streusel:* In a small bowl, using a wooden spoon, combine sugar, butter and cinnamon, until mixture forms moist crumbs. Set aside.
2. *Cupcakes:* In a small bowl, whisk together flour, baking powder and salt. Set aside.
3. In a medium bowl, whisk together melted butter, sugar, egg and vanilla. Using a wooden spoon, add flour mixture, stirring until smooth. Fold in apple. Divide batter evenly among prepared muffin cups. Sprinkle streusel evenly over batter.
4. Bake in preheated oven for 20 to 25 minutes or until tops spring back when lightly touched. Let cool in pan on a wire rack for 10 minutes, then remove from pan and cool completely on rack.

Variations

Add 2 tbsp (30 mL) chopped walnuts or pecans to the streusel.

For a stronger caramel flavor, use dark brown sugar.

Pear Crumble Cupcakes: Substitute an equal amount of diced peeled, cored pear for the apple.

Lemon Pound Cake

◆

Plain and simple is often the most delicious. Serve this cake unadorned, with coffee for an afternoon treat or with fresh fruit for dessert.

MAKES ONE 6-INCH (15 CM) CAKE (4 TO 6 SERVINGS)

- Preparation: 20 minutes
- Baking: 25 minutes
- Freezing: excellent

Tips

Use plain, vanilla or lemon yogurt. All work well.

Cooled cake will keep in an airtight container at room temperature for up to 3 days or can be frozen for up to 3 months. Thaw and bring to room temperature before serving.

Substitute orange or lime zest and juice for the lemon.

- Preheat oven to 350°F (180°C)
- 6-inch (15 cm) mini angel cake tube pan, greased and floured
- Electric mixer

CAKE

½ cup	all-purpose flour	125 mL
⅛ tsp	baking powder	0.5 mL
⅛ tsp	baking soda	0.5 mL
⅛ tsp	salt	0.5 mL
3 tbsp	butter, softened	45 mL
6 tbsp	granulated sugar	90 mL
1	egg	1
1 tsp	freshly grated lemon zest	5 mL
2 tbsp	plain yogurt (see Tip, left)	30 mL
1 tbsp	freshly squeezed lemon juice	15 mL

GLAZE (OPTIONAL)

3 tbsp	granulated sugar	45 mL
2 tbsp	freshly squeezed lemon juice	30 mL

1. *Cake:* In a small bowl, whisk together flour, baking powder, baking soda and salt. Set aside.
2. In a medium bowl, using electric mixer at high speed, beat together butter, sugar and egg, until very light and creamy, about 3 minutes. Add lemon zest. In alternating batches, at low speed, gradually mix in flour mixture, yogurt and lemon juice, until thoroughly blended. Spread batter evenly in prepared pan.
3. Bake in preheated oven for 20 to 25 minutes or until a toothpick inserted in the center comes out clean. Let cool for 10 minutes in pan, then remove from pan and place on a wire rack over a piece of waxed paper.
4. *Glaze (optional):* In a microwave-safe bowl, combine sugar and lemon juice. Microwave on Medium for about 1 minute, then stir until sugar is dissolved.
5. Using a fork, poke holes all over surface of warm cake. Brush glaze over top, letting it soak in. Cool completely on rack.

Carrot Layer Cake

◆

A no-muss, no-fuss recipe. Frost with Cream Cheese Frosting (page 185) if desired. Serve with a scoop of vanilla ice cream.

MAKES ONE 5-INCH (12.5 CM) LAYER CAKE (4 TO 6 SERVINGS)

- Preparation: 20 minutes
- Baking: 30 minutes
- Freezing: excellent

Tips

Peel carrots before grating. If they are not peeled, green flecks will appear in the baked cake.

This size of cake is ideal for a dinner party for four. There'll be no leftovers to worry about.

Cooled cake will keep in an airtight container in the refrigerator for up to 5 days or can be frozen for up to 3 months. Thaw and bring to room temperature before serving.

- **Preheat oven to 325°F (160°C)**
- **Two 5-inch (12.5 cm) round cake pans, greased and floured**

½ cup	all-purpose flour	125 mL
½ tsp	baking powder	2 mL
½ tsp	ground cinnamon	2 mL
¼ tsp	baking soda	1 mL
Pinch	salt	Pinch
½ cup	granulated sugar	125 mL
¼ cup	vegetable oil	60 mL
1	egg	1
¾ cup	grated peeled carrots (see Tips, left)	175 mL
¼ cup	finely chopped walnuts	60 mL

1. In a large bowl, whisk together flour, baking powder, cinnamon, baking soda and salt. Set aside.
2. In another large bowl, whisk together sugar, oil and egg, until smooth. Using a wooden spoon, stir in flour mixture until thoroughly combined. Stir in carrots and walnuts. Divide batter evenly between prepared pans.
3. Bake in preheated oven for 25 to 30 minutes or until a toothpick inserted in the center comes out clean. Let cool for 10 minutes in pans, then remove from pans and cool completely on a wire rack.
4. *Assembly:* spread a layer of frosting over one cake layer. Place second cake layer on top. Spread remaining frosting over sides and top of cake.

> ## Variations
>
> Substitute an equal amount of raisins or dried cranberries for the nuts.
>
> Try pecans instead of walnuts.

Chocolate Raspberry Torte

◆

Tender, moist and chocolaty, this is one of the best chocolate cakes I've ever made. If serving to company, add fresh raspberries (see Variations, opposite). For everyday, simply top with the chocolate frosting.

MAKES ONE 6-INCH (15 CM) LAYER CAKE (4 TO 6 SERVINGS)

- Preparation: 25 minutes
- Baking: 30 minutes
- Freezing: not recommended

Tips

Sift cocoa powder before using, to remove any lumps that have formed during storage.

Seedless raspberry jam and homemade versions have more flavor than regular store-bought raspberry jam.

- **Preheat oven to 350°F (180°C)**
- **Two 6-inch (15 cm) round cake pans, greased and floured**
- **Electric mixer**

CAKE

1 cup	all-purpose flour	250 mL
1 cup	granulated sugar	250 mL
1/3 cup	unsweetened cocoa powder, sifted (see Tips, left)	75 mL
3/4 tsp	baking powder	3 mL
3/4 tsp	baking soda	3 mL
1/4 tsp	salt	1 mL
1	egg	1
1/2 cup	milk	125 mL
1/4 cup	vegetable oil	60 mL
1 tsp	pure vanilla extract	5 mL
1/2 cup	boiling water	125 mL

FILLING

1 cup	heavy or whipping (35%) cream	250 mL
2 tbsp	confectioners' (icing) sugar, sifted	30 mL
1/3 cup	raspberry jam (see Tips, left)	75 mL

FROSTING

3/4 cup	semisweet chocolate chips, melted	175 mL
6 tbsp	sour cream	90 mL
	Fresh raspberries, optional	

1. *Cake:* In a large mixing bowl, whisk together flour, sugar, cocoa powder, baking powder, baking soda and salt. Add egg, milk, oil and vanilla. Using electric mixer, beat at medium speed for 1 minute. Reduce speed to low and add boiling water, mixing just until combined (batter will be thin). Divide batter evenly between prepared pans.

2. Bake in preheated oven for 25 to 30 minutes or until a toothpick inserted in the center comes out clean. Let cool for 10 minutes in pans, then remove from pans and cool completely on a wire rack. Cut each layer in half horizontally so you end up with 4 layers.

Tips

Because it is so soft, the chocolate sour cream frosting spreads beautifully. It firms up as it cools.

Cake will keep in an airtight container in the refrigerator for up to 3 days.

3. *Filling:* In a small bowl, beat cream and confectioners' sugar until stiff peaks form.
4. *Frosting:* In a bowl, combine sour cream and warm melted chocolate. Stir well.
5. *Assembly:* Place one cake layer, cut side up, on a serving platter. Spread with one-third of the jam, then one-third of the whipped cream (see Quick Tip, below). Top with another cake layer, cut side up. Repeat topping and layering, ending with the top cake layer cut side down. Cover top and sides of cake with frosting. Refrigerate until ready to serve. Decorate with fresh raspberries, if desired.

Variations

For special occasions, top with fresh raspberries and chocolate curls or shavings.

Make a chocolate layer cake using Sour Cream Fudge Frosting (page 187) or Milk Chocolate Frosting (page 188).

QUICK TIP

When spreading a whipped cream filling between cake layers, leave a small border around the edges so the cream doesn't spread into the frosting on the sides of the cake.

Best Ever Banana Cake

◆

This is a tender, light, moist cake with a mild banana flavor. Cover with Banana Butter Frosting (page 186) and it's doubly delicious.

MAKES ONE 6-INCH (15 CM) LAYER CAKE (4 TO 6 SERVINGS)

- Preparation: 30 minutes
- Baking: 30 minutes
- Freezing: excellent

Tips

The riper the bananas, the better the flavor.

Buttermilk and yogurt both work well in this cake. Use whichever you have on hand.

Cooled cake will keep in an airtight container in the refrigerator for up to 5 days or can be frozen for up to 3 months. Thaw and bring to room temperature before serving.

- Preheat oven to 350°F (180°C)
- Two 6-inch (15 cm) round cake pans, greased and floured
- Electric mixer

1 cup	all-purpose flour	250 mL
1 tsp	baking powder	5 mL
¼ tsp	baking soda	1 mL
¼ tsp	salt	1 mL
⅔ cup	granulated sugar	150 mL
½ cup	mashed ripe banana (1 large; see Tips, left)	125 mL
¼ cup	butter, softened	60 mL
¼ cup	buttermilk or plain yogurt	60 mL
1	egg	1

1. In a large bowl, whisk together flour, baking powder, baking soda and salt. Add sugar, banana, butter and buttermilk. Using electric mixer at medium speed, beat for 1½ minutes. Add egg. Beat for 1 minute longer. Divide batter evenly between prepared pans.
2. Bake in preheated oven for 25 to 30 minutes or until a toothpick inserted in the center comes out clean. Let cool for 10 minutes in pans on a wire rack, then remove from pans and transfer to rack to cool completely.
3. *Assembly:* spread a layer of frosting over one cake layer. Place second cake layer on top. Spread remaining frosting over sides and top of cake.

Variations

If you are going to eat the whole cake the same day it is baked, add a layer of sliced bananas between the cake layers.

Try icing with Sour Cream Fudge Frosting (page 187) or Basic Vanilla Frosting (page 184).

Quick 'n' Easy Apple Cake

◆

This cake is moist and delicious, with a hint of cinnamon. No icing is required, so it's a great breakfast cake, too.

MAKES ONE 6-INCH (15 CM) CAKE (4 TO 6 SERVINGS)

- Preparation: 20 minutes
- Baking: 35 minutes
- Freezing: excellent

Tips

Use a tart, firm apple, such as Granny Smith.

Chop apple just before using, to prevent browning.

To get an even covering of batter on top, drop it by teaspoonfuls (5 mL) over the apples, which makes it easier to spread.

Cooled cake will keep in an airtight container in the refrigerator for up to 3 days or can be frozen for up to 3 months. Thaw and bring to room temperature before serving.

- Preheat oven to 350°F (180°C)
- 6-inch (15 cm) square cake pan, greased and floured

TOPPING

2 tbsp	granulated sugar	30 mL
½ tsp	ground cinnamon	2 mL

CAKE

¾ cup	all-purpose flour	175 mL
¾ tsp	baking powder	3 mL
Pinch	salt	Pinch
½ cup	granulated sugar	125 mL
¼ cup	vegetable oil	60 mL
1	egg	1
2 tbsp	apple juice	30 mL
1 tsp	pure vanilla extract	5 mL
1	large apple, peeled, cored and chopped (see Tips, left)	1

1. *Topping:* In a small bowl, stir together sugar and cinnamon. Set aside.
2. *Cake:* In a small bowl, whisk together flour, baking powder and salt. Set aside.
3. In a medium bowl, whisk together sugar, oil, egg, apple juice and vanilla. Gradually whisk in flour mixture until smooth. Spread half the batter evenly in prepared pan. Sprinkle apple overtop. Sprinkle half the topping over apple. Spread remaining batter on top. Sprinkle with remaining topping.
4. Bake in preheated oven for 30 to 35 minutes or until a toothpick inserted in the center comes out clean. Let cool in pan on a wire rack. Serve warm or cold.

Variations

Add 2 tbsp (30 mL) chopped pecans or almonds to the topping.

Substitute a pear for the apple.

Maple-Frosted Applesauce Spice Cake

A carbon copy of the old-fashioned Spanish Bar Cake, this cake is dense, moist and delicious.

MAKES TWO MINI LOAVES

- Preparation: 25 minutes
- Baking: 27 minutes
- Freezing: excellent

Tips

Either canned or bottled applesauce works well.

There is no need for an electric mixer when making small batches of cake. You can get the butter-sugar mixture to a light, creamy consistency by beating it with a wooden spoon.

- **Preheat oven 350°F (180°C)**
- **Two 5½- by 3¼-inch (14 by 8 cm) mini loaf pans, greased and floured**

CAKE

¾ cup	all-purpose flour	175 mL
½ tsp	baking soda	2 mL
¼ tsp	salt	1 mL
⅛ tsp	baking powder	0.5 mL
¼ tsp	ground cinnamon	1 mL
⅛ tsp	ground allspice	0.5 mL
⅛ tsp	ground cloves	0.5 mL
⅓ cup	granulated sugar	75 mL
⅓ cup	unsweetened applesauce (see Tips, left)	75 mL
2 tbsp	water	30 mL
2 tbsp	butter, melted	30 mL
1	egg	1
3 tbsp	raisins	45 mL
2 tbsp	chopped walnuts	30 mL

MAPLE FROSTING

1 tbsp	butter, softened	15 mL
⅔ cup	confectioners' (icing) sugar, sifted	150 mL
2 tbsp	pure maple syrup	30 mL

1. *Cake:* In a small bowl, whisk together flour, baking soda, salt, baking powder, cinnamon, allspice and cloves. Set aside.
2. In a large bowl, whisk together sugar, applesauce, water, melted butter and egg. Gradually stir in flour mixture until thoroughly blended. Fold in raisins and walnuts. Divide batter evenly between prepared pans.
3. Bake in preheated oven for 22 to 27 minutes or until a toothpick inserted in the center comes out clean. Let cool for 10 minutes in pans, then remove to a wire rack and cool completely.

Tip

Frosted loaves will keep in an airtight container in the refrigerator for up to 5 days or can be frozen for up to 3 months. Thaw and bring to room temperature before serving.

4. *Maple Frosting:* In a small bowl, using a wooden spoon or electric mixer, beat butter until smooth. In alternating batches, add confectioners' sugar and maple syrup, beating until smooth and spreadable. Divide icing into two equal portions and spread evenly over cakes.

Variations

Omit raisins and nuts, if desired.

Substitute ground nutmeg for the allspice or cloves.

QUICK TIP

Foil loaf pans are excellent. They are great for gift-giving, too.

Apricot Hazelnut Torte

◆

"Heaven in a nutshell" perfectly describes this melt-in-your-mouth dessert.

MAKES ONE 6-INCH (15 CM) LAYER CAKE (4 TO 6 SERVINGS)

- Preparation: 25 minutes
- Baking: 22 minutes
- Freezing: not recommended

Tips

Be sure your bowls are grease-free, or the egg yolks will not beat to full volume and the whites won't be stiff.

For easy spreading, press the jam through a fine-mesh sieve with the back of a spoon to remove any lumps of fruit.

- Preheat oven to 350°F (180°C)
- Two 6-inch (15 cm) round cake pans, greased and floured or lined with parchment paper
- Electric mixer

CAKE

6 tbsp	all-purpose flour	90 mL
1 tsp	baking powder	5 mL
¼ tsp	salt	1 mL
½ cup	ground hazelnuts	125 mL
2	eggs, separated	2
1 tbsp	water	15 mL
½ tsp	pure vanilla extract	2 mL
8 tbsp	granulated sugar, divided	120 mL

FILLING

1 cup	heavy or whipping (35%) cream	250 mL
2 tbsp	confectioners' (icing) sugar, sifted	30 mL
½ cup	apricot junior baby food	125 mL

GLAZE AND DECORATION

¼ cup	strained apricot jam (see Tips, left)	60 mL
1 tbsp	chopped hazelnuts, optional	15 mL

1. *Cake:* In a small bowl, whisk together flour, baking powder, salt and ground hazelnuts. Set aside.
2. In a medium bowl, using electric mixer at high speed, beat together egg yolks, water and vanilla, until thick and light. Gradually add 6 tbsp (90 mL) sugar, beating until thick and light, about 5 minutes.
3. In a large bowl, using electric mixer at high speed, beat together egg whites and 2 tbsp (30 mL) sugar until stiff peaks form. In 4 equal batches, fold flour mixture into egg yolk mixture, mixing well after each addition. Fold in one-quarter of the meringue, then gently fold in remaining meringue. Divide batter evenly between prepared pans.

Tip

4. Bake in preheated oven for 18 to 22 minutes or until a toothpick inserted in the center comes out clean. Let cool in pans for 5 minutes, then remove from pans and cool completely on a wire rack.

5. *Filling:* In a small bowl, beat together cream and confectioners' sugar until stiff peaks form. Gently fold in apricot baby food.

6. *Assembly:* Cut cooled cakes in half horizontally so you end up with 4 layers. Place one layer, cut side up, on a serving platter. Spread one-third of filling on top. Top with another layer of cake. Repeat topping and layering, ending with the top cake layer cut side down. Brush top layer with apricot jam. If desired, sprinkle chopped hazelnuts around top edges. Refrigerate until ready to serve.

Variations

Substitute walnuts, almonds or pecans for the hazelnuts.

Almond Dacquoise

Crunchy almond meringue layered with whipped cream makes an elegant light dessert, perfect for special occasions.

MAKES 4 TO 6 SERVINGS

- Preparation: 25 minutes
- Baking: 55 minutes
- Chilling: 1 to 8 hours
- Freezing: not recommended

Tips

Be sure to bring the eggs to room temperature before using, so they beat to maximum volume.

Make sure bowls and beaters are grease-free, or the egg whites won't beat to stiff peaks.

- Preheat oven to 350°F (180°C)
- 2 baking sheets, lined with parchment paper
- Rimmed baking sheet
- Food processor
- Electric mixer

MERINGUE

1 cup	sliced almonds, divided	250 mL
¾ cup	granulated sugar, divided	175 mL
1 tbsp	cornstarch	15 mL
4	egg whites, at room temperature (see Tips, left)	4
¼ tsp	pure almond extract	1 mL

FILLING

1 cup	heavy or whipping (35%) cream	250 mL
⅓ cup	confectioners' (icing) sugar, sifted	75 mL
1 tsp	freshly grated lemon zest	5 mL
1 tbsp	freshly squeezed lemon juice	15 mL

1. *Meringue:* Draw two 5-inch (12.5 cm) circles on each piece of parchment paper, for a total of 4 circles. Set aside.
2. Spread almonds on rimmed baking sheet. Bake in preheated oven, stirring occasionally, for 8 to 10 minutes or until light golden. Let cool.
3. Reduce oven temperature to 275°F (140°C).
4. In food processor fitted with the metal blade, process ¾ cup (175 mL) toasted almonds with ¼ cup (60 mL) sugar and the cornstarch, until almonds are very finely chopped. Set aside.
5. In a large bowl, using electric mixer at high speed, beat egg whites until soft peaks form. Gradually add remaining sugar, 1 tbsp (15 mL) at a time, beating until stiff, glossy peaks form. Beat in almond extract. Sprinkle half the ground almond mixture over egg whites and fold in thoroughly. Gently fold in remaining ground almond mixture. Divide meringue evenly among the 4 parchment paper circles, spreading evenly to fill circles. Transfer to baking sheets.

Tip
. . . .

Dacquoise will keep in an airtight container in the refrigerator for up to 3 days.

6. Bake in 275°F (140°C) oven, rotating pans halfway through, for 40 to 45 minutes or until firm. Using a spatula, transfer to a wire rack and let cool completely.

7. *Filling:* In a small bowl, using electric mixer at high speed, beat together cream and confectioners' sugar until stiff peaks form. Stir in lemon zest and lemon juice. Set aside 1 cup (250 mL) for the topping.

8. *Assembly:* Place one meringue layer on a serving plate. Spread one-third of remaining whipped cream evenly overtop. Repeat with 2 more meringue layers. Top with remaining meringue layer. Spread reserved whipped cream over top and sides of torte. Press remaining toasted almonds onto sides of torte. Refrigerate for 1 hour or up to 8 hours before serving.

Variations

Substitute an equal amount of hazelnuts for the almonds.

Instead of coating the top and sides of the cake, divide the filling into 4 equal portions and spread one-quarter over each meringue layer, leaving the sides uncovered. Sprinkle the top layer with almonds.

Basic Vanilla Frosting

◆

A velvety smooth, creamy frosting that goes well with almost any cake or cupcake.

MAKES ENOUGH FROSTING FOR ONE 6-INCH (15 CM) LAYER CAKE OR 8 CUPCAKES

- Preparation: 10 minutes

Tip
. . . .
For a festive frosting on cupcakes, beat in a few drops of food coloring.

- **Electric mixer**

½ cup	unsalted butter, softened	125 mL
1½ cups	confectioners' (icing) sugar, sifted	375 mL
1 tbsp	milk	15 mL
½ tsp	pure vanilla extract	2 mL

1. In a large bowl, using electric mixer at low speed, beat together butter and half of the confectioners' sugar. In alternating batches, gradually add remaining confectioners' sugar, milk and vanilla, mixing well after each addition. Increase speed to high and beat until light and fluffy.

Variations

Lemon or Orange Frosting: Substitute an equal amount of lemon or orange juice for the milk and 1 tsp (5 mL) freshly grated lemon or orange zest for the vanilla.

Chocolate Frosting: Add 1 oz (30 g) melted and cooled chocolate along with the butter.

Cocoa Frosting: Replace 3 tbsp (45 mL) of the confectioners' sugar with sifted unsweetened cocoa powder.

Coffee Frosting: Add 2 tsp (10 mL) instant coffee granules to the butter.

Mint Frosting: Add 2 to 3 drops of pure peppermint extract and green food coloring to the butter.

Rocky Road Frosting: Break 2 to 3 chocolate sandwich cookies into small pieces and beat into the finished frosting.

Cream Cheese Frosting

◆

Don't limit this classic frosting to carrot cake. It's delicious on almost anything.

MAKES ENOUGH FROSTING FOR ONE 6-INCH (15 CM) LAYER CAKE OR 6 CUPCAKES

- Preparation: 10 minutes

Tips

· ·

To ease mixing, bring cream cheese to room temperature before using.

Sift confectioners' sugar to remove any lumps that may have formed during storage.

- **Electric mixer**

4 oz	cream cheese, softened (see Tips, left)	120 g
2 tbsp	butter, softened	30 mL
½ tsp	freshly squeezed lemon juice	2 mL
1⅓ cups	confectioners' (icing) sugar, sifted	325 mL

1. In a small bowl, using electric mixer at medium speed, beat together cream cheese, butter and lemon juice. Gradually add confectioners' sugar, beating until smooth.

Variation
Substitute an equal amount of pure vanilla extract for the lemon juice.

Banana Butter Frosting

This frosting on a banana cake or cupcake is outrageously good.

MAKES ENOUGH FROSTING FOR ONE 6-INCH (15 CM) LAYER CAKE OR 8 CUPCAKES

- Preparation: 10 minutes

Tips

Try this frosting on a chocolate or white cake or cupcakes.

Decorate with dried banana chips.

• **Electric mixer**

¼ cup	butter, softened	60 mL
¼ cup	mashed ripe banana (1 small)	60 mL
2 cups	confectioners' (icing) sugar, sifted	500 mL
1½ tsp	milk	7 mL

1. In a large bowl, using electric mixer at low speed, beat together butter, mashed banana and half of the confectioners' sugar. In alternating batches, gradually add remaining confectioners' sugar and milk, beating until creamy.

Sour Cream Fudge Frosting

◆

This frosting is smooth and creamy, with a unique chocolate flavor that will keep everyone guessing about the ingredients.

MAKES ENOUGH FROSTING FOR ONE 6-INCH (15 CM) LAYER CAKE OR 6 CUPCAKES

• Preparation: 10 minutes

Tips
. . . .

To ensure a smooth frosting, sift the confectioners' sugar before using.

Either low-fat or regular sour cream works well in this frosting. Use whichever you prefer.

• **Electric mixer**

½ cup	semisweet chocolate chips, melted and cooled	125 mL
2 tbsp	butter, softened	30 mL
1⅓ cups	confectioners' (icing) sugar, sifted (see Tips, left)	325 mL
¼ cup	sour cream (see Tips, left)	60 mL

1. In a large bowl, using electric mixer at low speed, beat together melted chocolate chips and butter. In alternating batches, gradually add confectioners' sugar and sour cream, beating until smooth. Increase speed to medium and beat until smooth and creamy.

Variation
Add 1 tsp (5 mL) instant coffee granules along with the chocolate.

Milk Chocolate Frosting

A milk chocolate flavor that's great on chocolate cake and cupcakes.

MAKES ENOUGH FROSTING FOR ONE 6-INCH (15 CM) LAYER CAKE OR 8 CUPCAKES

• Preparation: 10 minutes

Tip

Both salted and unsalted butter work well in this recipe. Use whatever you have on hand.

• **Electric mixer**

6 tbsp	butter, softened (see Tip, left)	90 mL
1¼ cups	confectioners' (icing) sugar, sifted	300 mL
3 tbsp	unsweetened cocoa powder, sifted	45 mL
2 tbsp	milk	30 mL

1. In a large bowl, using electric mixer at low speed, beat butter until smooth. In alternating batches, add confectioners' sugar, cocoa powder and milk, beating well after each addition. Increase speed to medium and beat until smooth and spreadable.

Variation
For a more intense chocolate flavor, increase the amount of cocoa powder to ¼ cup (60 mL).

Chocolate Glaze

◆

When you don't have time to make a frosting, this glaze is an easy alternative.

MAKES ABOUT ¼ CUP (60 ML) OR ENOUGH FOR 6 CUPCAKES

• Preparation: 5 minutes

Tips

Substitute chopped semisweet chocolate for the chocolate chips.

Heat the mixture until the chocolate has almost melted (but not quite), then stir until completely smooth.

| ¼ cup | semisweet chocolate chips (see Tips, left) | 60 mL |
| 2 tbsp | heavy or whipping (35%) cream | 30 mL |

1. In a small microwave-safe bowl, combine chocolate chips and cream. Microwave on Medium for 30 seconds. Stir well, then heat for another 30 seconds. Stir until smooth. Set aside for a few minutes to thicken before pouring over cupcakes.

Chocolate Overload Cheesecake

◆

As this cheesecake proves, you can never have too much chocolate. Serve plain or with a dollop of whipped cream.

MAKES ONE 6-INCH (15 CM) CAKE (4 TO 6 SERVINGS)

- Preparation: 30 minutes
- Baking: 45 minutes
- Chilling: overnight
- Freezing: excellent

Tips

Don't skimp on the chocolate. The better the quality of chocolate you use, the better the flavor of your cheesecake.

Cheesecake will keep in an airtight container in the refrigerator for up to 5 days or can be frozen for up to 3 months. Thaw in refrigerator overnight and bring to room temperature before serving.

- Preheat oven to 325°F (160°C)
- 6-inch (15 cm) springform pan, greased
- Electric mixer

CRUST

¾ cup	chocolate wafer crumbs	175 mL
2 tbsp	butter, melted	30 mL

FILLING

12 oz	cream cheese, softened	375 g
½ cup	granulated sugar	125 mL
4 tsp	unsweetened cocoa powder, sifted	20 mL
1	egg	1
1	egg yolk	1
3 oz	white chocolate, coarsely chopped	90 g
3 oz	semisweet chocolate, coarsely chopped	90 g

1. *Crust:* In a small bowl, combine chocolate wafer crumbs and melted butter. Press mixture evenly into bottom of prepared pan.
2. Bake in preheated oven for 5 minutes. Set aside.
3. *Filling:* In a medium bowl, using electric mixer at medium speed, beat together cream cheese, sugar and cocoa powder, until smooth and creamy, about 2 minutes. Add egg and egg yolk, beating well. Fold in white chocolate and semisweet chocolate. Spread evenly over baked crust.
4. Bake for 35 to 40 minutes or until softly set. Let cool completely in pan on a wire rack, then refrigerate overnight. To unmold cake, run a knife around edge of pan and remove ring.

Variations

Mocha Chocolate Overload Cheesecake: Add 2 tsp (10 mL) instant espresso powder to the filling along with the cocoa powder.

Substitute bittersweet chocolate for the semisweet chocolate.

Chocolate Almond Cheesecake

◆

Remember to serve cheesecake at room temperature for the best flavor and a creamy texture.

MAKES ONE 6-INCH (15 CM) CAKE (4 TO 6 SERVINGS)

- Preparation: 30 minutes
- Baking: 40 minutes
- Chilling: overnight
- Freezing: excellent

Tips

Run a knife around the edge of the pan when it comes out of the oven, then cool. This will help prevent the surface of the cake from cracking.

Cheesecake will keep in an airtight container in the refrigerator for up to 5 days or can be frozen for up to 3 months. Thaw in refrigerator overnight and bring to room temperature before serving.

- Preheat oven to 325°F (160°C)
- 6-inch (15 cm) springform pan, greased

CRUST

⅔ cup	chocolate wafer crumbs	150 mL
2 tbsp	finely chopped almonds	30 mL
1 tbsp	granulated sugar	15 mL
2 tbsp	butter, melted	30 mL

FILLING

8 oz	cream cheese, softened	250 g
¼ cup	granulated sugar	60 mL
1	egg	1
3½ oz	semisweet chocolate, melted and cooled	105 g
⅓ cup	sour cream	75 mL
2 tbsp	almond liqueur	30 mL
⅓ cup	sliced almonds, toasted	75 mL

1. *Crust:* In a small bowl, combine chocolate wafer crumbs, almonds, sugar and melted butter. Stir well. Press mixture evenly into bottom of prepared pan.
2. Bake in preheated oven for 5 minutes. Set aside.
3. *Filling:* In a medium bowl, using electric mixer at medium speed, beat together cream cheese and sugar until light and creamy. Beat in egg. Add melted chocolate, sour cream and liqueur. Mix well. Spread evenly over baked crust.
4. Bake for 30 to 35 minutes or until softly set. Let cool completely in pan on a wire rack, then refrigerate overnight.
5. To unmold cake, run a knife around edge of pan and remove ring. Garnish with toasted sliced almonds before serving.

> ## Variation
> Substitute coffee liqueur for the almond liqueur and sprinkle crushed chocolate-covered coffee beans on top of the cake.

Chocolate Toffee Candy Bar Cheesecake

Rich and decadent, a small slice of this cheesecake goes a long way.

MAKES ONE 6-INCH (15 CM) CAKE (4 TO 6 SERVINGS)

- Preparation: 30 minutes
- Baking: 42 minutes
- Chilling: overnight

Tips

I like to use Skor bars, which are available in bulk food stores. Heath bars are also great.

Run a knife around the edge of the pan when it comes out of the oven, then cool. This will help prevent the surface of the cake from cracking.

When baking, it is a good idea to place the pan on a piece of aluminum foil to catch any drips.

- **Preheat oven to 325°F (160°C)**
- **6-inch (15 cm) springform pan, greased**

CRUST

⅓ cup	all-purpose flour	75 mL
1½ tbsp	packed brown sugar	22 mL
1½ tbsp	finely chopped almonds	22 mL
3 tbsp	butter, softened	45 mL

FILLING

8 oz	cream cheese, softened	250 g
¼ cup	granulated sugar	60 mL
1 tsp	all-purpose flour	5 mL
1	egg	1
2 tbsp	sour cream	30 mL
⅓ cup	chopped crunchy chocolate toffee bar (1 bar, 1.4 oz/39 g; see Tips, left)	75 mL

1. *Crust:* In a small bowl, using a wooden spoon, stir together flour, brown sugar, almonds and butter, until crumbly. Press mixture firmly into bottom of prepared pan.
2. Bake in preheated oven for 8 to 12 minutes or until light golden. Set aside.

Tips

Refrigerating cheesecakes overnight improves their texture. If overnight isn't an option, chill for at least 3 hours, if possible.

Cheesecake will keep in an airtight container in the refrigerator for up to 5 days or can be frozen for up to 3 months. Thaw in refrigerator overnight and bring to room temperature before serving.

3. *Filling:* In a medium bowl, using electric mixer at medium speed, beat together cream cheese, sugar and flour until light and creamy. Beat in egg, then sour cream, mixing well. Stir in chopped candy bar. Spread evenly over baked crust.

4. Bake in preheated oven for 25 to 30 minutes or until softly set. Let cool in pan on a wire rack, then refrigerate overnight.

5. To unmold cake, run a knife around edge of pan and remove ring.

Variations

For added decadence, serve with a drizzle of caramel or chocolate sauce.

Mix 'n' Match Mini Vanilla Cheesecakes

This versatile recipe can be served in several different ways: top with fruit pie filling, lemon curd, fresh fruit or fruit jam.

MAKES 6 MINI CHEESECAKES

- Preparation: 25 minutes
- Baking: 28 minutes

Tips

For a creamy texture and taste, serve cheesecakes at room temperature.

Cheesecake will keep in an airtight container in the refrigerator for up to 5 days or can be frozen for up to 3 months. Thaw in refrigerator overnight and bring to room temperature before serving.

- **Preheat oven to 325°F (160°C)**
- **6-cup muffin pan, lined with paper liners**
- **Electric mixer**

CRUST

½ cup	graham wafer crumbs	125 mL
1 tbsp	granulated sugar	15 mL
4 tsp	butter, melted	20 mL

FILLING

8 oz	cream cheese, softened	250 g
¼ cup	granulated sugar	60 mL
½ tsp	freshly grated lemon zest	2 mL
1½ tsp	freshly squeezed lemon juice	7 mL
1	egg	1

1. *Crust:* In a small bowl, combine graham wafer crumbs, sugar and melted butter. Press a rounded tablespoonful (20 mL) of crumb mixture into bottom of each cup.
2. Bake in preheated oven for 5 minutes. Set aside.
3. *Filling:* In a medium bowl, using electric mixer at medium speed, beat together cream cheese, sugar, lemon zest and lemon juice, until light and creamy. Beat in egg. Divide mixture evenly between prepared crusts.
4. Bake for 18 to 23 minutes or until set. Let cool completely in pan on a wire rack. Top as desired.

Variations

Omit the lemon zest and juice. Add 1 tsp (5 mL) pure vanilla or almond extract in Step 3.

No-Bake Raspberry Cheesecake

◆

This no-fuss cheesecake highlights the flavor of fresh raspberries.

MAKES ONE 6-INCH (15 CM) CAKE (4 TO 6 SERVINGS)

- Preparation: 25 minutes
- Chilling: 2 hours
- Freezing: not recommended

Tips

Unflavored gelatin is sold in a box of envelopes (0.25 oz/7 g each) or in bulk at bulk food stores. This recipe uses half an envelope.

You can use frozen berries, but be sure to thaw them first and drain off excess liquid.

Cheesecake will keep in an airtight container in the refrigerator for up to 5 days.

- **6-inch (15 cm) springform pan**
- **Electric mixer**

CRUST

½ cup	graham wafer crumbs	125 mL
4 tsp	granulated sugar	20 mL
2 tbsp	butter, melted	30 mL

FILLING

1½ tsp	unflavored gelatin (see Tips, left)	7 mL
2 tbsp	water	30 mL
4 oz	cream cheese, softened	125 g
¼ cup	granulated sugar	60 mL
½ cup	heavy or whipping (35%) cream	125 mL
1 cup	fresh raspberries, slightly crushed (see Tips, left)	250 mL

1. *Crust:* In a small bowl, combine graham wafer crumbs, sugar and melted butter. Press mixture evenly into bottom of pan. Refrigerate while preparing filling.
2. *Filling:* In a small bowl, stir together gelatin and water. Set aside for 5 minutes, then warm in microwave for about 30 seconds, until gelatin has dissolved. Set aside.
3. In a medium bowl, using electric mixer at medium speed, beat together cream cheese and sugar until light and creamy.
4. In another small bowl, using electric mixer at high speed, beat cream until stiff peaks form.
5. Gently fold whipped cream, prepared gelatin and crushed raspberries into cream cheese mixture until combined. Spread evenly over chilled crust. Refrigerate until set, about 2 hours.
6. To unmold cake, run a knife around edge of pan and remove ring.

Variation

Substitute an equal amount of strawberries for the raspberries.

Mini Chocolate Cheesecakes

◆

Elevate these yummy cheesecakes from family treat to special-occasion dessert with the simple addition of shaved chocolate or chocolate curls.

MAKES 6 MINI CHEESECAKES

- Preparation: 25 minutes
- Baking: 28 minutes
- Freezing: excellent

Tip
. . . .
Try topping each cheesecake with a sprinkling of toasted sliced almonds.

- **Preheat oven to 325°F (160°C)**
- **Electric mixer**
- **6-cup muffin pan, lined with paper liners**

CRUST

½ cup	vanilla or chocolate wafer crumbs	125 mL
4 tsp	butter, melted	20 mL

FILLING

8 oz	cream cheese, softened	250 g
¼ cup	packed brown sugar	60 mL
1	egg	1
½ cup	semisweet chocolate chips, melted and cooled	125 mL
1 tbsp	almond liqueur	15 mL

TOPPING (OPTIONAL)

⅓ cup	sour cream	75 mL
1 tsp	granulated sugar	5 mL
¼ tsp	pure vanilla extract	1 mL

1. *Crust:* In a small bowl, combine wafer crumbs and melted butter. Press a rounded tablespoonful (20 mL) of crumb mixture into bottom of each cup.
2. Bake in preheated oven for 5 minutes. Set aside.
3. *Filling:* In a medium bowl, using electric mixer at medium speed, beat together cream cheese and brown sugar until light and creamy. Beat in egg. Mix in melted chocolate chips and liqueur. Divide mixture evenly between prepared crusts.
4. Bake for 18 to 23 minutes or until set. Let cool in pan on a wire rack for 10 minutes.

Tips

If not serving the same day, these are better without the sour cream topping.

Cheesecakes will keep in an airtight container in the refrigerator for up to 5 days or can be frozen for up to 3 months. Thaw in refrigerator overnight and bring to room temperature before serving.

5. *Topping (optional):* In a small bowl, stir together sour cream, sugar and vanilla. Spoon over warm cheesecakes and bake for 5 minutes longer.

6. Let cool completely in pan on a wire rack before removing from pan.

Variations

Substitute an equal amount of coffee liqueur or Irish cream liqueur for the almond liqueur.

QUICK TIP

Dress these up with chocolate curls or shavings.

Mini Pies and Tarts

PASTRY

TWO-CRUST PIES

ONE-CRUST PIES AND TARTS

Basic Pastry

A tender, flaky crust is not difficult to achieve once you master the technique.

MAKES ONE OR TWO 6-INCH (15 CM) PIE CRUSTS

- Preparation: 15 minutes
- Chilling: 30 minutes

Tips

Although shortening is shelf stable, it is better to chill it before using in pastry.

Use a pastry blender to cut in the shortening. Be careful not to blend the mixture too finely. Flaky pastry is the result of lumps of fat melting during baking.

SINGLE PIE CRUST

¾ cup	all-purpose flour	175 mL
¼ tsp	salt	1 mL
6 tbsp	cold shortening (see Tips, left)	90 mL
1½ to 2 tbsp	ice water	22 to 30 mL

DOUBLE PIE CRUST

1½ cups	all-purpose flour	375 mL
½ tsp	salt	2 mL
⅔ cup	cold shortening	150 mL
4 to 5 tbsp	ice water	60 to 75 mL

1. In a medium bowl, using a fork, stir together flour and salt. Using a pastry blender or two knives, cut in shortening until mixture resembles large peas. Don't overblend; the mixture should be crumbly.

2. Sprinkle with ice water, 1 tbsp (15 mL) at a time, mixing lightly with a fork after each addition. Add just enough water to hold dough together. Press into a ball. Refrigerate for 15 to 30 minutes (for easy rolling).

3. Follow instructions for making either a single or double pie crust. *For a single crust:* Flatten dough into a round disk. Transfer to a floured surface or pastry cloth. *For a double crust:* Divide dough into 2 equal portions. Flatten dough into round disks. Transfer 1 disk to a floured surface or pastry cloth; keep remaining disk covered until ready to use.

4. Roll out dough to a uniform thickness (about ⅛ inch/3 mm), starting in the center and rolling, spoke-fashion, toward the edge with light, even strokes. If dough sticks, lightly dust the bottom of the pastry or the board with flour. Roll pastry loosely around the rolling pin, then unroll over a pie plate, easing dough into plate without stretching. Trim dough, leaving ½ inch (1 cm) overhang.

Tips

A pastry cloth and rolling pin cover are worthwhile investments. The dough doesn't stick and you don't have to worry about it getting tough because you've added too much flour to keep it from sticking. You can find them in specialty stores that carry baking equipment.

For best results, make pastry as needed.

5. *For a single crust:* Fold overhang under and flute the edge. *For a double crust:* Fill bottom crust, then roll out remaining dough and unroll over filling. Fold edge of top crust under overhang of bottom crust; seal and flute edge. Cut slits in center of top crust to allow steam to escape.

Variations

Replace half of the shortening with butter. The butter will add a nice flavor and give you a slightly crisper crust.

For a pastry that is more forgiving of overhandling, add cake and pastry flour in Step 1:
For single crust, add 2 tbsp (30 mL).
For double crust, add 3 tbsp (45 mL).

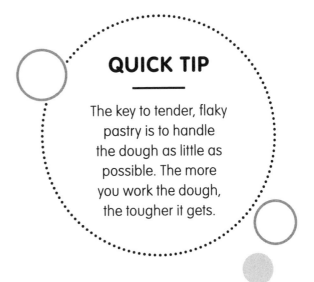

QUICK TIP

The key to tender, flaky pastry is to handle the dough as little as possible. The more you work the dough, the tougher it gets.

All-Butter Pastry

While the result is not as flaky as a shortening-based pastry, butter adds color and flavor to a tender, crisp pastry.

MAKES TWO 6-INCH (15 CM) PIE CRUSTS

- Preparation: 15 minutes
- Chilling: 30 minutes

Tips

Using ice water keeps the dough cool while mixing.

You can add the water to the food processor, but the pastry will not be as tender.

Halve the recipe to make a 6-inch (15 cm) single crust.

Butter pastry is a nice match for fruit pies.

For best results, make pastry as needed.

• Food processor

1½ cups	all-purpose flour	375 mL
1½ tsp	granulated sugar	7 mL
¼ tsp	salt	1 mL
½ cup	cold unsalted butter, cubed	125 mL
6 tbsp	ice water	90 mL
1 tsp	vinegar	5 mL

1. In food processor fitted with the metal blade, combine flour, sugar and salt; pulse to combine. Scatter butter over flour mixture and pulse until butter is the size of peas. Transfer mixture to a medium bowl.
2. In a small bowl, combine ice water and vinegar. Add half the liquid to flour mixture, stirring with a fork to combine. Add remaining liquid, 1 tbsp (15 mL) at a time, just until dough begins to hold together. Shape dough into a ball. Wrap in plastic wrap and flatten into a disk. Refrigerate for about 30 minutes before using in your favorite recipe.

Mini Peach Pies

◆

One of the best ways to enjoy fresh peaches when they are in season is in a wedge of pie served warm with vanilla ice cream.

MAKES TWO 4-INCH (10 CM) PIES (2 TO 4 SERVINGS)

- Preparation: 30 minutes
- Baking: 40 minutes
- Freezing: excellent

Tips

If peaches are tart, add 1 tbsp (15 mL) sugar in Step 1.

To ease rolling, use a pastry cloth and cover or roll dough between two sheets of plastic wrap.

Baking on the lower shelf to start seals the crust so the bottom won't be soggy.

For a shiny golden crust, brush the top pastry with an egg wash, made by beating together 1 egg and 1 tbsp (15 mL) water.

For a nice finish, sprinkle granulated sugar over top of crust before baking.

Cooled pies will keep in an airtight container in the refrigerator for up to 3 days or can be frozen for up to 3 months. Thaw overnight in refrigerator and bring to room temperature before serving.

- **Preheat oven to 425°F (220°C)**
- **Two 4-inch (10 cm) mini pie pans**

1½ cups	sliced peeled, pitted peaches	375 mL
3 tbsp	granulated sugar	45 mL
1 tbsp	cornstarch	15 mL
½ tsp	ground cinnamon	2 mL
1½ tsp	freshly squeezed lemon juice	7 mL
1	batch Double Pie Crust (page 200) or All-Butter Pastry (page 202)	1

1. In a medium bowl, combine peaches, sugar, cornstarch, cinnamon and lemon juice. Stir well. Set aside.
2. Divide dough into two equal portions. On a lightly floured surface, roll out one portion to a thickness of ⅛ inch (3 mm); keep other portion covered until ready to use. Cut out two 6½-inch (16.5 cm) circles and transfer to pie pans, easing pastry into pans without stretching. Trim crust, leaving a ¾-inch (2 cm) overhang. Spoon filling into crust.
3. Repeat with remaining portion of dough and place crusts over filling. Seal and flute or crimp edges. Cut a few small holes in the top to let steam escape.
4. Bake in preheated oven on lower rack for 10 minutes, then reduce temperature to 350°F (180°C). Bake for 25 to 30 minutes longer or until crust is golden and peaches are tender. Let cool on a wire rack.

Variations

Substitute an equal amount of sliced peeled, cored apples for the peaches.

Try making this with a combination of half peaches and half pears.

Strawberry Rhubarb Pie

◆

This pie boasts a pleasing combination of sweet and tart that tastes even better with vanilla ice cream.

MAKES ONE 6-INCH (15 CM) PIE (4 SERVINGS)

- Preparation: 30 minutes
- Baking: 40 minutes
- Freezing: excellent

Tips

If the berries and rhubarb are unusually sweet or tart, adjust the sugar accordingly to suit your tastes.

Sealing the top and bottom crusts with water before fluting ensures a good seal on the pastry edge, which helps keep the filling from leaking out.

Cooled pie will keep in an airtight container in the refrigerator for up to 3 days or can be frozen for up to 3 months. Thaw overnight in refrigerator and bring to room temperature before serving.

- Preheat oven to 425°F (220°C)
- 6-inch (15 cm) pie plate

½ cup	granulated sugar	125 mL
¼ cup	all-purpose flour	60 mL
1½ cups	chopped rhubarb (see Tips, left)	375 mL
1 cup	halved or sliced strawberries	250 mL
1	recipe Double Pie Crust (page 200) or All-Butter Pastry (page 202)	1
1 tbsp	butter	15 mL
1	egg yolk	1
2 tsp	water	10 mL
1 tbsp	coarse white sugar	15 mL

1. In a medium bowl, combine granulated sugar and flour. Add rhubarb and strawberries. Toss to coat thoroughly. Set aside.
2. Divide dough into two equal portions. On a lightly floured work surface, roll out one portion into a ⅛-inch (3 mm) thick circle; keep other portion covered until ready to use. Carefully transfer to pie plate, easing pastry into pan without stretching. Trim crust, leaving a ¾-inch (2 cm) overhang. Spoon filling into crust. Dot with butter.
3. Roll out remaining portion of dough into a ⅛-inch (3 mm) thick circle. Moisten rim of bottom with water and place top crust over filling. Trim crust, leaving a ¾-inch (2 cm) overhang. Fold overhang under bottom crust. Seal and flute edge.
4. In a small bowl, whisk together egg yolk and water. Brush over top crust. Sprinkle with coarse sugar. Cut small slits in top crust to let steam escape.
5. Bake on lower rack of preheated oven for 10 minutes, then reduce temperature to 350°F (180°C). Bake for 25 to 30 minutes longer or until crust is golden and fruit is bubbly and tender. Let cool on a wire rack.

Variation

Vary the proportions of strawberries to rhubarb to suit your taste, keeping the total amount to 2½ cups (625 mL).

Bumbleberry Pie

This mixture of apples and berries nestled in flaky pastry is heaven.

MAKES ONE 6-INCH (15 CM) PIE (4 SERVINGS)

- Preparation: 30 minutes
- Baking: 45 minutes
- Freezing: excellent

Tips

Letting the mixed filling stand while you prepare the crust gives the flour and sugar a chance to meld with the fruit, which helps the mixture thicken during baking. Stir just before filling the pastry shell.

The egg wash glaze and sugar make for an attractive presentation, but you can omit them and still have great flavor.

Cooled pie will keep in an airtight container in the refrigerator for up to 3 days or can be frozen for up to 3 months. Thaw in refrigerator overnight and bring to room temperature before serving.

Substitute an equal amount of sliced peeled, pitted peaches for the apples.

Use only one type of berry rather than two. Choose your favorite.

- **Preheat oven to 425°F (220°C)**
- **6-inch (15 cm) pie plate**

$1/3$ cup	granulated sugar	75 mL
3 tbsp	all-purpose flour	45 mL
2 cups	sliced peeled, cored apples	500 mL
$1/2$ cup	fresh raspberries	125 mL
$1/2$ cup	fresh blueberries	125 mL
1 tsp	freshly squeezed lemon juice	5 mL
1 tbsp	butter	15 mL
1	batch Double Pie Crust (page 200) or All-Butter Pastry (page 202)	1
1	egg yolk	1
2 tsp	water	10 mL
1 tbsp	coarse white sugar	15 mL

1. In a medium bowl, combine granulated sugar and flour. Add apples, raspberries, blueberries and lemon juice. Toss gently until fruit is thoroughly coated. Set aside.

2. Divide dough into two equal portions. On a lightly floured work surface, roll out one portion into a $1/8$-inch (3 mm) thick circle; keep other portion covered until ready to use. Carefully transfer to pie plate, easing pastry into pan without stretching. Trim crust, leaving a $3/4$-inch (2 cm) overhang. Spoon filling into crust. Dot with butter.

3. Roll out remaining portion of dough into a $1/8$-inch (3 mm) thick circle. Moisten rim of bottom crust with water and place top crust over filling. Trim crust, leaving a $3/4$-inch (2 cm) overhang. Fold overhang under bottom crust. Seal and flute edge.

4. In a small bowl, whisk together egg yolk and water. Brush over top crust. Sprinkle with coarse sugar. Cut small slits in top crust to let steam escape.

5. Bake on lower rack of preheated oven for 10 minutes, then reduce temperature to 350°F (180°C). Bake for 30 to 35 minutes longer or until crust is golden and fruit is tender and bubbly. Let cool on a wire rack.

Free-Form Berry Tarts

◆

This is summer at its best. The open single crust makes preparation easy.

MAKES 2 TARTS (2 SERVINGS EACH)

- Preparation: 35 minutes
- Baking: 25 minutes
- Standing: 45 minutes
- Freezing: not recommended

Tips

An all-shortening pastry works best for this tart, as it holds in the fruit juices.

Be careful to leave enough pastry around the fruit filling that you can pleat it over the edges.

- **Preheat oven to 400°F (200°C)**
- **Baking sheet, lined with parchment paper**

TARTS

3 tbsp	granulated sugar	45 mL
1½ tbsp	cornstarch	22 mL
½ cup	sliced fresh strawberries	125 mL
½ cup	fresh raspberries	125 mL
½ cup	fresh blueberries	125 mL
1 tsp	freshly grated lemon zest	5 mL
1	batch Double Pie Crust (page 200)	1
1	egg yolk	1
2 tsp	water	10 mL
1 tbsp	coarse white sugar	15 mL

BERRY TOPPING

¼ cup	sliced fresh strawberries	60 mL
¼ cup	fresh raspberries	60 mL
¼ cup	fresh blueberries	60 mL
1 tbsp	granulated sugar	15 mL
1 tbsp	freshly squeezed lemon juice	15 mL

1. *Tarts:* In a medium bowl, combine sugar and cornstarch. Add strawberries, raspberries, blueberries and lemon zest. Toss gently until well coated. Set aside.
2. Divide dough into two equal portions. On a lightly floured surface, roll each portion into an 8-inch (20 cm) circle. Place side by side on prepared baking sheet.
3. Spoon equal amounts of berry mixture into center of each pastry round, leaving a 1½-inch (4 cm) border of pastry around edge of fruit. Fold up pastry around filling, pleating every 1 to 2 inches (2.5 to 5 cm), as needed. Pinch pleated dough to secure.

Tip

Cooled tarts will keep in an airtight container in the refrigerator for up to 3 days. Add the berry topping just before serving.

4. In a small bowl, whisk together egg yolk and water. Brush over pastry. Sprinkle with coarse sugar.

5. Bake on lower rack of preheated oven for 20 to 25 minutes or until pastry is golden. Let cool on pan on a wire rack for 45 minutes.

6. *Berry Topping:* Meanwhile, in a medium bowl, toss together strawberries, raspberries, blueberries, sugar and lemon juice, until berries are well coated. Set aside for 45 minutes.

7. *Assembly:* Spoon berry mixture evenly over cooled tart and serve.

Variations

Substitute an equal amount of blackberries for the blueberries.

Vary the fruit to suit your own personal taste, keeping the total amount to $1\frac{1}{2}$ cups (375 mL).

Apple Puff Squares

Here crunchy cinnamon almonds and apples top a tender, flaky puff pastry. These can bake while you enjoy dinner.

MAKES 4 SQUARES

- Preparation: 15 minutes
- Baking: 12 minutes
- Cooling: 15 minutes
- Freezing: not recommended

Tips

Look for small apples so the slices will fit nicely on the pastry squares.

Some packages of puff pastry come pre-rolled into 10-inch (25 cm) squares. This makes preparation even easier.

You can assemble these up to 3 hours ahead. Cover and refrigerate before baking.

Cooled squares will keep in an airtight container in the refrigerator for up to 3 days.

- **Preheat oven to 425°F (220°C)**
- **Baking sheet, lined with parchment paper**

½	package (1 lb/450 g) frozen butter puff pastry, thawed as directed	½
1	egg	1
1 tbsp	water	15 mL
⅓ cup	chopped almonds	75 mL
¼ cup	granulated sugar, divided	60 mL
½ tsp	ground cinnamon	2 mL
2	small apples, peeled, cored and thinly sliced (see Tips, left)	2
1 tbsp	freshly squeezed lemon juice	15 mL
2 tbsp	strained apricot jam	30 mL

1. On a lightly floured surface, roll out pastry into a 10-inch (25 cm) square. Cut into 4 squares. Place on prepared baking sheet.
2. In a small bowl, whisk together egg and water. Brush over pastry.
3. In another small bowl, combine almonds, 3 tbsp (45 mL) sugar and cinnamon. Sprinkle evenly over pastry squares.
4. Arrange about 12 apple slices in an overlapping circle on each square. Brush apples with lemon juice. Sprinkle with remaining 1 tbsp (15 mL) sugar.
5. Bake in preheated oven for 10 to 12 minutes or until pastry is puffed and golden. Let cool on baking sheet on a wire rack for about 15 minutes, then brush jam over apples.

Variations

Substitute an equal amount of sliced peaches, pears, nectarines or plums for the apples.

Open Apple Plum Tart

Two fall fruits combine in this easy-to-make open pie.

MAKES ONE 6-INCH (15 CM) PIE (4 SERVINGS)

- Preparation: 20 minutes
- Baking: 40 minutes
- Freezing: excellent

Tips

Use firm apples such as Granny Smith, Golden Delicious, Gala or Courtland.

Red, black and prune plums all work well. The biggest difference will be in the color.

Dotting the fruit filling with butter makes a big difference in flavor.

For an attractive finish, brush pastry edges with milk or an egg wash and sprinkle with coarse white sugar before baking.

Cooled pie will keep in an airtight container in the refrigerator for up to 3 days or can be frozen for up to 3 months. Thaw in refrigerator overnight and bring to room temperature before serving.

- **Preheat oven to 450°F (230°C)**
- **6-inch (15 cm) pie plate**

⅓ cup	granulated sugar	75 mL
3 tbsp	all-purpose flour	45 mL
½ tsp	ground cinnamon	2 mL
¼ tsp	ground nutmeg	1 mL
1¾ cups	sliced peeled, cored apples (see Tips, left)	425 mL
1¼ cups	sliced pitted plums (see Tips, left)	300 mL
1½ tsp	freshly squeezed lemon juice	7 mL
1 tbsp	butter	15 mL
1	batch Single Pie Crust (page 200)	1

1. In a small bowl, combine sugar, flour, cinnamon and nutmeg. Add apples and plums and toss until fruit is well coated. Set aside.
2. On a lightly floured work surface, roll out pastry into a 9-inch (23 cm) circle. Transfer to pie plate, easing pastry into pan without stretching. Trim crust, leaving a ¾-inch (2 cm) overhang. Spoon prepared fruit into crust. Dot with butter. Fold pastry edges over fruit, pleating about every 2 inches (5 cm). Pinch pleated dough to secure.
3. Bake on lower rack of preheated oven for 10 minutes, then reduce temperature to 350°F (180°C). Bake for 25 to 30 minutes longer or until pastry is golden and apples are tender.

Variations

Substitute an equal amount of sliced peeled, pitted peaches or nectarines for the apples.

Fresh Fruit Flan

◆

You can change up this flan, using whatever fruit is in season. Use a variety of fruits for color and texture or keep it simple with one or two. Store in the refrigerator but serve at room temperature for maximum flavor.

MAKES ONE 6-INCH (15 CM) FLAN (4 SERVINGS)

- Preparation: 25 minutes
- Chilling: 15 minutes
- Baking: 12 minutes
- Freezing: not recommended

Tips

The crust can be prepared a few days ahead of the filling.

When choosing your fruit topping, pick a variety of shapes and colors for an attractive presentation.

Try strawberries, raspberries, blueberries, kiwifruit, grapes, apricots, mandarins, pineapple and/or peaches. You will need to slice or dice larger fruits.

- **Preheat oven to 425°F (220°C)**
- **6-inch (15 cm) fluted tart pan with removable bottom**

CRUST

⅔ cup	all-purpose flour	150 mL
1 tbsp	confectioners' (icing) sugar, sifted	15 mL
⅓ cup	butter, softened	75 mL

FILLING

4 oz	cream cheese, softened	125 g
¼ cup	confectioners' (icing) sugar, sifted	60 mL
½ tsp	pure vanilla extract	2 mL
¼ cup	heavy or whipping (35%) cream	60 mL
1½ cups	fruit	375 mL

GLAZE (OPTIONAL)

¼ cup	strained apricot jam	60 mL
1½ tsp	freshly squeezed lemon juice	7 mL

1. *Crust:* In a small bowl, whisk together flour and confectioners' sugar. In another bowl, using a wooden spoon, cream butter. Gradually add flour mixture, stirring until combined. With floured hands, work dough into a smooth ball. Press evenly into bottom and up sides of pan. Using the tines of a fork, prick crust all over. Refrigerate for 15 minutes.

2. Bake crust on lower rack of preheated oven for 8 to 12 minutes or until golden. Let cool completely in pan on a wire rack.

Tips

If using canned or juicy fruits, drain well on paper towels before using.

Cooled flan will keep in an airtight container in the refrigerator for up to 3 days.

3. *Filling:* In a medium bowl, using a wooden spoon, beat together cream cheese, confectioners' sugar and vanilla, until smooth. Whip cream until stiff peaks form; fold into cheese mixture.

4. *Assembly:* Spread filling evenly in cooled crust. Arrange fruit in a pleasing pattern overtop.

5. *Glaze (optional):* In a small bowl, stir together jam and lemon juice. Brush over fruit.

Variation

Using seasonal berries and fruits is ideal, but canned fruit also works well.

Key Lime Pie

There are many different recipes for Key lime pie. This one is for a more traditional version of the popular pie.

MAKES ONE 6-INCH (15 CM) PIE (4 SERVINGS)

- Preparation: 15 minutes
- Baking: 35 minutes
- Freezing: not recommended

Tips

Half a 10 oz (300 mL) can of sweetened condensed milk equals $2/3$ cup (150 mL).

Serve with whipped cream, or prepare a meringue using the 2 egg whites (see Lemon Meringue Pie, page 218).

Cooled pie will keep in an airtight container in the refrigerator for up to 5 days.

- **Preheat oven to 325°F (160°C)**
- **6-inch (15 cm) pie plate**

CRUST

⅔ cup	graham wafer crumbs	150 mL
2½ tbsp	butter, melted	37 mL

FILLING

2	egg yolks	2
⅔ cup	sweetened condensed milk (see Tips, left)	150 mL
¼ cup	fresh lime juice	60 mL
1 tbsp	water	15 mL
	Few drops green food coloring, optional	

1. *Crust:* In a medium bowl, combine graham wafer crumbs and melted butter. Stir well. Press mixture evenly into bottom and up sides of pie plate.
2. Bake in preheated oven for 12 to 15 minutes or until set. Let cool on a wire rack.
3. *Filling:* In a medium bowl, whisk together egg yolks, condensed milk, lime juice, water and food coloring, if desired. Mix well. (Mixture will thicken.) Spoon into prepared crust.
4. Bake for 15 to 20 minutes longer or just until filling is set. Let cool completely in pan on wire rack.

> ## Variations
>
> If desired, you can use a baked pie shell in place of the graham wafer crust.
>
> Add 2 tbsp (30 mL) flaked coconut to the crust.

Creamy Peach Crumble Pie

◆

You'll find this pie, with its crunchy oat crumble topping paired with a creamy fresh peach filling, absolutely addictive.

MAKES ONE 6-INCH (15 CM) PIE (4 SERVINGS)

- Preparation: 20 minutes
- Baking: 40 minutes
- Freezing: not recommended

Tips

Substitute an equal quantity of Greek yogurt for the sour cream.

To peel peaches, immerse in a bowl of boiling water for about 1 minute, then transfer to a bowl of ice water. This will loosen the skin and make it easier to peel off.

Always bake fruit pies on a piece of aluminum foil to catch any juices that might leak.

Cooled pie will keep in an airtight container in the refrigerator for up to 3 days.

- **Preheat oven to 350°F (180°C)**
- **6-inch (15 cm) pie plate**

TOPPING

1/3 cup	all-purpose flour	75 mL
1/4 cup	packed brown sugar	60 mL
2 tbsp	large-flake (old-fashioned) rolled oats	30 mL
1/2 tsp	ground cinnamon	2 mL
2 tbsp	butter, softened	30 mL

FILLING

6 tbsp	sour cream (see Tips, left)	90 mL
1/4 cup	granulated sugar	60 mL
2 tbsp	all-purpose flour	30 mL
1 1/2 cups	sliced peeled, pitted peaches (see Tips, left)	375 mL
1	batch Single Pie Crust (page 200)	1

1. *Topping:* In a medium bowl, using a fork, mix together flour, brown sugar, oats, cinnamon and butter, until mixture resembles coarse crumbs. Set aside.
2. *Filling:* In a medium bowl, whisk together sour cream, sugar and flour. Stir in peaches.
3. On a lightly floured work surface, roll dough into a 1/8-inch (3 mm) thick circle. Carefully transfer to pie plate, easing pastry into pan without stretching. Trim crust, leaving a 3/4-inch (2 cm) overhang. Flute edge. Spread prepared filling evenly in pie shell. Sprinkle topping evenly over filling.
4. Bake on lower rack of preheated oven for 35 to 40 minutes or until pastry is golden and fruit is tender. Let cool completely on a wire rack.

Variations

Add 2 tbsp (30 mL) chopped nuts to the topping.

Replace half of the peaches with pears or apples.

Use quick-cooking rolled oats for a less "oaty" taste and appearance.

Dutch Apple Pie

My sister is famous for this pie. The recipe was given to her by a Mennonite friend.

MAKES ONE 6-INCH (15 CM) PIE (4 SERVINGS)

- Preparation: 20 minutes
- Baking: 45 minutes
- Freezing: excellent

Tips

Smaller apples are better for small pie plates. Fit them snugly into the shell. I usually start by arranging slices in a circle around the edge, then fill in the center. Cut the center piece to fit, if necessary.

Cooled pie will keep in an airtight container in the refrigerator for up to 3 days or can be frozen for up to 3 months. Thaw in refrigerator overnight and bring to room temperature before serving.

- **Preheat oven to 425°F (220°C)**
- **6-inch (15 cm) pie plate**

1	recipe Single Pie Crust (page 200)	1
2	small apples, peeled, cored and quartered (see Tips, left)	2
6 tbsp	granulated sugar	90 mL
3 tbsp	all-purpose flour	45 mL
1 tbsp	butter, softened	15 mL
½ tsp	ground cinnamon	2 mL
¼ cup	heavy or whipping (35%) cream	60 mL

1. On a lightly floured work surface, roll dough into a ⅛-inch (3 mm) thick circle. Carefully transfer to pie plate, easing pastry into pan without stretching. Trim crust, leaving a ¾-inch (2 cm) overhang.

2. In a small bowl, using a fork, stir together sugar, flour, butter and cinnamon, until mixture resembles coarse crumbs. Sprinkle half of the mixture evenly into pastry shell. Arrange apple quarters, cut side down and packed tightly together, on top. Sprinkle with remaining flour mixture. Pour cream evenly over filling.

3. Bake in preheated oven for 10 minutes, then reduce oven temperature to 350°F (180°C). Bake for 30 to 35 minutes longer or until pastry is golden and apples are tender. Let cool slightly on a wire rack. Serve warm or cool.

Variation

Add 2 tbsp (30 mL) finely chopped almonds to the topping.

Mini Pecan Pies

◆

Pecan has always been one of my favorite pies. Now I can enjoy it more often in mini form. Serve warm with ice cream or whipped cream.

MAKES 6 MINI PIES

- Preparation: 15 minutes
- Baking: 20 minutes
- Freezing: excellent

Tips

Toast nuts for optimum flavor. Place on a baking sheet in a preheated 350°F (180°C) oven for about 5 minutes. Let cool completely before using.

Do not fill the muffin cups more than three-quarters full, or they may boil over.

Let the pies cool completely before trying to remove them from the pan. If they are still warm they will be too fragile and could break.

Cooled pies will keep in an airtight container in the refrigerator for up to 10 days or can be frozen for up to 3 months. Thaw in refrigerator overnight and bring to room temperature before serving.

- Preheat oven to 425°F (220°C)
- 6-cup jumbo muffin pan, ungreased
- 4- to 5-inch (10 to 12.5 cm) round pastry cutter

1	batch Double Pie Crust (page 200)	1
½ cup	pecan halves (see Tips, left)	125 mL
1	egg	1
3 tbsp	granulated sugar	45 mL
Pinch	salt	Pinch
⅓ cup	corn syrup	75 mL
2 tbsp	butter, softened	30 mL

1. On a lightly floured work surface, roll out dough until $\frac{1}{8}$ inch (3 mm) thick. Using pastry cutter, cut into 6 rounds. Gently press rounds into bottoms and up sides of muffin cups.
2. Scatter pecans into pastry-lined cups, dividing evenly.
3. In a medium bowl, whisk together egg, sugar, salt, corn syrup and butter. Pour evenly over pecans, filling each cup about three-quarters full (see Tips, left).
4. Bake on lower rack of preheated oven for 5 minutes, then reduce oven temperature to 350°F (180°C). Bake for 15 minutes longer or just until set. Let cool completely in pan on a wire rack, then remove from pan (see Tips, left).

Variations

Substitute an equal amount of maple syrup for the corn syrup, or use half maple and half corn syrup.

Maple Walnut Tarts: Substitute an equal amount of walnuts for the pecans and maple syrup for the corn syrup.

Lemon Almond Custard Tarts

◆

If you like lemon you'll love these refreshingly light and lemony tarts.

MAKES THREE 4-INCH (10 CM) TARTS OR ONE 6-INCH (15 CM) TART (SEE VARIATION)

- Preparation: 20 minutes
- Chilling: 15 minutes
- Baking: 32 minutes
- Freezing: not recommended

Tips

Be sure to zest lemons before juicing. Warm them in the microwave for about 10 seconds to yield maximum juice.

If you prefer an exceptionally tart lemon flavor, increase the quantity of lemon juice to ⅓ cup (75 mL).

Just before serving, sprinkle with confectioners' sugar.

A garnish of fresh berries is attractive and delicious.

Cooled tarts will keep in an airtight container in the refrigerator for up to 5 days.

- **Preheat oven to 375°C (190°F)**
- **Three 4-inch (10 cm) tart pans with removable bottoms**

CRUST

½ cup	all-purpose flour	125 mL
1 tbsp	confectioners' (icing) sugar, sifted	15 mL
¼ cup	butter, softened	60 mL

FILLING

1	egg	1
3 tbsp	granulated sugar	45 mL
1 tsp	freshly grated lemon zest	5 mL
¼ cup	freshly squeezed lemon juice	60 mL
3 tbsp	ground almonds	45 mL
1 tbsp	butter, melted and cooled	15 mL

1. *Crust:* In a small bowl, whisk together flour and confectioners' sugar. In another bowl, using a wooden spoon, cream butter. Gradually add flour mixture and stir until combined. With floured hands, work dough into a smooth ball. Divide into 3 equal portions. Press each portion into bottoms and up sides of tart pans. Using the tines of a fork, prick pastry all over. Refrigerate for 15 minutes.

2. Bake on lower rack of preheated oven for 12 to 16 minutes or until light golden. Let cool on a wire rack.

3. *Filling:* Meanwhile, in a medium bowl, whisk together egg and sugar. Add lemon zest, lemon juice, almonds and melted butter, whisking until smooth. Divide mixture evenly among cooled shells.

4. Bake in preheated oven for 12 to 16 minutes or just until filling is set. Let cool completely on wire rack.

Variation

Prepare tart in a 6-inch (15 cm) tart pan. Bake for 18 to 22 minutes.

Marvelous Butter Tarts

◆

This recipe underwent several versions to achieve what I think is an amazing butter tart. (My neighbors didn't mind the large number of taste tests.) Serve these warm with ice cream for dessert.

MAKES 6 TARTS

- Preparation: 15 minutes
- Baking: 14 minutes
- Freezing: excellent

Tips

If you don't have a 4-inch (10 cm) pastry cutter, use the lid from a jar.

If you prefer a runny filling, bake for only 10 minutes.

Let tarts cool completely in the pan for easy removal. If they are still warm, the pastry can easily break (although they will still taste great eaten with a spoon).

Cooled tarts will keep in an airtight container at room temperature for up to 7 days or can be frozen for up to 3 months. Thaw in refrigerator overnight and bring to room temperature before serving.

- **Preheat oven to 425°F (220°C)**
- **6-cup muffin pan**
- **4-inch (10 cm) round pastry cutter**

1	batch Double Pie Crust (page 200)	1
1/4 cup	packed brown sugar	60 mL
1/4 cup	corn syrup	60 mL
2 tbsp	butter, melted	30 mL
1	egg	1
1/2 tsp	pure vanilla extract	2 mL
Pinch	salt	Pinch
1/3 cup	raisins	75 mL

1. Divide pastry into two equal portions. On a lightly floured work surface, roll out one portion to 1/8 inch (3 mm) thick; keep other portion covered until ready to use. Cut out six 4-inch (10 cm) circles (you may have a little pastry left over). Carefully press circles into bottoms and up sides of muffin cups.
2. In a medium bowl, whisk together brown sugar, corn syrup, melted butter, egg, vanilla and salt. Set aside.
3. Divide raisins evenly among pastry shells. Fill shells two-thirds full with syrup mixture.
4. Bake on lower rack of preheated oven for 10 to 14 minutes or just until filling is set (be careful not to overbake). Let cool completely in pan on a wire rack, then remove from pans (see Tips, left).

Variations

Substitute an equal amount of chopped pecans or dried cranberries for the raisins.

Omit the raisins, if desired, for a plain butter tart.

Lemon Meringue Pie

◆

In our family, this pie was preferred to a birthday cake. Once you've tried it, a store-bought pie just won't do.

MAKES ONE 6-INCH (15 CM) PIE (4 SERVINGS)

- Preparation: 25 minutes
- Cooking: 5 minutes
- Cooling: 15 minutes
- Baking: 40 minutes
- Freezing: not recommended

Tips

Bring egg whites to room temperature before using, to obtain the greatest volume when beating to stiff peaks.

Be sure the mixing bowl is completely clean (free of grease) or the egg whites will not reach stiff peaks when beaten.

- **Preheat oven to 425°F (220°C)**
- **6-inch (15 cm) pie plate**

1	batch Single Pie Crust (page 200)	1
FILLING		
½ cup	granulated sugar	125 mL
2 tbsp	cornstarch	30 mL
¼ tsp	salt	1 mL
⅔ cup	cold water	150 mL
2	egg yolks	2
1 tbsp	butter	15 mL
1 tsp	freshly grated lemon zest	5 mL
¼ cup	freshly squeezed lemon juice	60 mL
MERINGUE		
2	egg whites (see Tips, left)	2
¼ tsp	cream of tartar	1 mL
¼ tsp	pure vanilla extract	1 mL
2 tbsp	granulated sugar	30 mL

1. On a lightly floured work surface, roll out pastry into a 9-inch (23 cm) circle. Carefully transfer to pie plate, easing pastry into pan without stretching. Trim crust, leaving a ¾-inch (2 cm) overhang. Fold edge under and flute.
2. Cut a 10-inch (25 cm) circle of parchment paper. Place over pastry shell. Fill with pie weights or dried beans.
3. Bake on lower rack of preheated oven for 10 minutes. Let cool on a wire rack for 5 minutes, then remove weights. Reduce oven temperature to 350°F (180°C) and bake for 12 to 15 minutes or until golden. Set aside.

To help prevent meringue from shrinking when baked, spread it over the hot filling and over the top edge of the pastry to seal.

Any meringue-topped pie is best eaten the same day it is made.

4. *Filling:* In a small saucepan over medium heat, whisk together sugar, cornstarch and salt. Gradually whisk in water until smooth. Bring to a boil, stirring constantly. Boil for 1 minute. Remove from heat.

5. In a small bowl, whisk together egg yolks. Add about $\frac{1}{4}$ cup (60 mL) hot filling, whisking well. Gradually add yolk mixture to hot filling. Reduce heat to medium-low and cook, stirring constantly, until mixture returns to a boil; boil for 1 minute. Remove from heat. Add butter, lemon zest and lemon juice, stirring until smooth. Let cool for 15 minutes, then pour into baked shell.

6. *Meringue:* In a small bowl, using an electric mixer at high speed, beat egg whites, cream of tartar and vanilla until soft peaks form. Gradually add sugar, 1 tbsp (15 mL) at a time, beating until stiff peaks form. Spoon meringue over warm filling. Spread to edges of pastry to prevent shrinkage.

7. Bake in preheated oven for 12 to 15 minutes or until meringue is golden. Let cool on a wire rack for at least 3 hours, until filling is set.

Variations

Spread a thin layer of melted chocolate or raspberry jam over the baked crust before adding the filling.

Cream Puffs

Homemade cream puffs or éclairs filled with real whipped cream are divine. They are next to impossible to buy because of their short shelf life.

MAKES 3 CREAM PUFFS

- Preparation: 15 minutes
- Baking: 37 minutes
- Freezing: not recommended

Tips

The only difference between a cream puff and an éclair is the shape.

To ease mixing, bring the egg to room temperature before using.

- **Preheat oven to 400°F (200°C)**
- **Baking sheet, greased**

PASTRY

¼ cup	water	60 mL
2 tbsp	butter	30 mL
¼ cup	all-purpose flour	60 mL
Pinch	salt	Pinch
1	egg (see Tips, left)	1

FILLING

½ cup	heavy or whipping (35%) cream	125 mL
1 tbsp	confectioners' (icing) sugar, sifted	15 mL

TOPPING

½ cup	chocolate, dulce de leche or fruit sauce, warm or cool	125 mL

1. *Pastry:* In a small saucepan over medium heat, bring water and butter to a full boil. Add flour and salt all at once. Reduce heat to low. Using a wooden spoon, stir vigorously for 1 minute or until mixture pulls away from the sides of the pan and forms a smooth ball. Remove from heat and let cool for 5 minutes.
2. Add egg, beating vigorously with wooden spoon or electric mixer at high speed, until smooth and glossy. Drop dough in 3 mounds, each about ¼ cup (60 mL), onto prepared baking sheet, spacing about 2 inches (5 cm) apart.
3. Bake in preheated oven for 30 to 35 minutes or until puffed and golden. Using a sharp knife, cut a small slit in the side of each puff to let steam escape. Bake for 2 minutes longer. Transfer puffs to a wire rack to cool completely.

Tips

Fill puffs just before serving, as the pastry will get soggy fairly quickly. Unfilled puffs will keep in an airtight container at room temperature for up to 3 days.

For bite-size puffs, drop by tablespoonfuls (15 mL) onto baking sheet. Bake for about 15 minutes, until puffed and golden.

4. *Filling:* In a small bowl, using an electric mixer at high speed, beat cream and confectioners' sugar until stiff, moist peaks form. Cut cooled puffs in half lengthwise. Fill with whipped cream.
5. Top with warm or cool sauce. Serve immediately.

Variations

To make éclairs, pipe the dough into 4-inch (10 cm) strips, using a pastry bag fitted with a large round tip.

Fill the puffs with ice cream instead of whipped cream.

Spoonable Desserts

COBBLERS, CRISPS AND CRUMBLES

PUDDINGS

Apple Crisp

Apple crisp is a comfort-food classic. Serve with a scoop of vanilla ice cream or a dollop of whipped cream. Greek yogurt also makes a great topping.

MAKES 3 TO 4 SERVINGS

- Preparation: 15 minutes
- Baking: 35 minutes
- Freezing: not recommended

Tips

If the apples are very tart, increase the amount of sugar in the filling to taste.

Almost any kind of apple will work in apple crisp. The more flavorful the apple, the more flavorful your crisp.

Cooled crisp will keep in an airtight container in the refrigerator for up to 3 days.

- **Preheat oven to 375°F (190°C)**
- **4-cup (1 L) baking dish, greased**

TOPPING

⅔ cup	packed brown sugar	150 mL
½ cup	all-purpose flour	125 mL
¾ tsp	ground cinnamon	3 mL
¼ cup	butter, softened	60 mL

FILLING

4 cups	sliced peeled, cored apples (see Tips, left)	1 L
2 tbsp	granulated sugar	30 mL
½ tsp	ground cinnamon	2 mL
1 tbsp	freshly squeezed lemon juice	15 mL

1. *Topping:* In a small bowl, using a fork, stir together brown sugar, flour, cinnamon and butter, until crumbly. Set aside.
2. *Filling:* In a medium bowl, toss together apples, sugar, cinnamon and lemon juice, until apples are well coated. Arrange evenly in prepared baking dish. Sprinkle topping evenly over apples.
3. Bake in preheated oven for 30 to 35 minutes or until apples are tender and topping is golden. Serve warm.

Variations

For a pop of color and a tarter taste, add ½ cup (125 mL) fresh or frozen cranberries to the filling.

A combination of half peaches and half apples also tastes great. Keep the total quantity to 4 cups (1 L).

Peach, Apple and Blueberry Crisp

◆

This is a tasty combination, but you can vary the fruits to suit your personal tastes as well as what's in season. Serve with frozen yogurt or ice cream.

MAKES 3 TO 4 SERVINGS

- Preparation: 20 minutes
- Baking: 35 minutes
- Freezing: not recommended

Tips

Large-flake (old-fashioned) rolled oats will give a more "oaty" flavor and appearance.

If the apples are sour and juicy, you may want to add a little more sugar and flour to the filling.

To ensure that the filling bakes uniformly, cut soft fruits into larger chunks and firm fruits into smaller pieces.

Cooled crisp will keep in an airtight container in the refrigerator for up to 3 days.

- **Preheat oven to 375°F (190°C)**
- **4-cup (1 L) baking dish, greased**

TOPPING

⅓ cup	quick-cooking rolled oats (see Tips, left)	75 mL
¼ cup	packed brown sugar	60 mL
3 tbsp	all-purpose flour	45 mL
½ tsp	ground cinnamon	2 mL
¼ tsp	ground nutmeg	1 mL
2 tbsp	cold butter	30 mL

FILLING

1 cup	sliced peeled, cored apples (see Tips, left)	250 mL
1 cup	sliced peeled, pitted peaches (see Tips, left)	250 mL
½ cup	fresh blueberries	125 mL
¼ cup	granulated sugar	60 mL
1½ tbsp	all-purpose flour	22 mL
2 tsp	freshly squeezed lemon juice	10 mL

1. *Topping:* In a small bowl, whisk together oats, brown sugar, flour, cinnamon and nutmeg. Using a pastry blender or two knives, cut in butter until mixture resembles coarse crumbs. Set aside.
2. *Filling:* In a medium bowl, toss together apples, peaches, blueberries, sugar, flour and lemon juice, until fruit is well coated. Spread evenly in prepared baking dish. Sprinkle topping over fruit.
3. Bake in preheated oven for 30 to 35 minutes or until fruit is tender and topping is golden. Serve warm.

Variations

Substitute an equal amount of raspberries for the blueberries.

Pear, Apple and Blueberry Crisp: Substitute an equal amount of sliced peeled, cored pears for the peaches.

Strawberry Rhubarb Crisp

◆

Rhubarb is a sure sign of spring. Couple it with fresh strawberries and you have a winning crisp.

MAKES 3 TO 4 SERVINGS

- Preparation: 20 minutes
- Baking: 30 minutes
- Freezing: not recommended

Tips

The cups will be full. Bake them on a baking sheet to catch any drips that may boil over.

To make one large crisp, make in a 5-cup (1.25 L) baking dish and bake for about 35 minutes or until fruit is tender and topping is golden.

Cooled crisp will keep in an airtight container in the refrigerator for up to 3 days.

- **Preheat oven to 375°F (190°C)**
- **Three 10 oz (300 mL) ramekins or custard cups, greased**

TOPPING

⅓ cup	packed brown sugar	75 mL
¼ cup	all-purpose flour	60 mL
2 tbsp	quick-cooking rolled oats	30 mL
2 tbsp	chopped pecans	30 mL
½ tsp	ground cinnamon	2 mL
3 tbsp	cold butter	45 mL

FILLING

2½ cups	fresh strawberries, halved	625 mL
¾ cup	chopped fresh rhubarb	175 mL
2 tbsp	all-purpose flour	30 mL
2 tbsp	granulated sugar	30 mL

1. *Topping:* In a small bowl, using a wooden spoon, combine brown sugar, flour, oats, pecans and cinnamon. Using a pastry blender or two knives, cut in butter until mixture is crumbly. Set aside.
2. *Filling:* In a large bowl, toss together strawberries, rhubarb, flour and sugar. Spoon into prepared ramekins, dividing evenly. Sprinkle topping over fruit.
3. Bake in preheated oven for 25 to 30 minutes or until fruit is tender and topping is golden. Serve warm.

> ## Variations
>
> Use your favorite nut. Walnuts, hazelnuts and almonds all work great.
>
> *Raspberry Rhubarb Crisp:* Substitute an equal amount of raspberries for the strawberries.

Bumbleberry Cobbler

Bumbleberry is simply a mixture of fruits. Customize this dessert by using your favorite fruit or whatever's in season.

MAKES 3 TO 4 SERVINGS

- Preparation: 20 minutes
- Baking: 30 minutes
- Freezing: not recommended

Tips

Place pan on a baking sheet or a piece of aluminum foil when baking, to catch any drips.

The biscuit topping is best when warm. A scoop of vanilla ice cream is a nice finishing touch, especially when the cobbler is still warm.

Cooled cobbler will keep in an airtight container in the refrigerator for up to 3 days.

- Preheat oven to 400°F (200°C)
- 6-cup (1.5 L) baking dish, greased

FILLING

3 cups	sliced peeled, cored apples	750 mL
½ cup	cranberries (fresh or frozen)	125 mL
½ cup	blueberries (fresh or frozen)	125 mL
⅓ cup	granulated sugar	75 mL
2 tbsp	all-purpose flour	30 mL
¼ cup	water	60 mL

TOPPING

¾ cup	all-purpose flour	175 mL
2 tbsp	granulated sugar, divided	30 mL
2 tsp	baking powder	10 mL
⅛ tsp	salt	0.5 mL
¼ cup	cold butter	60 mL
⅓ cup	milk	75 mL

1. *Filling:* In a large bowl, toss together apples, cranberries, blueberries, sugar and flour, until fruit is well coated. Add water and stir well. Spread evenly in prepared baking dish.
2. *Topping:* In a medium bowl, whisk together flour, 1 tbsp (15 mL) sugar, baking powder and salt. Using a pastry blender or two knives, cut in butter until mixture resembles coarse crumbs. Add milk all at once, stirring with a fork until ingredients are moistened. Drop mixture by teaspoonfuls (5 mL) over fruit, covering surface evenly. Sprinkle with remaining 1 tbsp (15 mL) sugar.
3. Bake in preheated oven for 25 to 30 minutes or until topping is golden (see Tips, left). Serve warm.

Variations

Substitute an equal amount of raspberries for either the blueberries or the cranberries.

Substitute an equal amount of sliced peeled, pitted peaches for the apples.

Pear Cranberry Crumble

A crumbly oat topping makes any combination of fruit special. Pears and cranberries are especially nice together.

MAKES 3 TO 4 SERVINGS

- Preparation: 20 minutes
- Baking: 35 minutes
- Freezing: not recommended

Tips

Large-flake (old-fashioned) rolled oats are not rolled as thinly as quick-cooking rolled oats, so they have a crunchy, slightly chewy texture. You can use whichever oats you have on hand.

The baking dish will seem very full but the fruits will sink while cooking. Place the pan on a baking sheet or a piece of aluminum foil when baking, to catch any drips.

Cooled crumble will keep in an airtight container in the refrigerator for up to 3 days.

- **Preheat oven to 350°F (180°C)**
- **4-cup (1 L) baking dish, greased**

TOPPING

3 tbsp	all-purpose flour	45 mL
3 tbsp	packed brown sugar	45 mL
½ tsp	ground cinnamon	2 mL
2 tbsp	butter, softened	30 mL
⅓ cup	large-flake (old-fashioned) rolled oats (see Tips, left)	75 mL

FILLING

3 cups	diced peeled, cored pears	750 mL
1 cup	cranberries (fresh or frozen)	250 mL
3 tbsp	granulated sugar	45 mL
1½ tbsp	all-purpose flour	22 mL

1. *Topping:* In a small bowl, whisk together flour, brown sugar and cinnamon. Using a fork, mash in butter until mixture is crumbly. Stir in oats. Set aside.
2. *Filling:* In a medium bowl, using a wooden spoon, stir together pears, cranberries, sugar and flour. Spread evenly in prepared baking dish. Sprinkle with topping.
3. Bake in preheated oven for 30 to 35 minutes or until fruit is tender and topping is golden. Serve warm.

Variations

Apple Cranberry Crumble: Substitute an equal amount of sliced peeled, cored apples for the pears.

Peach Blueberry Crumble: Substitute an equal amount of sliced peeled, pitted peaches for the pears and blueberries for the cranberries.

Chocolate Bread Pudding

◆

This is a rich, custardy, chocolaty dessert.
Serve with a dollop of whipped cream for a nice finishing touch.

MAKES 4 SERVINGS

- Preparation: 20 minutes
- Standing: 1 hour
- Baking: 35 minutes
- Freezing: not recommended

Tips

I prefer to remove the crusts from the bread, but leave them on if you prefer.

For a decadent dessert, pour custard sauce (see Raspberry Trifle, page 233) over individual servings.

Cooled bread pudding will keep in an airtight container in the refrigerator for up to 3 days.

- **Preheat oven to 325°F (160°C)**
- **4-cup (1 L) baking dish, greased**

¾ cup	table (18%) cream or milk	175 mL
2 oz	bittersweet chocolate, chopped	60 g
2	eggs	2
2 tbsp	granulated sugar	30 mL
3 cups	cubed egg bread	750 mL

1. In a small saucepan over medium heat, combine cream and chocolate, stirring until chocolate is melted. Set aside.
2. In a small bowl, whisk together eggs and sugar. Whisk in chocolate mixture.
3. Arrange bread in prepared baking dish. Pour egg mixture overtop, pressing down lightly to submerge bread. Let stand for 30 minutes.
4. Place dish in a larger shallow baking pan. Pour enough boiling water into pan to come halfway up sides of pudding dish.
5. Bake in preheated oven for 30 to 35 minutes or until set. Transfer dish to a wire rack and let cool for about 30 minutes before serving.

Variation
Add ⅓ cup (75 mL) dried cherries to the bread cubes.

Raspberry Clafouti

♦

If you have fresh raspberries on hand, this is very quick, very easy and very delicious. Great for when unexpected guests arrive!

MAKES 2 MINI PIES (2 SERVINGS EACH)

- Preparation: 10 minutes
- Baking: 25 minutes
- Freezing: not recommended

Tips

For best results, bring all the ingredients to room temperature before using.

Clafouti is best enjoyed the same day it's made.

- **Preheat oven to 350°F (180°C)**
- **Two 4½-inch (11.5 cm) mini pie dishes (1 cup/250 mL each)**

1 cup	fresh raspberries	250 mL
2 tbsp + 1 tsp	granulated sugar, divided	30 mL + 5 mL
1	egg	1
¼ cup	milk	60 mL
1 tbsp	raspberry or orange liqueur	15 mL
2 tsp	butter, melted	10 mL
¼ cup	all-purpose flour	60 mL
⅛ tsp	baking powder	0.5 mL
Pinch	salt	Pinch

1. Divide raspberries evenly between pie dishes. Sprinkle with 1 tbsp (15 mL) sugar, dividing equally.
2. In a small bowl, whisk together egg, milk, liqueur and melted butter. In another small bowl, whisk together flour, 1 tbsp (15 mL) sugar, baking powder and salt. Add to egg mixture, whisking until smooth. Pour over fruit, dividing evenly between dishes.
3. Bake in preheated oven for 20 to 25 minutes or until puffed, set and golden. Let cool in pan on a wire rack for 10 minutes. Sprinkle each with ½ tsp (2 mL) sugar and serve warm.

Variations

Substitute ¾ cup (175 mL) fresh blueberries or pitted cherries for the raspberries.

Serve with a dollop of whipped cream or a drizzle of lemon juice for a nice finishing touch.

This recipe can easily be doubled or tripled for unexpected guests.

Berry Gratin

◆

This is one of the easiest fruit desserts you can make but it's impressive enough to serve to guests.

MAKES 2 SERVINGS

- Preparation: 10 minutes
- Chilling: 30 minutes
- Broiling: 3 minutes
- Freezing: not recommended

Tips

For a lighter dessert, use milk or a lighter cream in place of the heavy cream.

You may find it easier to use a wooden spoon to stir the cheese mixture to start, then switch to a whisk and whisk until smooth.

When broiling, keep an eye on the oven. The sugar will burn quickly.

Berry gratin is best enjoyed the same day it's made.

- **5½-inch (14 cm) square shallow baking dish, greased**

½ cup	each fresh blueberries, raspberries and blackberries	125 mL
2 oz	cream cheese, softened	60 g
1½ tbsp	heavy or whipping (35%) cream (see Tips, left)	22 mL
1 tsp	freshly squeezed lemon juice	5 mL
2 tbsp	packed brown sugar	30 mL

1. Place berries in prepared dish. Gently toss to combine.
2. In a small bowl, whisk together cream cheese, cream and lemon juice, until smooth (see Tips, left). Spread evenly over fruit. Refrigerate for 30 minutes or until cold. Sprinkle brown sugar evenly overtop.
3. With oven rack positioned about 4 inches (10 cm) from the element, broil until sugar is melted and caramelized, about 3 minutes. Let cool for 10 minutes, then serve warm.

Variations

Substitute halved strawberries for one of the berries.

Use ¾ cup (175 mL) each of your favorite two berries.

Substitute an equal amount of Neufchâtel or mascarpone cheese for the cream cheese.

Crème Brûlée

◆

The contrast of crunchy caramelized topping against velvety custard is simply luscious.

MAKES 2 SERVINGS

- Preparation: 20 minutes
- Baking: 30 minutes
- Cooling: 2½ hours
- Freezing: not recommended

Tips

If you have one, you can use a kitchen torch to caramelize the sugar topping in Step 4.

Crème brûlée will keep in an airtight container in the refrigerator for up to 2 days. The topping may soften with storage; if desired, recrisp under the broiler for 1 minute.

- **Preheat oven to 300°F (150°C)**
- **Two 5 oz (150 mL) shallow baking dishes**

CUSTARD

1 cup	heavy or whipping (35%) cream	250 mL
3 tbsp	granulated sugar, divided	45 mL
½	vanilla bean, split lengthwise	½
2	egg yolks	2
Pinch	salt	Pinch

TOPPING

3 tbsp	granulated sugar	45 mL

1. *Custard:* In a small saucepan, combine cream and 2 tbsp (30 mL) sugar. Scrape vanilla bean seeds into milk (save pod for another use). Heat mixture over medium heat just until it starts to bubble around the edges of the pan.
2. In a small bowl, whisk together egg yolks, remaining 1 tbsp (15 mL) sugar and salt. Pour 2 tbsp (30 mL) hot cream into egg mixture, whisking constantly. Repeat, whisking after each addition, until all the cream is added. Strain mixture through a fine-mesh sieve into a measuring cup. Divide custard evenly between dishes and place them in a small roasting pan. Place pan in oven. Pour enough boiling water into pan to come halfway up sides of dishes.
3. Bake in preheated oven for 25 to 30 minutes, just until set around the edges but slightly soft in the center. Remove pan from oven and carefully transfer dishes to a wire rack. Let cool for 30 minutes. Cover with plastic wrap and refrigerate until cold, at least 2 hours or up to 2 days.
4. *Topping:* Sprinkle 1½ tbsp (22 mL) sugar evenly over each custard. With oven rack positioned about 4 inches (10 cm) from element, broil until sugar is melted and caramelized, about 3 minutes. Serve immediately.

Variation

Substitute 1 tsp (5 mL) pure vanilla extract for the vanilla bean seeds.

Raspberry Trifle

◆

This dessert looks very elegant but is simple to make and very comforting.

MAKES 4 SERVINGS

- Preparation: 25 minutes
- Cooking: 10 minutes
- Chilling: 4 hours
- Freezing: not recommended

Tips

Seedless raspberry jam has a more intense flavor than regular raspberry jam.

Trifles can be made ahead and refrigerated up to 12 hours. Add whipped cream and berry garnish when ready to serve.

Try other berries such as strawberries or blueberries.

Substitute an equal amount of ladyfingers for the pound cake.

- **4 mini trifle dishes or wineglasses**

CUSTARD

2	egg yolks	2
¾ cup	milk, divided	175 mL
2 tbsp	granulated sugar	30 mL
2 tbsp	cornstarch	30 mL
1 tsp	pure vanilla extract	5 mL

PUDDING

5 oz	prepared pound cake	150 g
2 tbsp	raspberry jam (see Tips, left)	30 mL
¾ cup	heavy or whipping (35%) cream	175 mL
1⅔ cups	fresh raspberries	400 mL
	Fresh raspberries for garnish	

1. *Custard:* In a medium bowl, combine egg yolks, ¼ cup (60 mL) milk, sugar and cornstarch. Whisk until smooth.
2. In a small saucepan over medium heat, heat remaining milk just until bubbles start to form around the edges. Gradually add hot milk to egg yolk mixture, whisking constantly. Cook, stirring often, for about 5 minutes or until thickened.
3. Strain custard through a fine-mesh sieve into a bowl. Stir in vanilla. Cover surface of custard with plastic wrap (to avoid a skin forming) and refrigerate for 4 hours, until cold, or overnight.
4. *Pudding:* Cut cake into slices ½ inch (2 cm) thick. Spread jam on one side of each slice. Cut slices into cubes. Set aside.
5. In a small bowl, beat cream until stiff peaks form. Fold about one-third of the whipped cream into cooled custard.
6. *Assembly:* Divide half of the cake cubes evenly between dishes. Top with one-third of the berries, then one-third of the custard. Repeat layers. Top with remaining whipped cream. Refrigerate until ready to serve. Garnish with fresh berries.

Mixed Berry Meringue Nests

◆

Take advantage of whatever berries are in season to make this light and lovely summertime dessert.

MAKES 4 SERVINGS

- Preparation: 15 minutes
- Baking: 2 hours
- Standing: 2 hours
- Freezing: not recommended

Tips

. . . .

Separate egg whites from yolks while the eggs are cold. When yolks are cold, they are less likely to break.

For best results, bring egg whites to room temperature before using.

Meringue nests can be prepared up to 5 days in advance. Store in an airtight container at room temperature.

- **Preheat oven to 200°F (100°C)**
- **Baking sheet, lined with parchment paper**

MERINGUE NESTS

1 tsp	cornstarch	5 mL
1 tsp	white vinegar	5 mL
2	egg whites (see Tips, left)	2
½ cup	granulated sugar	125 mL

TOPPING

½ cup	fresh blueberries	125 mL
½ cup	fresh raspberries	125 mL
½ cup	fresh strawberries, halved	125 mL
1 tbsp	confectioners' (icing) sugar, sifted	15 mL
½ cup	lemon-flavored Greek yogurt	125 mL

1. *Meringue Nests:* In a small bowl, stir together cornstarch and vinegar until cornstarch dissolves. Set aside.
2. In a small bowl, beat egg whites until frothy. Gradually add sugar, beating until stiff peaks form. Gently fold in cornstarch mixture.
3. Drop 4 equal mounds of meringue onto parchment paper. Using the back of a spoon, make a well in the center of each to form a nest shape.
4. Bake in preheated oven for 2 hours, then turn off oven and leave door slightly ajar. Let meringues dry in oven for 2 hours. Remove from oven and let cool completely on a wire rack.
5. *Topping:* In a small bowl, combine berries and confectioners' sugar, stirring until sugar dissolves.
6. Spoon yogurt into centers of meringue nests, dividing evenly. Top with berries. Serve immediately.

Variations

Make this using your favorite combination of berries, or simply one type of berry.

Substitute an equal amount of plain yogurt or whipped cream for the lemon Greek yogurt.

Baked Custard

◆

Something about this simple dessert is so comforting. The feeling could be sentimental—it's one of my mom's favorites. Serve with a sprinkle of nutmeg on top.

MAKES 3 SERVINGS

- Preparation: 10 minutes
- Baking: 30 minutes
- Freezing: not recommended

Tips

Be careful not to overcook custard. The top should be set around the edges but still a bit soft in the center. The custards will continue to cook while cooling.

Cooled custard will keep in an airtight container in the refrigerator for up to 3 days.

- **Preheat oven to 350°F (180°C)**
- **Three 6 oz (175 mL) custard cups**

½ cup	evaporated milk	125 mL
½ cup	milk	125 mL
¼ cup	granulated sugar	60 mL
2	eggs	2
½ tsp	pure vanilla extract	2 mL

1. In a small saucepan over medium heat, heat evaporated milk, regular milk and sugar, just until sugar has dissolved and bubbles start to form around edges of pan. Set aside to cool slightly.

2. In a small bowl, whisk together eggs and vanilla. Gradually whisk in milk mixture. Strain through a fine-mesh sieve into a measuring cup to remove any bits of egg white (discard solids). Pour into custard cups.

3. Place cups in a shallow baking pan and pour in enough boiling water to come halfway up sides of cups.

4. Bake in preheated oven for 25 to 30 minutes or just until almost set. Transfer to a wire rack and let cool. Serve at room temperature or chilled.

Variations

For a lighter custard, omit the evaporated milk and double the amount of regular milk.

For a richer, more caramel flavor, omit the regular milk and use double the amount of evaporated milk.

Gluten-Free Desserts

Gluten-Free Cranberry Almond Muffins

Who knew a gluten-free muffin could taste so good?

MAKES 6 MUFFINS

- Preparation: 20 minutes
- Baking: 40 minutes
- Freezing: excellent

Tips

Almond flour is available in most bulk food and health food stores.

Because these muffins do not contain any gluten, they won't rise as much as a regular muffin, and the tops will be slightly concave rather than rounded.

Cooled muffins will keep in an airtight container at room temperature for up to 3 days or can be frozen for up to 3 months. Thaw and bring to room temperature before serving.

- **Preheat oven to 300°F (150°C)**
- **6-cup muffin pan, greased or lined with paper liners**

1 cup	almond flour (see Tips, left)	250 mL
½ tsp	baking soda	2 mL
¼ tsp	sea salt	1 mL
1 tsp	ground cinnamon	5 mL
1	egg	1
3 tbsp	olive oil	45 mL
3 tbsp	liquid honey	45 mL
½ cup	cranberries (fresh or frozen)	125 mL
3 tbsp	chopped almonds	45 mL

1. In a small bowl, whisk together almond flour, baking soda, salt and cinnamon. Set aside.
2. In a medium bowl, whisk together egg, oil and honey. Add flour mixture, stirring well. Fold in cranberries and almonds. Divide batter evenly among prepared muffin cups, filling three-quarters full.
3. Bake in preheated oven for 35 to 40 minutes or until tops spring back when lightly touched. Let cool in pan on a wire rack for at least 10 minutes, then remove from pan.

Variations

Substitute an equal amount of hazelnut flour for the almond flour and hazelnuts for the almonds.

Try blueberries instead of the cranberries.

Gluten-Free Banana Bread

This gluten-free version of an all-time favorite quick bread is super easy to make.

MAKES 1 LOAF (4 SERVINGS)

- Preparation: 15 minutes
- Baking: 35 minutes
- Freezing: excellent

Tips

The riper the bananas, the better the flavor

If the loaf is browning too quickly while baking, cover the top with a piece of foil after 20 minutes.

Cooled loaf will keep in an airtight container at room temperature for up to 3 days or can be frozen for up to 3 months. Thaw in refrigerator overnight and bring to room temperature before serving.

- **Preheat oven to 350°F (180°C)**
- **5½- by 3¼-inch (14 by 8 cm) foil loaf pan, greased**

¾ cup	mashed ripe bananas (2 medium; see Tips, left)	175 mL
2 tbsp	milk	30 mL
1 tsp	pure vanilla extract	5 mL
½ tsp	vinegar	2 mL
⅓ cup	soy flour	75 mL
¼ cup	packed brown sugar	60 mL
1½ tsp	gluten-free baking powder	7 mL
1 tsp	xanthan gum	5 mL
½ tsp	baking soda	2 mL
¼ tsp	salt	1 mL
1	egg	1
2 tbsp	vegetable oil	30 mL

1. In a medium bowl, whisk together banana, milk, vanilla and vinegar. Set aside.
2. In a small bowl, whisk together soy flour, brown sugar, baking powder, xanthan gum, baking soda and salt. Set aside.
3. Add egg and oil to banana mixture, whisking well. Add flour mixture, stirring just until combined. Pour batter evenly into prepared pan.
4. Bake in preheated oven for 30 to 35 minutes or until a toothpick inserted in the center comes out clean. Let cool in pan on a wire rack for 10 minutes, then remove from pan and let cool completely on rack.

Variations

Add ⅓ cup (75 mL) chopped walnuts or pecans to the egg-oil mixture.

Gluten-Free Oatmeal Cranberry Cookies

This is a new twist on an old-fashioned favorite. You can make these with raisins, too.

MAKES 8 MEDIUM OR 6 LARGE COOKIES (SEE TIPS, BELOW)

- Preparation: 15 minutes
- Chilling: 15 minutes
- Baking: 12 minutes
- Freezing: excellent

Tips

For a somewhat less "oaty" taste and appearance, use quick-cooking rolled oats.

If you like chewy cookies, bake for 8 minutes. For crisp cookies, bake for 12 minutes.

Always use regular (not nonstick) baking sheets for cookies. Cookies tend to bake faster and brown more quickly on nonstick pans.

To make large cookies, drop dough by large spoonfuls (2 tbsp/30 mL). Bake for 10 to 14 minutes, as directed.

Cooled cookies will keep in an airtight container at room temperature for up to 1 week or can be frozen for up to 3 months. Thaw and bring to room temperature before serving.

- **Preheat oven to 350°F (180°C)**
- **Baking sheet, lightly greased or lined with parchment paper**

¼ cup	gluten-free oat flour	60 mL
1 tbsp	tapioca starch	15 mL
1 tsp	ground cinnamon	5 mL
¼ tsp	baking soda	1 mL
¼ tsp	xanthan gum	1 mL
¼ cup	butter, melted	60 mL
¼ cup	packed brown sugar	60 mL
2 tbsp	granulated sugar	30 mL
1	egg	1
⅔ cup	gluten-free large-flake (old-fashioned) rolled oats	150 mL
½ cup	dried cranberries	125 mL

1. In a small bowl, whisk together oat flour, tapioca starch, cinnamon, baking soda and xanthan gum. Set aside.
2. In a medium bowl, whisk together melted butter, brown and granulated sugars and egg. Stir in flour mixture, oats and cranberries. Stir well. Refrigerate batter for 15 minutes.
3. Drop by heaping tablespoonfuls (22 mL) onto prepared cookie sheet, spacing 2 inches (5 cm) apart.
4. Bake in preheated oven for 8 to 12 minutes or until set and light golden. Let cool on pan on a wire rack for 2 minutes. Transfer cookies to rack and cool completely.

Make Ahead: Dough can be refrigerated in an airtight container for up to a week or frozen for up to 3 months. Thaw and bring to room temperature before baking.

Variation

Substitute an equal amount of raisins or chopped pitted dates for the cranberries.

Gluten-Free Peanut Butter Chocolate Chip Cookies

You don't have to have celiac disease to enjoy these classic cookies.

MAKES ABOUT 8 COOKIES

- Preparation: 20 minutes
- Baking: 10 minutes
- Freezing: excellent

Tips

Dip the fork in flour to prevent it from sticking to the dough.

Cooled cookies will keep in an airtight container at room temperature for up to 1 week or can be frozen for up to 3 months. Thaw and bring to room temperature before serving.

- **Preheat oven to 350°F (180°C)**
- **Baking sheet, lightly greased or lined with parchment paper**

2/3 cup	soy or amaranth flour	150 mL
4 tsp	tapioca starch	20 mL
1/4 tsp	xanthan gum	1 mL
1/8 tsp	baking soda	0.5 mL
2/3 cup	crunchy peanut butter	150 mL
1	egg	1
1/4 cup	packed brown sugar	60 mL
1/4 tsp	pure vanilla extract	1 mL
1/4 cup	chopped peanuts	60 mL
1/4 cup	semisweet chocolate chips	60 mL

1. In a small bowl, whisk together flour, tapioca starch, xanthan gum and baking soda. Set aside.
2. In a medium bowl, using a wooden spoon, stir together peanut butter, egg, brown sugar and vanilla, until smooth. Add flour mixture, stirring until combined. Stir in peanuts and chocolate chips.
3. Using your hands, roll dough into $1\frac{1}{2}$-inch (4 cm) balls. Place on prepared baking sheet, spacing 2 inches (5 cm) apart. Using a fork, flatten slightly (see Tips, left).
4. Bake in preheated oven for 8 to 10 minutes or until firm. Let cool on pan on a wire rack for 2 minutes. Transfer cookies to rack and cool completely.

Make Ahead: Dough can be refrigerated in an airtight container for up to a week or frozen for up to 3 months. Thaw and bring to room temperature before baking.

Variations

Substitute additional chopped peanuts or peanut butter chips for the chocolate chips.

Gluten-Free Shortbread Cookies

◆

These melt-in-your-mouth shortbreads are always a hit during the holiday season.

MAKES ABOUT 8 COOKIES

- Preparation: 15 minutes
- Baking: 18 minutes
- Freezing: excellent

Tips

Dipping your fork into sugar helps to prevent the dough from sticking to it.

Decorate the cookies by pressing a piece of nut or candied cherry on top before baking.

Cooled cookies will keep in an airtight container at room temperature for up to 3 weeks or can be frozen for up to 3 months. Thaw and bring to room temperature before serving.

- **Preheat oven to 300°F (150°C)**
- **Baking sheet, ungreased or lined with parchment paper**

⅓ cup	rice flour	75 mL
¼ cup	cornstarch	60 mL
¼ cup	confectioners' (icing) sugar, sifted	60 mL
2 tbsp	potato starch	30 mL
1 tbsp	tapioca starch	15 mL
6 tbsp	salted butter, softened	90 mL
	Granulated sugar	

1. In a medium bowl, whisk together flour, cornstarch, confectioners' sugar, potato starch and tapioca starch. Add butter and, using a wooden spoon, stir just until combined. Using your hands, knead until a smooth dough forms.
2. Using your hands, roll dough into 8 balls about 1 inch (2.5 cm) in diameter. Place on prepared baking sheet, spacing 1 inch (2.5 cm) apart. Flatten each ball with a fork dipped in granulated sugar.
3. Bake in preheated oven for 14 to 18 minutes or until just starting to brown around the edges. Let cool for 5 minutes on pan, then transfer to a wire rack and cool completely.

Make Ahead: Dough will keep in the refrigerator for up to 1 week or in the freezer for up to 3 months. Thaw and bring to room temperature before baking.

Variation
Before baking, sprinkle the cookies with coarse white or colored sugar.

Gluten-Free No-Bake Apricot Snowballs

These bite-sized energy balls contain a fabulous mixture of dried fruits.

MAKES ABOUT 12 SNOWBALLS

- Preparation: 20 minutes
- Standing: 1 hour
- Freezing: excellent

Tips

The fruit mixture can be chopped after soaking, in a mini food processor fitted with the metal blade, pulsing just until finely chopped.

Snowballs will keep in an airtight container at room temperature for up to 2 weeks or can be frozen for up to 3 months. Thaw in refrigerator overnight and bring to room temperature before serving.

- **Baking sheet, lined with waxed or parchment paper**

¼ cup	very finely chopped dried apricots (see Tips, left)	60 mL
2 tbsp	very finely chopped dried figs	30 mL
2 tbsp	very finely chopped dried apples	30 mL
1 tbsp	very finely chopped prunes	15 mL
1 tbsp	very finely chopped dried cherries	15 mL
1 tsp	freshly grated orange zest	5 mL
2 tsp	freshly squeezed orange juice	10 mL
⅔ cup	unsweetened desiccated coconut, divided	150 mL
3 tbsp	finely chopped walnuts	45 mL

1. In a medium bowl, combine dried apricots, figs, apples, prunes and cherries and orange zest and orange juice. Cover and let stand for 1 hour, until softened (see Tips, left).
2. Add 3 tbsp (45 mL) coconut and the walnuts. Stir well, kneading with hands until mixture holds together.
3. Using your hands, roll into 1-inch (2.5 cm) balls. Place remaining coconut in a shallow dish. Roll each ball in coconut, then place on prepared baking sheet. Cover and let stand at room temperature overnight to mellow before serving.

Variations

Use your favorite dried fruits. A blend of sweet and tart dried fruits works best.

Gluten-Free Nanaimo Bars

For some people, these are a holiday favorite. For me, they are an anytime favorite.

MAKES 9 BARS

- Preparation: 30 minutes
- Chilling: 2 hours
- Freezing: excellent

Tip

If you don't have any unsweetened coconut on hand, you can use sweetened coconut.

- 9- by 5-inch (23 by 12.5 cm) loaf pan, lined with parchment paper

BASE

3 tbsp	butter	45 mL
1	egg	1
1 cup	hazelnut flour (see Tips, right)	250 mL
3 tbsp	unsweetened cocoa powder, sifted (see Quick Tip, right)	45 mL
1 tbsp	granulated sugar	15 mL
½ cup	unsweetened desiccated coconut (see Tip, left)	125 mL
¼ cup	chopped hazelnuts	60 mL

FILLING

2 tbsp	butter, softened	30 mL
1½ tbsp	milk or cream	22 mL
2 tbsp	gluten-free custard powder	30 mL
1 cup	confectioners' (icing) sugar, sifted	250 mL

TOPPING

1 tsp	butter	5 mL
2 oz	semisweet chocolate, chopped	60 g

1. *Base:* In a medium saucepan over medium heat, melt butter. Remove from heat. Using a wooden spoon, beat in egg. Add hazelnut flour, cocoa powder, sugar, coconut and nuts, stirring well. Spread mixture evenly in prepared pan, packing down firmly. Refrigerate until cold, about 30 minutes.

Tips

Substitute an equal amount of almond flour for the hazelnut flour and chopped almonds for the hazelnuts.

Bars will keep in an airtight container at room temperature for up to 2 weeks or can be frozen for up to 3 months (separate layers with waxed paper). Thaw and bring to room temperature before serving.

2. *Filling:* In a small bowl, using a wooden spoon, cream butter. Gradually add milk, custard powder and confectioners' sugar, stirring until smooth. Spread evenly over chilled base. Refrigerate until firm, about 1 hour.

3. *Topping:* In a small microwave-safe bowl, combine butter and chocolate. Microwave on Low for about 1 minute, stirring halfway through, until melted. Spread evenly over chilled filling. Refrigerate until set, about 30 minutes. Cut into bars.

Variations

To make cappuccino bars, add 1 tsp (5 mL) instant espresso powder to the filling.

For an orange twist, add 2 tsp (10 mL) freshly grated orange zest to the filling.

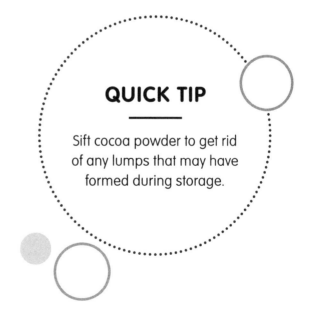

QUICK TIP

Sift cocoa powder to get rid of any lumps that may have formed during storage.

Gluten-Free Chocolate Banana Cake

◆

This moist cake is perfect for tucking into lunch boxes or as a pick-me-up afternoon snack.

MAKES 1 LOAF CAKE (4 SERVINGS)

- Preparation: 20 minutes
- Baking: 35 minutes
- Freezing: excellent

Tips

Press cocoa powder through a fine-mesh sieve before using, to get rid of any lumps.

Substitute an equal amount of brown rice flour for the quinoa flour.

If you have a sweet tooth, top with Banana Butter Frosting (page 186).

For an easy grab-and-go option, wrap individual slices in plastic wrap and freeze.

Cooled cake will keep in an airtight container at room temperature for up to 5 days or can be frozen for up to 3 months. Thaw in refrigerator overnight and bring to room temperature before serving.

- Preheat oven to 350°F (180°C)
- 9- by 5-inch (23 by 12.5 cm) loaf pan, greased and lined with parchment paper

⅓ cup	sorghum flour	75 mL
2½ tbsp	unsweetened cocoa powder, sifted (see Tips, left)	37 mL
2 tbsp	quinoa flour (see Tips, left)	30 mL
1 tbsp	tapioca starch	15 mL
¾ tsp	xanthan gum	3 mL
¼ tsp	baking soda	1 mL
⅛ tsp	salt	0.5 mL
1	egg	1
½ cup	mashed ripe banana (1 large)	125 mL
6 tbsp	granulated sugar	90 mL
2½ tbsp	vegetable oil	37 mL
2 tbsp	water	30 mL
½ tsp	pure vanilla extract	2 mL

1. In a small bowl, whisk together sorghum flour, cocoa powder, quinoa flour, tapioca starch, xanthan gum, baking soda and salt. Set aside.
2. In a medium bowl, whisk together egg, banana, sugar, oil, water and vanilla. Add flour mixture, stirring just until combined. Spread batter evenly in prepared pan.
3. Bake in preheated oven for 30 to 35 minutes or until a toothpick inserted in the center comes out clean. Let cool in pan on a wire rack for 15 minutes, then remove from pan and cool completely on rack.

Variations
Fold in ¼ cup (60 mL) chopped nuts or mini chocolate chips in Step 2.

Library and Archives Canada Cataloguing in Publication

Snider, Jill, 1947-, author
    175 best small-batch baking recipes : treats for 1 or 2 / Jill Snider.

Includes index.
ISBN 978-0-7788-0561-8 (softcover)

    1. Cookies. 2. Bars (Desserts). 3. Cookbooks. I. Title. II. Title:
One hundred and seventy-five best small-batch baking recipes.
III. Title: One hundred seventy-five best small-batch baking recipes.

TX772.S634 2017   641.86'54   C2017-901167-7

Index

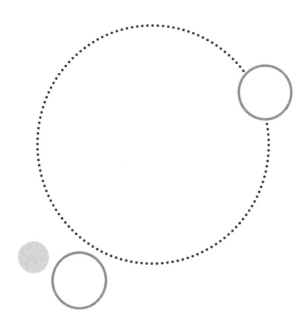